THE MAN WITH THE MIRACULOUS HANDS

The Man with the Miraculous Hands

BY JOSEPH KESSEL

*Translated from the French
by Helen Weaver and Leo Raditsa*

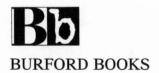

BURFORD BOOKS

Translation by Helen Weaver and Leo Raditsa published by
arrangement with Farrar, Straus and Giroux LLC.

Originally published in France by
Editions Gallimard as *Les Mains du Miracle*.

Printed in the United States of America.

10   9   8   7   6   5   4   3   2   1

Library of Congress Cataloging-in-Publication Data
Kessel, Joseph, 1898–
[Mains du miracle. English]
The man with the miraculous hands / Joseph Kessel.
p.   cm.
ISBN 1-58080-122-6
1. Kersten, Felix, 1898–1960.   2. Himmler, Heinrich,
1900–1945.   3. Physical therapists—Netherlands—Biography.
4. Nazis—Biography.   5. Germany—Politics and government—
1933–1945.   I. Title.

RM699.7.K4K413   2004
615.8'22'092—dc22

2004011961

CONTENTS

CHRONOLOGY

JANUARY 30, 1933:   Hitler comes to power

JUNE 30, 1934:   Hitler has Roehm, commander in chief of the S.A., assassinated by Himmler and the S.S.

MARCH 13, 1938:   The annexation of Austria

SEPTEMBER 29, 1938:   At Munich, the heads of the English and French governments, Chamberlain and Daladier, surrender part of Czechoslovakia to Hitler

MARCH 15, 1939:   Complete annexation of Czechoslovakia

SEPTEMBER 1, 1939:   Hitler attacks Poland

SEPTEMBER 3, 1939:   England and France declare war on Germany

MAY 10, 1940:   Invasion of Belgium and Holland

JUNE 22, 1940:   Defeat of France. Marshal Petain signs the armistice

APRIL 6, 1941:   Invasion of Yugoslavia

JUNE 22, 1941:   Hitler attacks Russia

DECEMBER 11, 1941:   U.S. declares war on Germany

AUGUST, 1942:   The German Army reaches Stalingrad

NOVEMBER 8, 1942:   Allied troops land in North Africa

JANUARY 31, 1943:   The Allies land in Sicily

JULY 10, 1943:   Germans surrender at Stalingrad

JUNE 6, 1944:   Allies land in Normandy

APRIL 29, 1945:   Hitler commits suicide

MAY 23, 1945:   Himmler commits suicide

PROLOGUE

Himmler committed suicide near Bremen in May, 1945, during that spring when a ravaged, tormented Europe at last found deliverance.

If one only counts years, that time is still not so distant from us. But so many and such momentous things have happened since, that already it seems very far away. Already an entire generation has sprung up, a generation for whom those miserable days are nothing but vague and confused memories. And to tell the truth, it is even becoming difficult for those who underwent the full experience of the war and the occupation to recall, without considerable mental effort, quite the extent of the terrible power which Himmler once had at his disposal.

Let us make that effort. . . .

The German Army occupied France, Belgium, and Holland, Norway and Denmark, Yugoslavia, Poland, and half of European Russia. And in these countries (not counting Germany itself, Austria, Hungary, and Czechoslovakia) Himmler had absolute authority over the Gestapo, the S.S., the concentration camps, and even the diet of the captured peoples.

He had his police force and his personal army, his spy and counter-spy services, his tentacle-like prison system, his organizations devoted to starvation, his immense private hunting and burial grounds. It was his job to watch over, round up, silence, arrest, torture, and put to death millions and millions of human beings. From the Arctic Ocean to the Mediterranean, from the Atlantic to the Volga and the Caucasus, all were at his mercy.

Himmler was a state within a state: a state of informing, inquisition, Gehenna, of death endlessly multiplied.

Only one man was higher than he: Adolf Hitler. From him Himmler accepted the lowest, most loathsome, most perverse tasks with a sort of blind, joyous devotion. For he worshiped, adored Hitler beyond all measure. It was his only passion.

Beyond this, there scarcely existed in the dull, mean, dogmatic, and incredibly methodical schoolmaster a lively feeling, a burning passion, a human weakness. For him it was enough to be the unchallenged expert in mass extermination, the greatest manufacturer of tortures and multiple death that history has ever known.

But a man came along who, during those awful years between 1940 and 1945, week by week, month by month, found a way of snatching his victims from the unfeeling and fanatical butcher. This man so worked on Himmler the all-powerful, Himmler the pitiless, that entire populations escaped the terror of deportation. He prevented the crematory ovens from receiving their full quota of corpses. And alone, unarmed, half prisoner, this man forced Himmler to deceive Adolf Hitler, to dupe his master, to betray his god.

I knew nothing of this story until a few months ago. It was Henri Torres who first sketched the main lines for me. He added that a friend of his, Mr. Jean Louviche, knew Kersten well, and suggested that we meet with him. Of course I agreed.

But I will confess that despite the assurances of the greatest lawyer of the day and of a distinguished, internationally known jurist, the story still left me more than skeptical. It was downright incredible.

It seemed even more so when I found myself in the presence of a man who was very stout, mild-mannered, with kind eyes and the sensual mouth of one who loves the good things of life: in short, Dr. Felix Kersten.

"Come now!" I said to myself. "This man against Himmler?" And yet, little by little, I don't know how or why, I sensed that from this calm mass of flesh, from this heavy good nature, there emanated a hidden and profound power which was steadying, reassuring. I noted that his glance, though kindly, was also extraordinarily level and shrewd. And the mouth, however sensual, also had sensitivity and vigor.

Yes, this man possessed a strange inner density. But even so, to have molded Himmler like a lump of soft clay? I looked at Kersten's hands. I had been told that it was their skill which explained the miracle. The doctor usually let them rest, the fingers interlaced, upon the curve of his stomach. They were large, short, plump, and heavy. Even in repose they seemed to have a life of their own, an assurance, a direction.

My doubts were still there but they were weaker. Jean Louviche then took me to another room in his apartment where there were tables and chairs loaded with documents, newspaper clippings, reports, and photostats.

"Here are the records," he said. "In German, Swedish, Dutch, and English."

I recoiled from this mass of paper.

"To be sure, I have selected the shortest and most critical ones," said Louviche, pointing to a separate pile.

In it, there was a statement by Prince Bernhardt of the Netherlands, every word of which was glowing, almost immoderate praise, listing the reasons why the Grand Cross of the Order of Orange Nassau, the highest decoration of the Netherlands, had been bestowed on Dr. Kersten.

6. *The Man with the Miraculous Hands*

There were photographic copies of letters addressed to Kersten by Himmler, granting him the human lives which the doctor had requested.

There was the preface to Kersten's *Memoirs*, written in English by H. R. Trevor-Roper, professor of contemporary history at Oxford and one of the greatest authorities of the British Secret Service on German affairs during the war. Mr. Trevor-Roper said, in part:

> *There is no man whose story seems at first glance as unbelievable as his. But on the other hand, there is no man whose story has been subjected to such minute investigation. It has been weighed by scholars, jurists, and even by political opponents, and has triumphed over all these tests.*

When I returned to the living room, I felt a little dizzy. The thing was true, then, it had been proved, undeniably: this fat man, this good-natured doctor who looked like a cross between a Flemish burgomaster and a Buddha of the West, had dominated Himmler to the extent of saving hundreds of thousands of human lives. But why? And how? By what incredible miracle? Now a boundless curiosity had replaced my disbelief.

Little by little, detail by detail, memory after memory, I managed to satisfy my curiosity. I spent hours with Kersten, asking questions and listening to his answers.

In spite of the incontestable proofs which I had seen with my own eyes, there were certain parts of the story which I still refused to accept. Such and such an incident could not be true; it was simply impossible. My doubts neither surprised nor upset Kersten; he must have been used to them. He would simply pull out, with a half smile, a letter, a paper, a testimonial, a photostat. And I would have to swallow that incident along with the rest.

DR. KO'S PUPIL

1

The great flood which ravaged Holland around the year 1400 swept
away the workshops and factories where the Kerstens, a rich bourgeois
family, had been making fine Flemish linen since the Middle Ages.

After this catastrophe, they established themselves at Göttingen, in
western Germany, and taking up their metier once more, regained their
fortune. When Charles V visited the city in 1544, Andreas Kersten
was a member of the municipal council, and to reward his achieve-
ments the emperor, without actually raising him to the rank of the
nobility, gave him a coat of arms: two beams surmounted by a knight's
helmet and sprinkled with fleurs-de-lis.

The family continued to prosper at Göttingen for 150 more years.
Then came a fire which ruined everything beyond repair.

The sixteenth century ended. Colonies were needed in the frontiers of Brandenburg. Margrave Johan Sigismund, the sovereign, granted a hundred hectares to the Kersten family. They worked it as peasants and farmers for two hundred years.

Brandenburg was no more than a province of the German Empire, and the nineteenth century was nearing its close, when Ferdinand Kersten was killed in the prime of life by a mad bull, on the land which the margrave had given to his ancestors from Göttingen.

His widow, who was left with small resources and a large family, sold the farm and settled in the small neighboring town, where she thought it would be easier for her to bring up her children.

Her younger son was raised to be a farmer, but he no longer had any land of his own. He looked for work and was offered a job as an administrator in the Baltic countries, which were part of czarist Russia. He yielded to the destiny which seemed to be pushing his family further and further east.

2

The estate of Lunia, in Liflande, was immense. It belonged to the Baron Nolke. The clan of which he was a member no longer exists, but it was quite large at that time in eastern and central Europe. The possessors of vast lands that were almost provinces in themselves, the Magnats, the Barines, lazy and pleasure-loving lords, left their property in the hands of stewards and went off to foreign countries, where they spent enormous sums of money.

Frederic Kersten was a man of great integrity, and so healthy that he was to reach the age of ninety-one without having known a day's illness. This honesty and vigor he placed entirely in the service of his passionate love of farming. He might have gone on supervising the estate indefinitely in his master's absence. However, during his frequent visits to Yurev, the principal town of the region, he met a Miss Olga Stubing, the postmaster's daughter, fell in love with her, won her, and married her. He left the Baron Nolke's employ in order to improve the property of his wife and father-in-law, who had a little piece of land outside Yurev and three houses surrounded with gardens in the same town.

Frederic Kersten and Olga Stubing were very happy.

The young wife was a very kind person. Almost every day she invited poor children into her home and fed and cared for them. Needy families came to her for help in times of trouble. Moreover, throughout the region she had the reputation of being able to cure fractures, rheumatism, neuralgia, and stomach-ache by simple massage, and much better than the doctors. When anyone remarked at this skill, which was not the result of study, she would reply humbly, "It's very simple, I get it from my mother."

3

One September morning in the year 1898, Olga Kersten gave birth to a son. He had a distinguished godfather: the French ambassador to Saint Petersburg. This diplomat, who had a passion for gardening, had become a close friend of agriculturist Frederic Kersten during the latter's rather frequent trips to the capital on business and in connection with his farm. The president of the French Republic at the time was Felix Faure. In his honor, the ambassador-godfather chose for his godson the name of Felix.

From his first years the baby was surrounded only by kindness, simplicity, honesty, and good sense. To the steady and unassuming virtues of old Germany were added the warmth and hospitality of a Russian home.

The town where the little boy grew up had all the charm of an old engraving. The houses were of wood, constructed with large, visible beams, except for the main street, which was called Nicolaievskaia, from the name of the czar in power. There the façades were of stone. On Sundays, carriages harnessed with splendid horses promenaded there: landaus and victorias in fine weather, fur-covered sleighs in winter. The River Emba passed through Yurev on its way to Lake Peipus. During the cold months there was skating on it, and the students in their military caps and tunics crowded around girls whose cheeks were rosy with the cold and who wore, from one end of Russia to the other, the same dresses and the same maroon aprons.

Yurev was the seat of the provincial government, and its governor, functionaries, magistrates, and police officers, with their hospitality, their good nature, and their venality, were just like the people one finds in Gogol, in *The Inspector General* or *Dead Souls*. And the merchants, with their bullnecks, their flowing beards, their squeaking boots, and their private language, were right out of the plays of Ostrowski. And the peasants fell to their knees when they passed in front of the cathedral. And when there were holy processions, all holy Russia shone on the garments and icons of the orthodox clergy which led the grand religious parades.

The samovar hummed from early dawn far into the night. Families were enormous, holidays numerous; the house and the table were always open.

In this bygone world of carefree ease, of leisure and plenty, the life of a child, provided, naturally, that his family was in comfortable circumstances and that he was unaware of the horrible poverty of the people, was one of almost magical sweetness.

In the life of little Felix Kersten the conspicuous events were the charity balls at which his mother sang in that delicious soprano voice and with that gift for music which had earned her the nickname "The nightingale of Liflande," while he secretly gorged himself with sweets. Then there were the holidays which he spent beside the sea, at Terioki, in Finland. There were the birthday presents, the Christmas presents, the Easter presents. . . .

However, his happiness was marred by his poor success at school. It was not ability that was lacking, but attention, application. His teachers said of him that he would never do anything serious. He was forgetful, dreamy, and inordinately fond of eating.

His father, tireless worker that he was, could not accept these defeats. He put them down to a home atmosphere that was too soft and permissive. When the boy was seven years old, he was sent to a boarding school a hundred kilometers from Yurev. He stayed there five years, without much improvement. Then he went to study at Riga, the great city in the Baltic known for the strictness and excellence of its courses and teachers. There, with considerable effort, Felix Kersten succeeded in finishing his secondary school studies.

At the beginning of the year 1914, his father sent him to Germany to enroll in the famous school of agriculture at Guenefeld in Schleswig-Holstein.

4

It was there that, six months later, the First World War took Felix Kersten by surprise. He found himself abruptly cut off from Russia and his family. As it turned out, he did not have much time to feel sorry. The czarist government did not have the slightest confidence in the large German-born population in the Baltic, at the borders of the empire, and so faithful to its origins. Thousands of families were deported to Siberia and Turkestan. Kersten's parents were included in this exodus, which took them to the other end of Russia. A lost village in the desolate country around the Caspian Sea was assigned to them as their residence for the duration of the war.

Felix Kersten, separated from his family at the age of sixteen by warring armies and vast spaces, could no longer count on the help or support of anyone. It was for him the moment of truth.

Up to now, this great pleasure-loving boy, rather fat, lazy, and dreamy, had understood nothing of his father's stubborn devotion to work. The instinct of self-preservation now taught him this virtue overnight. From that time, it became part of the pattern of his life.

Two years later, at Guenefeld, he received his degree in agricultural engineering. After this, he was to spend a period of probation on an estate in Anhalt. The authorities made no difficulties over the proposed change of residence of a student born of a German father. The administration considered Felix Kersten a subject of Kaiser Wilhelm II. But such privileges had their attendant duties. In 1917, Felix Kersten had to join the army.

He was now a young man of ample proportions, a temperate and peaceful disposition, and great emotional stability. While he admired the German people for their capacity for work, their methodicalness, their culture and their music, he hated uniforms, Prussian militarism, the fanatical love of discipline, and chauvinism. Moreover, he still had a secret and nostalgic fondness for the Russia of his childhood.

It was contrary to his nature to have to fight against her, with an army and for a cause that he could not admire. In the end, he found a compromise, a middle way.

Each of the great conflicts that have threatened to upset the structure of Europe had given to the little nations, occupied by giant empires, the hope and sometimes the means of winning their freedom. In the hope of doing so, they have always sided with whatever power threatened their overlords. Thus, in the First World War, the Czechs, who were being oppressed by Austria, deserted her to fight beside the Russians. By the same token, the Finns in Germany now formed a legion to throw off Russian domination. Felix Kersten enlisted with them.

Meanwhile, the Russian Revolution had broken out, and the czarist army was no more. The Baltic countries had also taken arms for their independence. A Finnish force was sent to aid the Estonians. Felix Kersten, who was now an officer, was with this force. He even got as far as Yurev, his native town which, now liberated, had taken its old name of Dorpat. In 1919 he was lucky enough to find his parents, repatriated from the shores of the Caspian Sea after the peace of Brest Litovsk.

His mother had lost neither her youthful spirit nor her goodness. His father, although he was almost seventy years old, was as robust and hard-working as ever. He had accepted the agrarian reform in favor of the peasants, which had been one of the first measures of the new Estonian government, with his customary philosophic resignation, although it deprived him of most of his wealth.

"A piece of land is always too big for one pair of hands," he told his son with a smile as the latter left with his regiment, which was still driving back the Russian guard.

Felix Kersten had to spend the entire winter in the marshes, without shelter. He contracted a rheumatism which paralyzed his legs, and was forced to leave on crutches for the military hospital at Helsinki.

5

While he was convalescing, Kersten thought about the future. He could stay in the Finnish Army; he belonged to the best regiment of the guard. But nothing about military life appealed to him. His agricultural training? He no longer had any land on which to apply it, and he had no desire to work for someone else.

After a great deal of thought, Kersten decided to become a surgeon. He confided his plan to the head doctor at the hospital, Major Ekman. The latter had taken a liking to the young officer with the nice manners and even temper who was so mature for his age.

"Believe me, my boy," he said, "I am a surgeon myself and I can assure you that the training is very long and difficult, especially for a young man like yourself who is without resources and must earn his living right away."

The old doctor took Kersten's wrist and went on, "If I were you, I would try to devote myself to the study of massage."

"Massage! But why?" demanded Kersten.

Major Ekman turned the wrist over, indicating the strong, plump palm and the broad, short fingers.

"This hand," said the major, "is ideally suited to massage, not to surgery."

"Massage . . ." repeated Kersten, half to himself. He was remembering how, when he was a child, the peasants and factory workers in the neighborhood used to come to his mother to be cured by her agile fingers of sprains, wrenched muscles, and even minor fractures. In fact, even his mother's mother had had the same skill. He told the head doctor about it.

"You see! It runs in the family," exclaimed Major Ekman. "Bring your crutches and follow me to the clinic; you will have your first lesson right now."

From this day the masseurs who were associated with the hospital began to instruct Kersten. And before a month had passed, the soldiers preferred the second-lieutenant student to the professionals. As for Kersten, he discovered to his astonishment and joy that his hands possessed the power to restore to the suffering bodies of men their flexibility, repose, and health.

In the northern countries, especially Finland, massage is a very old science, a much respected art. One of the greatest specialists then at Helsinki, a Dr. Kollander, came to the military hospital to treat difficult cases. There he met Kersten and, recognizing his gift, took him as a pupil.

The next two years were full of material hardships for the young man. He did not miss a single class or a single exercise, and at the same time to make ends meet he worked as a longshoreman, a waiter, and a dishwasher. But he had a strong constitution and a ferocious appetite which could put up with anything. Where another would have wasted away, he flourished.

In 1921 he received his degree in scientific massage. His teacher told him, "You must go to Germany to continue your studies."

Kersten agreed. Shortly afterwards he arrived in Berlin, completely penniless.

6

The problem of a lodging was the easiest to solve. Kersten's parents had an old friend in the German capital, the widow of a Professor Lube, who lived with her daughter, Elizabeth. The Lube family was not rich, but they were well-educated, cultured people. They were only too happy to provide refuge for the poor student. As for the other essentials—food, clothing, registration fees—Kersten got along as he had done at Helsinki, by doing whatever odd jobs he could find. He washed dishes, worked as a movie extra, and sometimes, at the recommendation of the Finnish Embassy, he acted as interpreter for Finnish tradesmen and industrialists who were passing through Berlin on business and did not speak German. There were good weeks and there were very bad ones. Kersten was not always able to satisfy his appetite, which was enormous. His clothing left much to be desired. The soles of his shoes often gaped. But he bore his poverty with patience. He was young, strong, proof against any test, and of a balanced and optimistic disposition.

Moreover, he had found someone to turn to in his worst moments: Elizabeth Lube, the younger lady of the house, but considerably older than he.

Their friendship was direct and spontaneous. Elizabeth was a very kind, intelligent, and active person. She needed an outlet for her inner resources, and this great young man who was so brave, healthy, cheerful, and poor, and who had landed on her mother's doorstep one morning, seemed the answer to her prayers. As for Felix Kersten, obliged once again to start life in a strange place, without money or family, how else could he respond to her unfailing devotion except with wholehearted gratitude and affection?

Then, too, Kersten had the liveliest appreciation for feminine companionship. He saw in the young ladies and women who attracted him the same creatures who graced the pages of the German and Russian romantics whom he had read so avidly. They were angels, they were poetic visions. He treated them with an old-fashioned gallantry and the most exalted respect. Perhaps this manner did not exactly go with his ruddy complexion, his premature stoutness, his calm and dignified bearing. But as it happened, the ladies adored him. He was a great success. Were his relations with them only platonic? It would be hard to believe; eating was not his only form of sensuality.

But with Elizabeth Lube his relations never went beyond the realm of pure friendship. It is possible that this reserve sprang from the difference in their ages, but it seems more likely that its real cause lay in a sort of unconscious prudence on the part of the two friends. Elizabeth Lube and Felix Kersten knew their friendship to be so rare and so precious that, by a kind of instinct, they kept it apart from the risks and upheavals which always threaten another sort of feeling. They were not mistaken, for their bond has lasted to this day, almost forty years. The wanderings of a lifetime, changes of fortune, of home, of family situation, the tragedy of Europe, and five terrible years for Kersten have only served to reinforce the strength and beauty of this spiritual tie formed in 1922 between the daughter of a good bourgeois family and the poor young student.

All this came about simply, day by day, without fancy words or gestures. Elizabeth Lube mended, washed, and ironed Kersten's linen and clothing. And when the day arrived that the young man was in desperate need of new shoes, Elizabeth Lube secretly sold (he did not know about it until much later) the one small diamond she had once inherited. While she darned and mended, Kersten told her of his hopes and dreams, or concentrated on his studies. He has said that for him she was both an older sister and a mother.

7

Professor Bier, the internationally known surgeon, was teaching in Berlin at that time. This distinguished master, who had received all the official honors, nonetheless took a passionate interest in certain medical techniques which the faculty looked upon as unorthodox: chiropractic, homeopathy, acupuncture, and above all, massage.

When Professor Bier heard that one of his students was trained in Finnish massage, he singled him out, became friendly with him, and told him one day, "Come to dinner tonight. I want you to meet someone who may interest you."

As Kersten made his way into the huge, brilliantly lighted rooms, he noticed sitting near his teacher a little old Chinese gentleman whose face, which was completely covered with tiny wrinkles, never stopped smiling above a scraggly gray beard.

"This is Dr. Ko," Professor Bier told Kersten.

The great surgeon had pronounced this name in a tone which surprised Kersten because of the deep respect it held. Dr. Ko did nothing, said nothing, at least at the beginning, to justify such a tone. Professor Bier carried the conversation almost singlehanded. The fragile old Chinese confined himself to shaking his head in short, rapid, polite nods and smiling interminably. From time to time the little black eyes that missed nothing would stop twinkling within the tiny slits of his half-shut lids, and survey Kersten with a remarkable intensity. Then wrinkles, smiles, and twinkling eyes would resume their lively and amiable little game.

Then all at once, in the most simple and unaffected way, Dr. Ko told the young man his story.

He was born in China, but he had grown up inside the walls of a monastery in northeastern Tibet. There he had been initiated from childhood not only in the teachings of philosophy, but also in the Chinese and Tibetan arts of healing as they have been handed down from generation to generation by the lama-doctors. And above all, the ancient and subtle art of massage. After he had devoted twenty years to these studies, the head of the monastery sent for him and said:

"We have nothing more to teach you in this part of the world. You will be given sufficient money to live in the Occident, so that you may study with the experts there."

The lama-doctor arrived in England, enrolled in one of the universities, and spent the time that was required to earn the degree of doctor. Then he set up practice in London.

"I treated my patients by using massage, as it is taught up there, in our Tibetan monasteries," said Dr. Ko. "It was not from pride that I did this. A lama, in his training, lays aside all vanities. It was because I thought that in Western science I was no better than a novice, surpassed by countless other excellent doctors. While on the other hand, I alone in that country was skilled in the methods of curing which have been practiced in China since the dawn of time."

"And Dr. Ko has done wonders," said Professor Bier. "His colleagues, of course, call him all sorts of names. I wrote him, and he has done us the honor of coming to work here in Berlin, under my absolute protection."

These words made a profound impression on Kersten. One of the foremost authorities in the world, a man with the best scientific training, had absolute confidence in this grotesque little creature, so wrinkled and yellow, from the rooftop of the world!

"I have told Dr. Ko about your studies in Finland," continued the professor, "and he asked me if he could meet you."

Dr. Ko rose, bowed, smiled, and announced, "We must leave our host. We have already imposed on his patience."

Professor Bier's home was in the neighborhood of the Tiergarten. Late strollers in the park that night might have seen, wandering among the dark groves and statues of royalty, two contrasting figures: one tall,

broad, and young, the other tiny, spare, and old. They were Dr. Ko
and Felix Kersten. The lama-doctor questioned the student exhaus-
tively. He wanted to know everything about him: his background, his
family, his temperament, his education, and above all, what he had
learned from his teachers at Helsinki.

"Very good, very good," said Dr. Ko at last. "I live not far from
here. Let us continue our conversation at my place."

As soon as they were in his apartment, Dr. Ko took off his clothes,
stretched out on the sofa, and asked Kersten, "Would you please
demonstrate your Finnish technique for me?"

Never had the young man concentrated so hard as he did on kneading this tiny yellow body, so fragile and parched. When at last he
straightened up from his work, he was very pleased with himself.

Dr. Ko dressed himself, regarded Kersten with his twinkling half-
shut eyes, and smiled.

"My young friend," said he, "you know nothing, absolutely nothing." He smiled again and went on, "But you are the one I have been
waiting for, for thirty years. According to my horoscope, fixed in Tibet
when I was still a novice, I was to meet this very year a young man
who would know nothing, and to whom I would teach everything. I
would like to take you for my pupil."

That was 1922.

The papers were beginning to speak of an inspired madman: Adolf
Hitler. And among his most fanatical supporters, they mentioned a
schoolmaster named Heinrich Himmler.

But these names meant nothing to Kersten, who was discovering
the wonderful art of Dr. Ko.

8

What Felix Kersten had learned at Helsinki and what Dr. Ko was revealing to him must both be described by the term "massage," since
the two schools had the common aim of giving the hands the power to
relieve and cure suffering. But as he absorbed the lessons of his new
teacher, Kersten came to realize that there was otherwise very little in
common between the Finnish school (which he knew, moreover, to be

unrivaled in Europe) and the tradition of the Far East whose basic principles and methods the old lama-doctor was passing on to him.

The Finnish method now began to seem like a primitive and almost blind groping in the dark, which could only hope to effect the most superficial, random, and temporary cures. The other method of manual therapy, the one with such ancient and distinguished origins, had at once the precision and versatility of wisdom and intuition. It went right to the core, to the marrow of the subject to be treated.

According to the Chinese and Tibetan science, as it was taught by Dr. Ko, the masseur's first duty was to find out, without any outside help and without paying any attention to the patient's complaints, the exact nature of the pain, and to ascertain its source. How, indeed, could one hope to cure an illness without knowing its origin?

To aid him in this crucial diagnosis, the practitioner had at his disposal the four pulses and nerve centers and networks of the human body which had been enumerated and recorded in Chinese medicine for centuries. But his only instrument of auscultation was the flesh on the tips of his fingers.

It was this flesh, then, that had to be trained, educated, refined, sensitized to the point where it could perceive the malady lurking under the skin, the fat, and the flesh, and determine which nerve group was affected. Only then was it of any use to know the outward gestures, that is the palm and finger movements which could influence the nerves in question and, thanks to the accuracy of the diagnosis, relieve or eliminate the pain.

Nevertheless, the mastering of these movements was not the most difficult part.

Obviously, to be completely familiar with the topography of the nervous system, to know just the degree of pressure, just the kneading action, just the delicate twists and turns necessary to correct a given weakness, and to be able to execute all these with the greatest efficacy, required a long and painstaking apprenticeship. Few pupils had the ability to succeed. But the essential secret of the art was the ability to locate with the tips of the fingers the essence of the malady, to measure its severity, and to know from what vital center it sprang.

20 . *The Man with the Miraculous Hands*

The most refined, extensive knowledge of the epidermis was not enough. In order to render the tiny tactile antennae capable of recognizing all the nerves of the human organism and of responding, as it were, to their plea, the practitioner had virtually to leave his own body and enter that of his patient. This could only be attained through the age-old methods of the great religious disciplines of the Far East which, by means of spiritual concentration, special respiratory exercises, and inner states taken from Yoga, bring the mind and senses to a degree of acuteness and intuition otherwise unattainable.

What seemed like second nature to Dr. Ko, who had been dedicated from infancy to the training and meditations of the lamas, was terribly difficult for a Westerner, particularly one of Kersten's age. But he had the ability to work at it, tremendous will power and also, of course, the aptitude.

For three years he spent every minute with Dr. Ko when he was not attending courses or working at the odd jobs by which he earned his living. Only then did Dr. Ko say that he was satisfied with him.

Having assisted the old lama in his work, Kersten had seen him perform some remarkable cures, some of which seemed almost miraculous. Of course they were limited to a very definite area; Dr. Ko did not claim that his therapeutic massage could cure everything. But its range was so great (for the nerves play a role in the total organism whose extent and importance Kersten would never have known without studying Chinese medicine) that it was beyond the dreams of the most ambitious practitioner.

In spite of the great poverty in which he continued to live, these three years went very quickly for Kersten. Not only did he follow Dr. Ko's teachings with a joy and admiration which grew greater every day, but he came to feel for his teacher a fondness and respect which also deepened as time went by.

There was nothing of the ascetic about Dr. Ko. To be sure, he forbade the use of alcohol and tobacco, which dulled the sense of touch. But Kersten had never formed the taste for these stimulants. On the other hand, the lama-doctor approved of eating well. He did his own cooking and often invited Kersten to share his excellent chicken broth with rice. As for physical relations with women, he considered them highly salutary for the proper balance of the nervous system.

Gentleness, courtesy, unselfishness, equanimity, and courage all contributed to Dr. Ko's calm and happy acceptance of life which never failed him. And Kersten, so big and robust, felt as if he were under the wing of the little old Chinese who never stopped smiling.

Thus the news he received one autumn morning in 1925 was quite a shock to him. Kersten had just arrived at his teacher's house. The latter told him very calmly, "I am leaving tomorrow to return to my monastery. I must begin to prepare myself for death. I have less than eight years to live."

Kersten stammered, "But that's impossible! You can't do it. . . . But how do you know?"

"From the most trustworthy source: the date was established long ago in my horoscope."

Dr. Ko's voice and smile had their habitual gentleness, but in his eyes Kersten saw an irrevocable decision.

It was only then, from the acuteness of his misery, from the internal uprooting he experienced, and the sense of isolation and exile that possessed him, that Kersten realized to what extent he was truly the disciple of this little yellowish, wrinkled man with his scrawny gray goatee.

"My mission is accomplished," continued Dr. Ko. "I have transmitted to you that which it was permitted to me to transmit. You are now ready to continue my work here. You will take over my patients."

There was nothing for Kersten to do but help his old teacher pack his bags. The following day Dr. Ko took the train for Le Havre, where he was to sail to Singapore, and from there return to his native Tibet.

And Kersten never heard of him again.

A HAPPY MAN

1

Kersten's material life was transformed almost overnight. Dr. Ko had a considerable practice, and his pupil's personality, his vigor, his substantial appearance, his natural charm and good manners, his kindliness, his youth, and the fact that he was a European who used the Eastern techniques with all the skill of an old lama—all this attracted so many patients that soon one had to sign up with Kersten three months in advance.

He rented a large apartment, filled it with fine furniture, bought a beautiful car, hired a chauffeur.

Elizabeth Lube supervised all these proceedings, and when all was in readiness, she came to keep house for him.

It was inevitable that such sudden and overwhelming success should arouse professional jealousy; but the spiteful words did not bother Kersten. He had the support of Professor Bier and other distinguished members of the faculty, and the results of his technique spoke for themselves.

His reputation began to spread outside Germany.

In 1928 Queen Wilhelmina of Holland summoned Kersten to The Hague to examine her husband, Prince Hendrik.

Kersten examined the prince with the tips of his fingers, according to the method he had learned from his Tibetan master, and found a very serious case of heart disease. To be sure, other physicians had given the same diagnosis. But the best of them had not been able to bring the prince out of his state of prostration and had given him only six months to live. Kersten restored him immediately, and for years to follow, to normal activity.

This trip had a strange effect on Kersten: he, who had never set foot in Holland before, found from the very first that he was wonderfully at ease, in complete harmony with the country and the people. He told himself it was impossible that this could be the call of race, of the blood. His family had left Holland more than five hundred years ago, then they had lived at Göttingen, then East Prussia, finally the Baltic. The blood could scarcely be pure. And yet it seemed to Kersten that in Holland he had found his true home, his natural habitat.

The favor he enjoyed with royalty and ordinary people alike after Prince Hendrik's recovery, hastened and justified this instinctive attraction. Accustomed as he was to weighing his decisions slowly and carefully, Kersten resolved then and there to settle in the Netherlands.

He kept his apartment in Berlin to receive his German patients, but he established his legal residence at The Hague.

From that time on, he divided his life between the two capitals. The domestic routine of both households was supervised by Elizabeth Lube. At once his housekeeper and his private secretary, she continued to be Kersten's most loyal and devoted friend.

It was not long before she had a third household to look after.

Numbered among Kersten's patients was one Auguste Rosterg, owner of potash mines and factories, one of the most powerful businessmen in Germany. His fortune at that time was estimated at 300,-000,000 marks.

He suffered from chronic headaches, vague shooting pains in the stomach, circulatory troubles, excruciating fatigue, exhausting insomnia—in short, from that malady peculiar to great businessmen, men consumed by their work, their ambitions, and their responsibilities.

Rosterg had been to the most celebrated specialists. He had taken medicine and followed cures of all kinds. Nothing had helped. The very rest which was prescribed to him as a last resort had become the worst torture of all. Kersten was his only hope.

Now, overwork in its extreme form, nervous collapse, was precisely the area in which Dr. Ko's therapy was most effective, because it operated on the nervous system itself. Kersten relieved, liberated, saved Auguste Rosterg.

When the treatment was over, the industrialist asked Kersten his fee.

Kersten named his standard figure for a successful cure: five thousand marks.

The industrialist made out a check. As he slipped it into his billfold, Kersten noticed that the first digit which appeared on it was the number 1. He started to bring it to Rosterg's attention, but a sort of embarrassment in the face of such pettiness restrained him. Leave it to the rich to be the worst misers of all. And after all, it won't ruin me, thought Kersten, philosophical as always.

The next day he took the check to his bank. Just as he was leaving the window, the clerk called him back:

"Doctor, doctor," he exclaimed, "you have left out two zeros on your deposit slip."

"I don't understand," said Kersten.

"This check is not for one thousand marks, but one hundred thousand marks," the clerk insisted.

"What are you talking about?" said Kersten.

"You have written one thousand marks," said the clerk.

"Well?"

"But, look for yourself, sir, the check is made out for one hundred thousand marks."

Forgetting his usual Olympian dignity, Kersten snatched the check. It was indeed made out for 100,000 marks.

For a few moments, Kersten stared dumfounded at this extravagant proof of a gratitude which he had mistaken for greed.

"Yes, of course . . . I am a little absent-minded today," he told the employee at last.

When he got home he told the story to Elizabeth Lube. She advised him to waste no time in using the money to acquire a piece of property. And so it was that Kersten came to own Hartzwalde: three hundred hectares of meadows and forests, sixty kilometers east of Berlin.

2

The year was 1931. By now Hitler had a large, powerfully organized and fanatical party. He had at his command inexhaustible resources and well-trained troops, ready to kill at a word from him.

Roehm was head of the S.A.

Himmler had the command of the S.S., the personal guard, janissaries, and executioners of the supreme ruler.

And Hitler shouted in a voice which became every day more hysterical and more confident that he would soon be lord of Germany, and then of Europe.

But people are such that the majority of them do not see, do not want to see, bad omens.

Kersten, moreover, had absolutely no interest in politics. He did not read the papers; it was through his patients that he learned of the news of the world. Good or bad, his philosophy about it was simply: why waste time worrying about what one can't do anything about?

His own time was taken up more and more every day by his profession. At The Hague, in Berlin, patients came to him in such numbers that his working day started at eight o'clock in the morning and lasted well into the night. He did not complain; he enjoyed his work and liked his patients. He treated many of them free of charge.

His reputation continued to grow. Since 1930, he had paid an annual visit to Rome, where he was called in the service of the royal family.*

In what little leisure time was left him by his activities in three capitals, Kersten filled his house in The Hague with the paintings of old Flemish masters, organized his estate at Hartzwalde,† and, in Berlin as well as The Hague, courted many beautiful women. Prolonged intrigues, momentary infatuations, more serious affairs, all these adventures became confused and blended together, but always pleasantly, freely, in an atmosphere of easy romanticism, sentimental grace, and good humor.

So engrossed was Kersten in his duties and pleasures that he was not even aware of Hitler's coming to power.

The idol of the Nazi party had held the post of chancellor of the Reich for three days before Kersten heard of it, by chance, in conversation with one of his patients. The news did not upset him very much. Was he not a Finnish citizen? Was not his legal residence in Holland? Were his patients about to desert him? Would the women stop smiling at him?

He was happy, and determined to remain that way.

The following year, 1934, in the month of June, Hitler, with a *sang-froid,* a savagery, and a perfection in the art of murder which terrified the world, had Roehm, the general of the S.A. who threatened to overshadow him, trapped and assassinated along with his most important officers.

The executioners on that bloody night were hand-picked S.S. men under their leader, Heinrich Himmler. From that day the name of this former schoolmaster, relatively obscure up to then, acquired an ominous ring. The Grand Inquisitor, the great butcher of Hitler's regime had begun to emerge into the light of day.

During his regular and frequent stays in Berlin, Kersten heard his patients and friends speak of Himmler more and more often, and each time with greater aversion and fear. He stood for the S.S., the Gestapo, torture, concentration camps.

* See Appendix, Note 1.
† See Appendix, Note 2.

The majority of Kersten's patients—intellectuals and upper middle-class liberals, or the poor people whom he treated for nothing—feared, despised, or were ashamed of Nazism. Kersten shared their feeling. His instinctive sense of justice, his deep-rooted, inborn goodness, his love of tolerance, decency, and moderation, everything in him was shocked and offended by the gross arrogance, the racial superstition, the police-state tactics, the fanatical adoration of the Führer, everything, in short, on which the Third Reich depended.

But, sensible and easygoing man that he was, he forced himself not to dwell on injustices he could do nothing about, and to get out of life as much pleasure as he could.

3

He succeeded admirably.

Well fed, ruddy with health, great eater, and favorite with the ladies, prudent but expansive, he systematically made his rounds: The Hague, Berlin, Rome, had his appointments fixed months in advance, saw, outside of his professional duties, only people he liked, took up with charming women, quietly did good and, with the help of his faithful friend, Elizabeth Lube, managed his property without ostentation.

The state of bachelorhood suited this type of life perfectly, and Kersten fully intended to remain single. When his friends pointed out to him that he was almost forty and ought to be thinking about marriage, he would answer that on this subject he had made a solemn vow. Then, over his amiable features would come that special smile which even today means he is dreaming of food.

"When I was a little boy at Dorpat," he would say, "my mother used to make a Russian dish called *rassol,* which I adored. I've never had it since. You can't get it in any restaurant. The day I taste it again . . . then, maybe, I'll get married out of sheer joy."

In 1937, at the end of February, Kersten, who had just finished a series of treatments at Berlin, was getting ready to return to The Hague.

On the eve of his departure he was invited to dine with friends—a retired German colonel and his wife, who was from Riga. It was an intimate party, planned only for Kersten and Elizabeth Lube. At the last minute, however, there arrived unexpectedly from Silesia a young girl whose family were very good friends of Kersten's host and hostess. Her name was Irmgard Neuschaffer.

In spite of his weakness for pretty faces, Kersten paid very little attention to the newcomer at first. And with good reason: for the first dish which was set before the speechless, unbelieving, overjoyed man was—the famous *rassol* of his childhood! At least, it looked exactly like it. Kersten tasted it. It was indeed a *rassol,* and an excellent one.

The hostess, who had been brought up in the Baltic, had remembered the recipe. Kersten filled his plate again and again. Nor did this prevent him from doing justice to the rest of the meal, which lasted a full three hours.

It was an unforgettable occasion. . . . Kersten was mellow, even lyrical. He looked at Irmgard Neuschaffer, who was charming, lively, and in the bloom of youth, and suddenly said to himself: "I'll marry that girl."

Without wasting a moment, he asked her whether or not she was engaged.

"No," was the reply. "But why?"

"Because in that case, we are free to marry."

"All the same, it's a little sudden," she answered, laughing. "Let us write to each other first."

Everything was arranged by letter. After two months of correspondence, they were engaged. Another two months, and they set the date. Kersten had not seen Irmgard since the night of the *rassol* when he arrived at the girl's home for the wedding.

Irmgard's father was the head of the forest rangers of the grand duchy of Hesse-Darmstadt. He lived in the middle of a huge, romantic forest, in a very old chateau belonging to the grand duke. Adjoining it was a splendid church which had been weathered by the centuries. It was here that the marriage took place.

After it was over, Kersten brought his young wife to Dorpat. His mother had died there some years before, but his father, robust and tireless for all his eighty-seven years, was still working his little plot of land with as much energy and good humor as if he were in the prime of life.

Next, the newlyweds traveled to Finland and to Berlin, where Kersten introduced Irmgard to his friends. The trip ended at The Hague.

There Kersten gave a magnificent party which brought together, amid the crystal, the massive chandeliers, and the paintings of old Flemish masters, everyone of importance in Dutch society, business, politics, or army.

The news spread through the town like wildfire: "The good Dr. Kersten is married." And many lovely women sighed.

4

In perfect health, rich, happy in his work, beloved by his patients, pampered by his young wife Irmgard, and by Elizabeth Lube, his old friend, plump, smiling, and confident, Kersten worked now at The Hague, now in Berlin, now in Rome, and relaxed at his estate, Hartzwalde.

It was there that his first son was born, with Kersten himself assisting at his wife's delivery.

Everything smiled on Kersten; his happiness was without flaw.

To be sure, during the year of the good doctor's marriage, Hitler had annexed Austria, and during the one in which his son was born, Hitler, having forced England and France to give way at Munich, had seized a piece of Czechoslovakia.

Looming over the invaded countries, as well as over Germany herself, around the figure of the lord of the swastika, was the sinister constellation of his right-hand men: Goering the fox, Goebbels the spreader of lies, Ribbentrop the villain, Streicher the scourge of the Jews. But above them all rose ever higher the star of that vile monster, the "faithful Heinrich," Himmler the executioner.

His name came to epitomize all the cruelty, the vileness, and the horror of the regime. The entire population was filled with loathing, terror, and hatred for the head of the secret police, the overseer of the concentration camps, the master of torture.

Even in his own party he was hated and despised.

30. *The Man with the Miraculous Hands*

Everything that Hitler and Himmler stood for was utterly repugnant to Felix Kersten. He did everything he could, in his prudent but generous way, to help the victims of Nazism whom he heard about or whom fate threw in his path. Both his mind and his heart rebelled against the reign of the brute.

But as greedy for happiness as he was for good food, he closed his eyes and ears to the warnings. He refused to let the banquet of his peaceful, pleasant existence be spoiled by the bitter taste of fear. He barricaded himself tightly behind the walls of his profession, his friendships, his family, and his happiness.

For if any man has ever known for ten years that rare thing, complete and perfect happiness, that man was Felix Kersten. And he knew it; he even boasted of it.

The gods have never stood for that.

THE BEAST IN HIS DEN

1

Rosterg, the German potash magnate whose generosity was responsible for Kersten's acquiring his estate Hartzwalde, was closely associated with a certain Auguste Diehn, a man of advanced years and of great intelligence and integrity. He was one of Kersten's oldest patients and also one of his dearest friends.

Toward the end of the year 1938, Diehn came to see the doctor, who was then in Berlin. Kersten noticed at once that his friend was nervous and ill at ease.

"You're overworked again?" he asked anxiously. "You've come for another treatment?"

"No, I am not here for myself," replied Diehn, averting his eyes.

"Rosterg?"

"No."

There was a silence.

"Would you be willing to examine Himmler?" Diehn asked abruptly.

"Who?" exclaimed Kersten.

"Himmler . . . Heinrich Himmler."

"Ah! No! Thank you very much," said Kersten. "I've been able to avoid having anything to do with that element, up to now, and I have no intention of starting with the worst of them."

There was another silence, a much longer one. Diehn took up the conversation with a visible effort.

"I have never asked you to do anything, Doctor," he said. "But today I am going to have to insist . . . for Rosterg's sake, as well as my own. You see, it seems that Himmler and Ley * are planning to nationalize the potash industry. Rosterg is the first target. Well, we know from experience, he and I, the influence you have over your patients, when you relieve their sufferings. . . . You can see, then . . ."

Auguste Diehn stopped speaking and bowed his head. Kersten said nothing, but silently studied the familiar, gray-haired profile. He remembered the complete confidence Diehn had had in him at the start of his career, the almost paternal feeling he had shown him, all the important patients, including Rosterg, whom he owed to this man. And above all, he guessed what it must have cost a man of his age, of his dignity and sensitivity, to make the request he had just heard. But on the other hand, how could he have anything to do with Himmler when, for his own peace of mind and inner security, he had forbidden himself even to think about the regime of which the head of the S.S. and the Gestapo was the most hateful personification?

"It would be a great service," whispered Auguste Diehn. "And then, is it not your professional duty to treat anyone who is sick?"

"Very well, I will do it," sighed Kersten.

* Minister of labor.

2

So religiously did he guard his own peace of mind that Kersten forced himself to forget his conversation with Diehn as soon as it was over. And for several months nothing happened to remind him of it.

He had been back at The Hague for some time when, in the first week of March, 1939, he received a telephone call from Germany. He recognized Rosterg's voice.

"You must come to Berlin immediately," the great industrialist told him briefly. "The time has come for the examination Diehn spoke to you about."

Kersten's system for banishing unpleasant thoughts was an efficient one. He did not understand what Rosterg was talking about and he asked anxiously, "Is Diehn sick? Does he need me?"

For several seconds Kersten heard only the buzzing of the telephone wires. Then he heard Rosterg's voice again, but this time it was much lower and had a guarded quality.

"No, this does not concern Diehn himself. It concerns a friend."

It was Rosterg's sudden reticence and his obvious fear of being overheard that jogged Kersten's memory: the name Rosterg did not dare pronounce was the name of Himmler.

Ah! thought Kersten. My promise . . . the moment has come. . . . I was hoping the thing had been forgotten, buried. . . .

The voice from Germany came through again:

"You remember . . . the important friend."

The tone of voice was more stifled than ever, and the manner more hurried.

Kersten gripped the receiver very hard with his broad fingers.

This secret fear on the part of a magnate, a powerful man, a giant of industry and finance was slightly chilling. In this voice, ordinarily so imperious, now so fearful, Kersten sensed the physical presence of a terrifying new world, a world of mistrust, of surveillance, of treachery, a world that lived in fear of the police; a world whose air was not fit for honest men to breathe.

So much the worse for me, he thought. I didn't have to give my word.

He drew a deep breath and said, "Very well. I will be there tomorrow."

3

In prewar Berlin, when the capital of the Third Reich was still undamaged, at number eight Prinz Albert Strasse, near Potsdam Square, there was a very large building over which floated a group of flags bearing swastikas.

There was nothing unusual about the flags; all public buildings were so decorated. And the house, except for its height, was very much like the others, heavy and gray, that surrounded it. However, when people walked by that particular house they hastened their steps, lowered their heads, or averted their eyes. For they knew that this dull-looking structure, which was guarded night and day by sentries as stiff as robots, housed a dread organization which worked day and night toward the enslavement and mutilation of the human mind and body. There were located the general headquarters and the Chancellery of the Reichsführer, Heinrich Himmler, head of the S.S., lord of the Gestapo.

On the tenth of March in the year 1939, a handsome civilian automobile pulled up in front of this house. A chauffeur in splendid livery got out to open the door and drew back to let a man of some forty years pass by. He was tall, stout, well dressed, measured in his movements, with pleasant features and a rosy complexion. For a moment he let his violet-blue eyes rest on the façade of the building. Then he made his way in a dignified manner to the front door. He was met by a soldier in the uniform of the S.S.

"What do you want?" demanded the sentinel.

"To see the Reichsführer," calmly replied the rosy-cheeked stranger.

"The Reichsführer in person?"

"In person."

If the soldier was surprised, he did not show it. He had been trained not to show his feelings.

"Write your name on this piece of paper," said the soldier. Then he disappeared into the building.

The other soldiers continued to stand guard. From time to time, out of the corners of their eyes, set in faces as impassive as blocks of wood and squeezed into helmets which came down to their eyebrows, they glanced at this man who asked so calmly to see—in person—their Reichsführer, the most dreaded man in all Germany.

Who could he be? He had nothing in common with the people who usually appeared at the headquarters of Prinz Albert Strasse: S.S. officers, high-ranking policemen, secret agents, informers, suspects called up for interrogation.

This man showed neither arrogance, nor haste, nor fear, nor servility, nor cruelty, nor cunning. He was simply a solid-looking citizen, well fed, poised, peaceable. With his hands folded across his plump stomach, he was waiting patiently, without anxiety.

"Heil Hitler!" said the officer, extending his arm in the standard Nazi salute.

The man with the pink cheeks and the blue eyes bordering on violet lifted his hat very politely and answered, "Good day, Lieutenant."

"Follow me," said the officer. In his tone and manner there was considerable respect.

The front door closed after the two men. The soldiers at attention could not refrain from exchanging a quick look of amazement.

4

The hall leading into the headquarters of the S.S. was very wide and high. There was a great deal of activity, but it was an ordered, precise activity. Officers of all ranks, messengers, couriers, orderlies went up and down the stairs leading to the floors above, emerged from or disappeared into corridors, exchanged salutes, gave or received orders. All these men wore the uniform of the S.S., and all the uniforms, from the generals down to the common soldiers, were spotless and precise, and worn with that peculiar insolence which one finds in the elite troops of a demanding leader.

Kersten, his hands in the pockets of his warm woolen overcoat and a felt hat on his head, the only civilian in this military crowd, crossed the hall of the S.S. headquarters. He stared in amazement at the guards who were stationed everywhere, rifles in their hands.

Does Himmler have to have all these arms for his security? wondered the doctor.

He was still unaware of the fact that the building was full of political prisoners. He did not know that, in the cellars below the very flagstones he was treading with his calm and dignified step, the executioners of the Gestapo were carrying on their merciless interrogations. Nevertheless, he found himself thinking, So this is the den of the beast. At the same time, he felt no fear. He was a man of good sense and steady nerves. He knew that Himmler could do nothing to him, and the machinery of his power aroused in the doctor's mind no more than a vague curiosity.

What is this interview going to be like? he wondered.

Following the officer who was conducting him, Kersten walked up an enormous marble staircase, then another. Next he was led to a sort of waiting room. He scarcely had time to say to himself, with a sort of philosophical amusement, "Look where Dr. Ko has brought me," when another officer, who wore the insignia of an aide-de-camp, came for him. They entered a corridor, but when they reached the middle of it, the officer stopped the visitor for a fleeting instant with a brief, barely perceptible gesture—just long enough for the X-ray mechanism hidden at that spot in the wall to reveal that the new arrival was unarmed.

Then the aide-de-camp led Kersten, who had noticed nothing, toward the door at the end of the corridor. He raised his hand to knock on the dark wood. But before he had a chance to do so, the door flew open, and a man in the uniform of a general of the S.S. appeared in the doorway. He was slight, with narrow shoulders. Steel-rimmed spectacles framed eyes of a deep gray. He had prominent, Mongoloid cheekbones. It was Himmler.

His face, which had deep hollows, was the color of beeswax, and his puny body was gnarled with pains which he could not succeed in controlling. With a clammy, thin, and bony hand, which was not without beauty, he seized the strong and plump hand of Kersten, and drawing the doctor inside the room, he burst out at once:

"Thank you for coming, Doctor. I have heard a great deal about you. Perhaps you will be able to relieve these excruciating stomach pains which permit me neither to walk or sit still."

Himmler released Kersten's hand. His unpleasant face became even more waxen. He continued:

"Not a single doctor in Germany has succeeded. But Messrs. Rosterg and Diehn have assured me that where others fail, you obtain results."

Without answering, arms at his sides, Kersten studied the Mongoloid cheekbones, the sparse hair, the receding chin.

So this is the head, he was thinking, which conceives, organizes, and puts into effect the measures which are a source of terror to the Germans and of horror to all civilized men. . . .

But Himmler was speaking again.

"Doctor, do you think you can help me?" he asked. "I would be infinitely grateful to you."

In those livid and flabby features, in the depths of these dull gray eyes, Kersten recognized the familiar appeal of suffering human flesh. Himmler was no more to him than a sick person like any other.

Kersten looked around the room. It was soberly furnished: a large desk covered with papers, a few chairs, and a long divan.

"Will you please remove your tunic and shirt and unbutton the top of your trousers, Reichsführer?" asked Kersten.

"At once, Doctor, at once," cried Himmler eagerly.

He stripped to the waist: he had round shoulders, narrower than the torso, flabby skin, poor muscles, and a prominent stomach.

"Please stretch out flat, on your back, Reichsführer," said Kersten.

Himmler lay down. Kersten drew a chair up to the divan and eased himself onto it. He placed his hands on the outstretched body.

5

If I seem to describe the following scene as if I had actually been present myself, the explanation is simple: an over-all fatigue sent me to Dr. Kersten, and every day for two weeks, under those hands which worked and revived my tired nerves, I observed him as closely as I could.

I even asked him once, "When you were treating Himmler, did you use the same method, the same manner, the same attitude?"

He looked at me with surprise, and answered, "But of course, exactly the same as with all my patients."

Of course, Kersten was twenty years younger then. But he belongs to that species of men who, because of some basic quality of their facial structure and general bearing remain, in spite of the signs of age, remarkably true to their youthful image. I had only to overlook a few lines in his face—and that was easy to do—and a certain heaviness in his limbs, and behold, I could visualize that first encounter.

6

Felix Kersten settled himself comfortably in a chair, which groaned under his weight, and extended his hands toward Himmler's bare and puny body.

Twenty years before, at Helsinki, the head doctor of the military hospital had called these hands "good." Indeed, it had been their strength, their size, and their skill which had virtually thrust upon Kersten the choice of his profession, the direction his life was to take. They were large, thick, fleshy, and warm. Each finger had, under its short, close-cut nail, a sort of swelling which was much more highly developed, much fleshier than is ordinarily the case. This was a kind of little antenna, and it was endowed with unusual acuteness and sensitivity.

The hands began to move. On one of them there sparkled, with a bluish light, the ring on which were inscribed the arms which in the sixteenth century Charles V had granted to the doctor's ancestor, Andreas Kersten, sheriff of Göttingen.

The fingers glided over the smooth skin. Their tips skimmed in turn over Himmler's throat, chest, heart, and stomach. At first their touch was light, barely perceptible. Then the antennae began to stop at certain spots, to press down, to seek, to listen. . . .

A natural gift, supplemented by a long and arduous period of training, had provided them with a clairvoyance unknown to ordinary men. And even that was not all. For in order for Dr. Ko's technique to be fully effective, in order for the finger tips to be able to tell the doctor that a certain tissue was dangerously enlarged or reduced, or that a certain nerve group was in a serious state of deficiency or fatigue, he had to have an absolute concentration, which cleared the consciousness and the senses of all but a single object and a single concern.

The doctor must no longer see or hear. The sense of smell likewise must cease to function. The tactile antennae, whose receptivity was marvelously strengthened by the temporary suspension of the other senses, became the sole means of communication with the world. And this world was limited to the body that was being examined, sounded, as it were, by the tips of the fingers. And their findings were in turn transmitted to a mind that had been emptied of every other preoccupation and closed to every other impression.

To arrive at this state no longer required any effort for Kersten, and the fact that the patient was Himmler in no way affected his facility. After three years of exercises and training with the lama-doctor, and fifteen years of daily practice, every hour of the day, he immediately attained the required degree of concentration.

However, in these moments his face underwent an extraordinary change. The features remained the same, to be sure. Kersten still had the same high, wide forehead, the same domelike head, the same glossy, dark blond hair that was just beginning to lighten. Just above the fine eyebrows, with the slightly devilish arch to them, the two parallel lines, like little furrows, were still there. The deep-set eyes retained their deep blue color, often turning to a brighter, more violet hue. Between the firm, rosy cheeks was the same mouth: small and delicate, sensitive and sensual. The long, unusually shaped ears were still closely fitted to the sides of the head.

Yes, the same features, the same patterns made up the face. But the tide that Kersten had released within himself and to which he had temporarily abandoned himself, had transformed its expression, its meaning, and, it almost seemed, its very substance. The lines disappeared, the flesh lost its heaviness, the mouth no longer had its sensual look. At last, the eyelids were shut; and he no longer resembled the good, solid Flemish burgomaster, painted by some old master, but one of those little Buddha figures from the Far East.

Himmler, rigid and contorted by the pain which tormented him without respite, never took his eyes off that oriental face. What an extraordinary doctor! Kersten had not asked him a single question. The other doctors—and Himmler had had so many of them that he had forgotten the number—had without exception asked him a great many questions. And he, with the willingness to oblige of all those who suffer from a chronic ailment, had described, each time in greater detail, the cramps which racked him and robbed him of all his energy. Each time, he had gone minutely into the causes which dated from his childhood: two paratyphoids, two attacks of pernicious dysentery, a bad case of food poisoning from fish. The doctors had taken notes, pondered, and discussed. Then there had been radiographs, examinations, analyses, blood tests. While this one . . . .

Suddenly, Himmler gave a cry. The fingers, up to now so light and velvety as they glided over the surface of his body, had just pressed brutally on a spot in the stomach from which the pain burst forth like a wave of fire.

"Very good . . . hold still," said Kersten softly.

Under the pressure of his hand, another tongue of pain burned, ravaged Himmler's intestines. Then another, and still another. The Reichsführer groaned and chewed his lips. His brow was wet with perspiration.

"That is very painful, isn't it?" asked Kersten each time.

"Terribly," answered Himmler between clenched teeth.

At last Kersten placed his hands on his knees, and opened his eyes.

"Now I see," said he. "It is the stomach, of course, but especially the sympathetic nervous system. There is nothing more painful than that . . . and your chronically overstrained nerves only serve to make your condition worse."

"Can you help me?" asked Himmler.

And again the wan and lusterless face expressed humble supplication, and the dull eyes begged for relief.

"We shall find that out right now," said Kersten.

He raised his arms, stretched his hands, worked his palms and fingers, to give them as much elasticity and vigor as possible, and went to work. This time he did not grope, for he knew exactly where to apply his effort. He thrust his fingers deep into his patient's stomach at the required spot, seized firmly and accurately the roll of flesh thus formed, and squeezed it, kneaded it, twisted it, knotted and unknotted it, in order to reach and waken the affected nerves through the skin, the fat, and the flesh.

At every movement, Himmler started with a stifled cry. But this time the pain was no longer blind, meaningless pain; it followed a definite course, as if it had a purpose.

After some manipulation, Kersten dropped his arms. His body slackened like that of a boxer between rounds, and he asked:

"How do you feel?"

Himmler paused a moment before answering. He seemed to be listening to what was taking place in his body, unable to believe what he heard. Finally he said hesitantly:

"I feel . . . yes, it's amazing . . . I feel better."

"Then let us continue," said Kersten.

His hands—those ruthlessly efficient hands—resumed their work. Once more, pain ran the length of the exhausted nerves like a cracking flame along an electric wire. But this time, even though too great a pressure or too violent a twist still caused him to gasp or cry out, Himmler had confidence. And this confidence helped the doctor.

After ten minutes Kersten stopped and said, "That will do for the first time."

Himmler appeared not to have heard him. He did not move; he scarcely breathed. He seemed to be afraid that the slightest movement, the shallowest breath would upset an inner balance of great fragility. His face expressed astonishment, disbelief.

"You can get up now," said Kersten.

Himmler raised his body slowly, carefully, as if it contained a priceless treasure. Then, in the same manner, he placed his feet on the floor. His trousers, which had been unbuttoned, slid down. He made an abrupt, instinctive movement to recover them. Then, frightened by the possible consequences of this movement, he remained frozen, clutching the trousers with paralyzed fingers. But his physical relief, the incomparable peace which follows the disappearance of unbearable pain, still remained.

Himmler fixed Kersten with a look which, behind the glass of the spectacles, revealed a kind of bewilderment.

"Am I dreaming? Is it possible? The pain is gone . . . completely gone."

He caught his breath and went on, more to himself than to Kersten, "No medicine works. . . . Even morphine has lost its effect . . . and now, in a few minutes— No, I would never have believed it."

With his free hand, Himmler stroked his stomach with the air of one who touches a miracle.

"Do you really think you can cure my cramps?" he cried.

"I believe so," said Kersten. "There are certain nerves which seem to be afflicted, and my treatment works directly on the nerves."

Himmler rose from the divan where he was sitting and came over to Kersten.

"Doctor," he said, "I want to keep you near me."

And without giving Kersten a chance to answer, he added:

"I will have you registered at once in the S.S. With the rank of colonel."

Kersten started. He looked uneasily at this puny, half-naked man who was still holding his trousers up. But this man, because he had ceased to suffer, had recovered the sense of his omnipotence. And he interpreted the doctor's surprise in his own way:

"It makes no difference that you are a foreigner. In the S.S., whatever I say goes. I am the Reichsführer. Just say the word, and you are a full colonel, with the rank, the pay, the uniform."

For a moment, the picture of himself as an S.S. officer flashed through Kersten's mind—he who was so big and easygoing, so fond of loose, comfortable clothing and soft materials—and it was all he could do to keep from laughing. But Himmler's eyes were fixed on him, and his whole manner indicated what an honor he was paying Kersten in making him this proposal.

"Yes, Doctor," he continued solemnly, "I give you my word: full colonel."

Kersten lowered his head slightly to show gratitude. He had the sense of entering a realm where the familiar values were reversed.

When one is with madmen, he thought, one must play their game.

He answered gravely, "Reichsführer, I am only too sensible of the honor you do me. But, unfortunately, it is impossible for me to accept it."

He went on to explain that he lived in Holland, that he had a home there, a family, an established routine, and a great many patients.

"But," he said, "should you have need of me, I can return. Moreover, I am not leaving at once, I am staying in Berlin for two weeks to see my patients here."

"Then, include me among them, Doctor. Come every day, I beg of you," cried Himmler.

He seized his shirt, put it on over his sloping shoulders, his prominent shoulder blades, and his protruding stomach, buttoned his trousers, tied his tie, put on his tunic with the insignia of an S.S. general, and pressed a buzzer.

The aide-de-camp entered and saluted.

"Dr. Kersten is always welcome here," Himmler told him. "It is an order. Let it be known by everyone."

7

Every morning the miracle was renewed. Every morning, the fangs and claws of the pain were removed by the hands which Himmler came to love even for the suffering they inflicted on him—just as the addict learns to cherish the prick of the needle which injects the drug he longs for.

But here it was not a question of a drug or an instrument. All the well-being, the felicity were lodged in the fingers of a man, of a big kindly doctor with a good face, a good smile, and good hands.

This is why the Reichsführer looked upon Kersten as a sort of magician, a sorcerer.

Accustomed as the doctor was to the surprise, the delighted gratitude of those whom he freed from torments of which they no longer expected to be cured, the behavior of Himmler left him dumfounded. Never had any one of his patients shown him such veneration, such exaltation that bordered on superstition. With Himmler, Kersten felt as if he were dealing with a sickly child.

And this man, second in power only to Hitler, and even more dreaded than Hitler, this man whose duty it was to keep the highest and most terrible secrets of state, proved to be unbelievably indiscreet. Relaxed and softened by the doctor's hands, in a drunken state of bliss in which the instinct of caution was suspended, Himmler was as free and abandoned as normally he was morbidly suspicious of everything and everyone.

These confessions were all made during the treatments. Kersten had established a pattern of stopping every five minutes or so to give the nerves a chance to rest. Thus each session, which lasted an hour, contained several intervals, and during these intervals Kersten encouraged conversation.

In order to understand the extraordinary story which begins to unfold here, one must try to imagine Himmler in those moments of calm.

Picture him, emerging from horrible whirlpools of pain to a miraculously calm surface. His bare, bruised body is bathed by and swims in a limitless sea of pleasure. He sees the hands which have rescued him from the depths: they are resting on the doctor's knees, or are crossed on his ample stomach. Above them, the calm, powerful chest and shoulders. And above that smiles the broad, rosy, and pleasant face, with its wise and kindly eyes. Everything about this good-natured magician invites friendship and confidence. And the Reichsführer, doubly overcome, first by the pain, and then by the pain's defeat, the Reichsführer whose whole life is devoted to the unthinking performance of the most secret, sordid, and brutal tasks, and who lives only among policemen, spies, fanatics, and hangmen, the Reichsführer

Heinrich Himmler has an unconquerable desire to talk, finally and for once in his life, without reserve, without fear, without design.

Naturally enough, he begins to chat about himself, about his illness. He has always been afraid of cancer; his father died of it. Kersten reassures him. Next, Himmler lets himself go a little further in confession. His suffering is not only physical; he is ashamed of himself. He fiercely hides his pains, his nausea, his agony. No one about him must even suspect his condition.

"But why?" wonders Kersten. "It is no disgrace to be sick."

"It is when one is in charge of the S.S., the elite of the German nation, which is in turn the elite of the world," answers Himmler, and he is off.

Kersten now listens to a long lecture on the Germanic race and the destined glory of the S.S., its purest essence. To this end, Himmler chooses the soldiers himself, and always on the same model: tall, athletic, blond, and blue-eyed. They must be tireless, inured to all hardships and, on the psychological level, as hard on themselves as they are on others. How could he, Himmler, the Reichsführer of these men whom he is training to be supermen, how could he let them see his own bodily misery?

All at once, his words take a dogmatic turn. He dwells interminably on the racial superiority of the Germanic people, and on the signs which prove it: tall stature, long skull, light hair, blue eyes. Whoever does not possess these attributes is not a German worthy of his race.

For all his considerable self-control, Kersten has a hard time concealing his surprise at these words when right under his nose is the wretched body which he has just finished kneading and to which he will soon return, the Mongoloid cheekbones, the round head, the black hair, and the dull gray eyes of his patient. Indeed, Himmler himself says:

"I am Bavarian, and the Bavarians, who are mostly dark, do not have the characteristics of which I speak. But they compensate for this deficiency by their singular devotion to the Führer. For the true German race, the purity of the Germanic blood are measured first of all by a man's love of Hitler."

The dull, spiritless eyes suddenly light up, and the monotonous voice vibrates with an extraordinary emotion. Himmler has pronounced the name of his demigod.

Now there is no stopping him. Hitler is a genius such as only appears once every thousand years, and the greatest among them. He is a predetermined being, one inspired. He is all-wise, all-powerful. The German people have only to follow him blindly in order to reach the zenith of their history.

At the end of a week Himmler had formed the habit of thinking out loud in front of his doctor.

At the beginning of the second week of the treatment, during one of the periods when Kersten was relaxing with his hands resting on his stomach, the Reichsführer, who was undressed and stretched out on the couch, said calmly:

"We will soon be at war. . . ."

Kersten's hands, which had been lightly interlaced, locked tightly together, but he did not move. In dealing with Himmler, he had learned to manipulate not only his patient's nerves, but also, sometimes, his psychological reactions.

"War!" he exclaimed. "Good heavens! But why?"

Himmler raised himself up slightly on his elbows and answered excitedly:

"When I make such an announcement, it is because I know it to be true. There will be a war because Hitler wants one."

The voice of this puny, half-naked man who was guardian of the most terrible secrets of the Third Reich, rose a few tones.

"The Führer wants war because he believes it is important for the good of the German people. War makes men stronger and more virile."

Himmler lay down full length again on the divan and added a trifle condescendingly, as if he were reassuring a frightened child:

"And anyway, it will be a little war: short, easy, and victorious. The democracies are rotten at the core. They will soon be brought to their knees."

It required something of an effort for Kersten to ask in an even, natural tone, "Don't you think that would be playing with fire?"

"The Führer knows very well just how far to go," said Himmler.

The rest period was over. The doctor's hands placed themselves once more on the spindly body, and the treatment continued.

By the time Kersten was ready to return to Holland, Himmler had no pain at all. He had not felt so well in years. He, who had been forced to follow an insipid and debilitating diet, and who was rather fond of eating—especially pork—could now eat whatever he pleased. The good-bys he said to his miraculous doctor were full of emotion and gratitude.

8

Three months passed. Hitler had seized Czechoslovakia, or at least what remained of it after the concessions made by England and France at Munich the preceding autumn. The world now sensed the impending catastrophe.

At the beginning of the summer of 1939, Kersten, who was at The Hague, received a telephone call from one of Himmler's aides-de-camp. The Reichsführer was in great pain. He begged the doctor to come to Munich as soon as possible.

At the station he was met by a military car driven by a chauffeur in the uniform of the S.S. He was driven to Gamund Tagan See, a place located forty kilometers from Munich, on a beautiful lake.

Himmler had a little house there with his wife, who was nine years his senior and very insignificant-looking, with an unpleasant, thin, dried-up face, and his daughter, a pale blonde of about twelve.

Kersten was lodged at a near-by hotel, but Himmler insisted on having the doctor present at all his meals, *en famille*. It was as if Himmler were trying to win over the magician who was once more delivering him from his torment, and to turn the sorcerer into a friend.

At table, he spoke with pleasure of Bavaria, his native province, and of the time when it was a sovereign kingdom. He was very proud of a great-grandfather who had served as a professional soldier in the

Bavarian guard under King Otto and then as commissioner of police at Lindau, on Lake Constance.

However, the real conversations between Himmler and Kersten, and the only ones that really interested the doctor, were those that took place during the treatments. Then Himmler was no longer the head of the house or the commander of the special troops and the secret police, but the half-naked patient who willingly, joyously abandoned himself to the miraculous hands.

These conversations sooner or later, one way or another, touched on the event which obsessed Himmler: the war; the imminent war; the war irrevocably decided upon by Hitler.

And Himmler would repeat like a litany the message from the most high:

"The Führer wants war. The world cannot know real peace until it has been purified by war. National Socialism must enlighten the world. After the war, the world will be National Socialist."

And again:

"Pacifism is weakness. Germany has the best army in the universe. And Hitler will remake the world with his army."

At first, Kersten made no reply to these speeches. He would have liked not to have heard them, not to believe them, to dismiss them as the results of delirium. But they had the ring of truth, of destiny. He was only playing back, like a phonograph record, what he heard every day from the sinister fanatic who was plotting to unleash the most frightful catastrophe. And Himmler himself was to be this man's right arm, and to play the lowest and most merciless part in the catastrophe.

Himmler—this pitiful weakling who groaned under the doctor's hands, and then gazed up at him with wondering, infantile gratitude.

Little by little, Kersten began to answer Himmler. It was not that he hoped to change the course of events in any way. But he did not want Himmler to be tempted to interpret his silence as approval or indifference.

So he said just what he thought: that the war was an outrage against humanity which would turn back against Germany herself; that one country could not triumph over all the others combined. Himmler had only one answer:

"The Führer says . . ."

9

In the middle of summer, as a vacation, Kersten took a trip to Estonia. His young wife and their little son, born the year before, accompanied him. The weather was magnificent. From The Hague they traveled in a leisurely manner to their estate, Hartzwalde; then they went to Stettin to set out by car for Tallinn, capital of Estonia. Once there, it was not a long trip to Dorpat, where Kersten was born and where his father was living still.

Driving through the countryside of his childhood, Kersten—was he thinking about what Himmler had said at Munich?—suddenly said to his wife:

"This may be the last trip we will ever make here in peace."

But it was not his nature to stay gloomy or anxious. He shook his head, shrugged his shoulders, and smiled.

They surprised Frederic Kersten bending over the soil of the little piece of land which had been granted him by Estonian laws. At eighty-eight he had the same love for the soil as in his youth, and the same stubborn devotion to work. He was still so robust that he asked his son innocently whether it was dangerous for a man his age to have sexual relations twice a week.

Kersten was proud of his father; the old man was delighted with his grandson; Irmgard was radiant with health and happiness. They were happy days.

As they were passing through Stettin on the way home, Kersten and his wife noticed a great change in the streets of the port and of the town: they were swarming with soldiers.

East Prussia, which the travelers went through next, looked like an army camp.

Kersten saw that the war which Himmler had predicted was now an open reality. The Germans were about to attack Poland.

Kersten returned to Berlin the twenty-sixth of August. Even before unpacking his bags, he telephoned Himmler to inform him of his arrival. Their relationship had assumed a familiarity which authorized such directness. Himmler seemed very happy to hear the doctor's voice.

"Please come to general headquarters at once," he said. "I have been waiting for you with great impatience. My cramps are starting up again. Unless you come, I will be very ill."

The attack was only in its initial stage; two treatments sufficed to check its course.

During the rest periods, Himmler and Kersten chatted as usual.

"Stettin and Prussia are overflowing with soldiers," said the doctor. "Is the war going to break out soon?"

"I am not permitted to tell you that," replied Himmler.

Kersten hid his embarrassment with a calculated smile and continued:

"You know, Reichsführer, I saw more than you think I did."

Himmler was in such a state of physical bliss at that moment, that he could no longer hold his tongue.

"It's true," he said. "We are going to take Poland to bring the English Jews to reason. They are closely allied with that country; they have promised to take its side."

"But," cried Kersten, "that means world war! If you attack Poland, the whole world will be involved."

A convulsive movement shook Himmler's bare body, and Kersten sat speechless. He had heard his patient groan, pant, grind his teeth, or sigh with relief during his treatments; he had never heard him laugh. But there he was, shaking with laughter. A grimace of pain temporarily checked his fit of mirth, but it soon started up again. And all the while, Himmler was saying:

"Oh! It hurts; but I can't help it. You talk like an utter fool. England and France are too weak and cowardly to bother to intervene. Return to The Hague with an easy mind: in ten days it will all be over."

10

Poland had fallen, but England and France had come to her defense. The war was still on.

In a neutral country like Holland the routine of existence was unaffected. Kersten continued to treat his patients, to see his friends; Irmgard, his wife, and Elizabeth Lube, his second mother, were still at his side. Although they were Germans, or perhaps because of it, both women hated Hitler passionately and prayed for his defeat.

On the first of October, 1939, Himmler had one of his aides-de-camp call Kersten on the telephone and request that he come to Berlin at once. The Reichsführer was very ill.

Elizabeth Lube and Kersten's wife were both against this trip. They felt that the doctor should stop treating Himmler. This man did not have the right to be considered a patient like all the others. In peacetime, well and good. But now that he was doing everything in his power as police officer and executioner to bring about the conquest of the world, to continue to *help* him was out of the question.

Kersten listened in silence and shook his head. Actually, he agreed with what they said. Nevertheless, he took the first express train for Berlin. He was impelled by something which he could not have explained himself.

This time Himmler was suffering a great deal. But he was susceptible to Kersten's influence in direct ratio to the severity of his pain, and when Kersten pointed out to him that, contrary to his prediction, Germany had not been able to avoid general hostilities, he tried to find excuses for this mistake.

Hitler had done everything in his power to avoid prolonging the conflict. But England and France closed their eyes to this. It was all Ribbentrop's fault; an hour before the English declared war, he was still saying they would not dare.

But a week later, thanks to Kersten's care, Himmler felt much better. Now he had recovered his confidence:

"The war with France and England does not frighten us. In fact, we are glad it happened. These two countries will be destroyed."

And when, at the end of the treatment, Kersten told Himmler that he would not be returning to Berlin until after the Christmas holidays (he always spent them at Hartzwalde), the Reichsführer exclaimed:

"By Christmas, it will all be over. You will celebrate the New Year in peace. You may count on it; Hitler has told me so."

Before leaving Berlin, Kersten carried out a plan which had been ripening in his mind unconsciously for some time: he went to the Finnish Embassy.

Finland: the country he had chosen for his own when he was less than twenty years old. He had fought for her independence; he was an officer in her reserve force. He still loved her very much.

When he met with the Finnish diplomats, whom he knew very well, Kersten told them all about his encounters with Himmler and how the Reichsführer, when he was in pain, indulged in front of his doctor in military and political confidences with unbelievable indiscretion.

Then Kersten confessed the doubts he had had about continuing to treat the head of the S.S. and the Gestapo in time of open war.

"But you should not hesitate a moment," they told him. "It is your *duty* to treat Himmler, as well and as often as you can. You must maintain and improve this astonishing confidence which he shows in you. And keep us informed, help us. It is of vital importance."

Kersten promised to do his best.

He marveled for a moment—he, who had always managed to maintain his precious privacy, his personal life, he, whose indifference and ignorance in the field of public affairs had been proverbial with his friends—to think that he was to play hereafter a role in the political game. And what a role! But he had no choice. Just as it had been impossible for him to remain silent when Himmler was insulting every decent human feeling, so now he had to place himself at the service of his country in such a terrible crisis.

Kersten felt neither pride, nor any particular satisfaction in thinking these thoughts. He was just a good, honest citizen, and he accepted the consequences of his honesty as if they were separate from and in spite of himself.

It was getting harder and harder to keep his life sealed up within its shell, or rather, the shell was no longer proof against the raging storms which were shaking Europe.

11

On the twentieth of December Kersten took his family to Hartzwalde.

He had telephoned Himmler on his way through Berlin, but the Reichsführer did not require his services.

At Christmas, at New Year's, the war with the Allies was still on, in spite of Himmler's predictions. And then something happened which affected Kersten very deeply: Russia attacked Finland.

Kersten had done everything humanly possible to help his country in a fantastically unequal contest. In Holland, he had raised money. In England, he had gotten warm clothing. In France, medicine and ambulances. In Italy, thanks to his old patient, Count Ciano, arms and airplanes. But in Germany there was nothing he could do. The Hitler-Stalin pact, signed a few days before the outbreak of World War II, imposed on the Third Reich a friendly neutrality toward Russia.

Once he had arrived at Hartzwalde, the doctor forced himself to forget all his worries. His training in mental concentration served him well.

Besides, there was the estate itself, spacious, rich with woods, laced with brooks of running water: here the protective shell formed itself again readily, automatically. What security, what peace there was in this countryside, in this house which Kersten had built and arranged for his own enjoyment! What an endless delight to stroll among its paths and glades, leaning on a big, heavy-headed cane, or to drive among its ancient trees in a little two-wheeled cart hitched to a peaceful horse. What a wonderful place it was to think, dream, eat, and sleep.

As for Irmgard, the estate was also her favorite place to be. She took a passionate interest in the kitchen and the poultry yard and also rode the thoroughbreds in the stable, for she was an accomplished horsewoman.

Finally, since autumn, Hartzwalde had entertained the guest who was closest of all to Kersten's heart: his father.

One of the provisions of the Hitler-Stalin treaty had granted the Baltic countries to Russia. Just as the czarist authorities had done in 1914, the Soviets deported the residents en masse to Turkestan and Siberia. However, those who were of German birth were permitted to return to their native country. Frederic Kersten took refuge in the home of his son.

This new ordeal had affected neither the health, the good humor, nor the industry of this astonishing old man, who was as gnarled and stocky as an indestructible peasant. Torn from his home at the beginning of the First World War, turned out of his new one at the beginning of the Second, this time without hope of return, he was fond of saying:

"I was no longer a young man at the time of the Russo-Japanese War, and that was before these last two. I learned one thing: wars pass, the earth remains. . . ."

But the Christmas holidays were over; it was time to emerge from the shell.

12

According to a schedule which had been established way in advance, Kersten was to treat his patients in Berlin for the first four months of the year 1940, after which he was to return to The Hague, where he was booked up solidly with appointments for the following period.

Until the end of April, Kersten treated Himmler and talked with him every morning.

The Reichsführer was at that time in full agreement with the pact between Germany and Russia. And with the same confidence with which he had declared that the war would be over by New Year's, he now predicted peace by summer.

In this, of course, he was only repeating the words of Hitler, whom he saw at least once and often twice a day.

Kersten's cycle of appointments at The Hague was scheduled to begin on the first of May. On April twenty-seventh, the doctor gave Himmler his passport, in order to get a visa more quickly. The Reichsführer had offered Kersten this service himself. Himmler promised that all the necessary steps would be taken to make Kersten's trip as convenient as possible. His last words were:

"You can relax at your estate for the rest of April. Everything will be in order."

The next day, the telephone rang out in the spacious study of Kersten's country home. It was Himmler.

Has he had a sudden crisis? wondered the doctor, as he waited for the call to come through.

But the now familiar voice contained no pain. On the contrary, it was lively, even cheerful.

"My dear Doctor," it said, "I must inform you that it is impossible, at the moment, for me to obtain your visa."

Kersten gave a little exclamation of surprise, but before he had a chance to say anything, Himmler was going on:

"The police are too busy. You must wait patiently at Hartzwalde."

"See here now, Reichsführer," said Kersten, who did not believe a word of what he had just heard, "how is it possible that you cannot get a visa, even if the police are over their ears? It is absolutely necessary that I be at The Hague on the first of May, that is, in two days. I have appointments with a dozen patients."

"I am sorry, I can do nothing to help you get out of Germany," said Himmler. His voice was still cheerful and friendly, but in it Kersten heard an irrevocable decision.

"But why not?" he asked all the same.

"Do not ask questions! It is impossible, that is all," said Himmler.

"Very well," replied Kersten. "In that case I will go to the Finnish Embassy."

At the other end of the wire, Kersten heard a burst of laughter, then the amused voice of Himmler:

"I guarantee you, my dear Dr. Kersten, that where I can do nothing, no embassy will be able to help you."

Then all at once the voice became serious:

"I request, I order you to remain at your estate for the coming week, and not to leave it."

Up to now Kersten had felt only surprise and annoyance; now he experienced a strange uneasiness. Meanwhile, he could not help thinking to himself, He would not speak to me this way if I had not restored him to health.

After a short silence, Kersten asked, "Then I am a prisoner?"

"Think whatever you choose," said Himmler. And he laughed again. "But rest assured—Finland will not declare war on us for your sake!"

And with that, he hung up. A few minutes later, all communication was cut between Hartzwalde and the outside world.

Twelve days of impatience, anxiety, and anger went by before the telephone again rang in Kersten's home. It was very early on the tenth of May. The call was from the S.S. headquarters. The doctor was to come to Berlin immediately to see the Reichsführer.

Rage was an emotion which Kersten experienced rarely. However, it was written all over his face and his massive body when he appeared before Himmler. His patient, smiling and friendly, seemed not even to notice it.

"My dear Dr. Kersten, forgive me if I have inconvenienced you, but surely you heard the radio this morning?'

"No," said Kersten between clenched teeth.

"What?" said Himmler. "You really don't know what has happened?"

"No," said Kersten.

Himmler exclaimed joyfully, with the look of one who tells his friend the best news in the world, "Our troops have entered Holland. They are going to free this brother nation of ours, this purely Germanic country, from the Jewish capitalists who have enslaved it."

During his enforced confinement, Kersten had had time to imagine many terrible things. But what he had just heard exceeded his worst suspicions.

Holland, the Dutch people . . . the country and people he loved above all others . . . that peace-loving country, with its easygoing men and women, treacherously attacked by all this senseless brute force.

The S.S. was there already, and the Gestapo was to follow, and the Mongoloid features of their great leader were contorted into a smile of triumph.

"In that case, I have no further business here. I am leaving for Finland," said Kersten.

He had lost all self-control. He who was ordinarily so calm and wary did not care, at that moment, if he made Himmler furious. He almost hoped he would.

But Himmler showed no resentment at all. The expression on his face was one of hurt surprise, of affectionate reproach. Without raising his voice, he said:

"I hope you will stay. I need you." Then, with mounting excitement, "Don't misunderstand me! If I prevented you from going to Holland, if I detained you in your country house, it was only out of concern and friendship for you. It was not only because of the dangers of war, bombardments, and so forth; an even greater one threatened you. You are very unpopular with our men there, the Dutch National Socialists and their leader, Mussert. And in the first hours of victory, executions are swift."

Himmler paused briefly before he went on, as if reluctantly, "Put yourself in their place. They know how closely you are connected with that court of Holland, completely overrun by Jews, from which we are going to liberate this purely Germanic people."

Kersten studied Himmler and thought, He believes it; he really believes it. For him, Queen Wilhelmina and her family and her ministers are Jewish agents. And the Dutch people, so liberal, so unprejudiced, so fiercely proud of their independence, he really believes that his Nazis and his S.S. will be their liberators. It's hopeless.

All he felt now was a bottomless grief. He said, "I will think it over, but in any case I will not stay in Germany much longer."

When he left the S.S. headquarters, Kersten went straight to the Finnish Embassy and told them he wished to leave as soon as possible. The diplomats who made up the upper echelon of the organization were silent for a moment. Kersten guessed from their faces what they were thinking. Finland was just emerging from a terrible war. She had had to surrender her cities and provinces to Russia. Her defenses were dismantled, her people exhausted. She could not survive without the support of Germany, and Kersten's proposed departure could well alienate one of the most powerful men in the Third Reich.

Their answer confirmed the doctor's suspicions.

"While it is true that you are the right age to be drafted into active service, as an officer and a doctor," they told him in substance, "it is much more important to your country that you remain with Himmler. There lies your duty as a citizen, there your real work."

They were right. However great his reluctance, or his mental anguish, he had to stay.

THE BATTLE BEGINS

1

On May 10, 1940, Kersten's situation was as follows:

His native country, Estonia, had been annexed by Soviet Russia, against whom he had fought in 1919; there he was liable to capital punishment.

His legal residence, Holland, had been invaded by Hitler's troops, and the Dutch Nazis were out to get him.

His adopted country, Finland, was closed to him, since its highest authorities had ordered him to continue treating Himmler.

Thus, Kersten found himself riveted to the man, and all at once he felt the full weight of the chain.

By May 15, Holland and Belgium were completely occupied. Kersten was told by Himmler's aides to pack his bags.

The Reichsführer was leaving for the front the next day and wanted his doctor to go with him. He was not actually sick, but might very well be in need of treatment en route. This time the invitation took the form not of a request, but of an order.

Himmler's private train, which was composed of sleeping cars, parlor cars, and dining cars, was a veritable headquarters on wheels. Every department under the Reichsführer—the Gestapo, the S.S., Intelligence, Counterespionage, Control of Occupied Territories— had its offices and its high officials. In the wake of this train came fear, hunger, torture, and death.

The private train stopped at Flamensfeld-in-Waterland. From there, Himmler and his agents spread out in all directions. Kersten watched as the horrible spider web was spun, and he had to take care of its originator and listen to his crows of triumph.

It was a terrible time for the doctor, for all his self-control. Nothing could save him from this moral enslavement but the defeat of Germany, and for this he looked to France. It was true that she had succumbed under the first blows, and that Nazi tanks were rolling along her beautiful roads, under the cloudless springtime sky. But Kersten remembered, with all the vividness of our memories of adolescence, the war of 1914. Then, too, the Germans had thought themselves the victors, and there had been the Marne, and there had been Verdun.

Alas, as the days went by, this hope dwindled. In vain Kersten closed his ears to the news reports. He could not ignore the evidence: Hitler's armies were advancing with terrifying speed.

One morning Himmler came into the compartment of the sleeping car which was reserved for the doctor, and said:

"My dear Dr. Kersten, come with me and watch us beat the French!"

Kersten could think of nothing more horrifying. He answered, "Thank you very much, but the French government has not given me a visa."

Himmler replied with a laugh, "In the future, it will not be the

French government that will grant visas for this country. It will be me. Come along!"

Kersten quietly shook his head. "I am not a military man," he said. "I do not enjoy seeing cities in flames."

"War is necessary. The Führer has said so."

The answer was short, automatic; but having given it, Himmler left without renewing his offer. To tell the truth, his cramps were beginning to bother him, and once again Kersten's hands were his only salvation.

June had arrived, bringing radiant weather. Never in his life had Kersten's heart been so heavy. He realized that France was done for. Apart from the possible consequences of her defeat for his own future, he suffered keenly for this country whose language his mother had spoken like a native, whose ambassador had been his godfather, and which represented in his eyes the finest culture, the most charming civilization, the proudest independence. It seemed to him that a great light which had illuminated the world had been extinguished.

Every day, in the dining car which served as mess for the officers of Himmler's general staff, Kersten had to endure the victorious libations, the pompous or crude toasts, the raucous howls celebrating the downfall of France. And he, who was so fond of eating, could hardly swallow a mouthful.

Naturally, this attitude only reinforced the hostility of Himmler's men toward him. When Kersten came into the dining car, the officers whispered, without caring whether or not he heard them,

"This strange doctor . . . this damned civilian . . . this Finn . . .

"He sees Himmler whenever he wants to, while we must follow the strictest protocol.

"He has been received at the court of Holland. He is a friend of our enemies. Only yesterday he said, 'Queen Wilhelmina is the soul of honesty,' although she has betrayed the German interests and is now in the pay of the Jews in England."

In the mess, however, was one man who did not share in the general animosity toward Kersten. He had the lowest rank, second lieutenant, but he held a very important position: private secretary to Himmler.

Of less than average height, peace-loving, unpretentious, obliging, Rudolph Brandt was, like Kersten, nothing but a stray civilian among the high officers, policemen, spies, and uniformed killers who filled the private train. A doctor of law, and one of the finest reporters in Germany, before the war Brandt had been first clerk to the state. One day Himmler had asked his men to find him a first-class secretary, and they chose Brandt. He had no sympathy for the Nazis but he dared not refuse. He was soon enlisted in the S.S. and given the uniform. His quick intelligence, his broad education, his quiet charm, and his great discretion had soon earned him the esteem and confidence of the Reichsführer.

Brandt suffered from stomach trouble, and Himmler had asked Kersten to treat him while on the train. Thus Brandt and Kersten were thrown together quite often.

In the beginning they were extremely cautious. In a world where informing was an everyday matter, and among men whose job it was to track down and root out the least trace of anti-Nazi feeling, one had to weigh every word when one was not thoroughly familiar with one's interlocutor. In conversations of this sort, intonations, pauses, tacit understandings, and looks were more important than words.

And so it was that Brandt and Kersten, in the midst of a pack of fanatics and unscrupulous *arrivistes,* gradually came to recognize each other for what they were: two lone men who had not yet forgotten what it was to be human. It was Brandt who warned Kersten through hints that some of Himmler's familiars, particularly those in charge of the Gestapo, had put the Reichsführer on his guard against the doctor. They had pointed to Kersten's low morale during these triumphant days and had accused him of lukewarmness toward Hitler's ideas. They had even insinuated that he might be a secret agent, a spy.

Kersten took advantage of Brandt's warning at the time he knew to be most favorable to him: during one of the pauses in the treatment.

"I have noticed that I am unpopular with your officers," he said to Himmler, who was stretched out on the bunk of his compartment.

"That's so," said Himmler.

"And I'm sure they must have told you some stories about me," the doctor went on.

"That's true, too," said Himmler. He shrugged his scrawny, bare shoulders and added, "They are fools; all the same, they do not wish to believe that it is possible to betray me!"

Himmler raised himself a little on his elbows. "I am a good judge of men," he said. "I see that you are devoted to me, and whatever they say, for you I have nothing but gratitude, trust, and wholehearted friendship."

So the matter was more or less settled, but neither the security guaranteed him by Himmler nor the sympathy which was beginning to draw him to Rudolph Brandt could pull Kersten out of his depression or dispel the overwhelming sense of solitude which he felt. He needed to be in familiar places again, to be with friends with whom he could share his burden. Berlin was too far away, but The Hague was near by, a few hours' drive. A trip there need not interrupt the daily treatments he was giving Himmler. During one of their sessions, Kersten told his patient:

"I am very anxious to see what state my house is in. All my beautiful furniture, my priceless paintings are there. One day would be enough."

But Himmler, despite, or perhaps because of the friendship he felt for Kersten, could not be persuaded.

"Absolutely not," he said. "The Dutch Nazis send me one accusation after another concerning you. You were the doctor and the intimate friend of Prince Hendrik, husband of Queen Wilhelmina. You are still in touch with members of the court remaining in the Netherlands. And the affection I feel for you also infuriates them: they feel it is dangerous for me to have near me a man with your connections and who, moreover, enjoys a certain freedom because he is Finnish. No, my dear Dr. Kersten, wait until the passions have died down."

He had to resign himself to living in the accursed train.

To escape from this landscape of rails and iron, Kersten took walks in the country. To escape from idleness, he began to keep a journal. And finally, to pass the time, he resorted to the little personal library which Himmler had brought with him and which he was delighted to place at his doctor's disposal.

As a result of this Kersten made an astonishing discovery. All the books belonging to the head of the S.S. and the Gestapo were on religion. Besides the great prophetic works like the Vedas, the Old Testament, the Gospels and the Koran, there were, either in the original German or translated from the French, English, Latin, Greek, or Hebrew, critical works and commentaries, theological tracts, mystical writings, and works on church government and law throughout the ages.

After he had discovered these volumes, he asked Himmler, "Haven't you told me that a true Nazi can have no religion?"

"Of course," said Himmler.

"Well?" asked Kersten, indicating the shelves of the makeshift library.

Himmler was much amused. "No, I have not been converted," said he. "These books are simply necessary for my work."

"I don't understand," said Kersten.

Himmler's face immediately became serious, exalted, and even before he opened his mouth, Kersten knew he was about to pronounce the name of his idol.

"Hitler has entrusted me with a highly important task," he said. "I am to prepare the new Nazi religion. I am to draft the new bible, the bible of the Germanic faith."

"I don't understand," Kersten repeated.

Himmler explained: "The Führer has decided that, after the victory of the Third Reich, he will abolish Christianity throughout Great Germany, that is to say, Europe, and establish the Germanic faith on its ruins. The latter will preserve the idea of God, but it will be very vague and indistinct. The Führer will replace Christ as the savior of humanity. Thus, millions and millions of people will say only Hitler's name in their prayers, and a hundred years from now nothing will be known but the new religion, which will endure for centuries."

Kersten listened with bowed head. He was afraid to let Himmler see from the expression on his face that for him this idea was pure insanity, and the men who had conceived it dangerous madmen. When he had succeeded in composing his features, he raised his eyes and looked at Himmler. Nothing had changed in that now familiar face of a pedantic schoolmaster with Mongoloid cheekbones.

"You see, for this new bible I need documents," Himmler concluded.

"I see," said Kersten.

That evening he wrote this conversation up in the journal he had started. These notes, first begun as a distraction, had become a habit, a necessity.

Meanwhile, the death agony of France was almost over. Marshal Petain was asking for armistice. Before going to Compiègne to attend the ceremony of the signing, Himmler offered to take Kersten with him. Again Kersten refused. He had no fondness, to begin with, for historic spectacles, still less for those which were so painful to him.

A few days later Himmler's private train was back in Berlin.

2

Outwardly, Kersten's life resumed its normal course. He returned to his apartment, his comforts and conveniences, and his work; he found his appetite. He saw his friends and family again. And at the end of every week, he again found peace in the fields and trees of Hartzwalde.

His wife, Irmgard, now lived there all the time. Kersten preferred this for her safety and that of his son. Moreover, she had loved the open air and country life from childhood. She enjoyed supervising the poultry yard and breeding cattle and pigs. Food restrictions were just beginning to be felt, and Irmgard knew how much good meat meant to her husband.

At Berlin, Elizabeth Lube kept house for him, and in his spare time, Kersten had love affairs, for his weakness for romance and his taste for variety were still very strong.

Everything was in its place, everything was just as it had been. But at the same time, everything was different. There was, for this epicurean, this sybarite, a painful awareness of and concern for what went on in the world. There was, for this doctor who had heretofore been so singlemindedly involved in his work and his profession, a strange new compulsion to write down in his journal what Himmler said about the Freemasons, the Jews, the "brood mares," the true German women destined to be used for the purity of the Aryan race.

There was, for this good bourgeois who loved his freedom, the necessity of living among police officers, detested by everyone, and the feeling of being their prisoner. And finally there was, for this greathearted man, the awful, unshakable conviction that the land dearest to him, the land he had chosen for his home and where he had found his best friends, was dying under the heel of a ruthless invader. He had already received letters from Holland from which he could guess the awful truth.

Kersten ate well, slept well, treated his patients as well and successfully as ever, kept his rosy complexion and good disposition. Those who met him thought to themselves, here is a happy man.

But beneath this exterior lay a deep anguish. Not only was Kersten obsessed by the misery that was in store for millions of his fellow men, about which he could do nothing, but the thought that he had to care for the man who was the chief instrument of this misery tormented him constantly.

Suppose he were to have nothing more to do with him?

But things had now come to such a point that it was impossible for him to refuse.

Suppose he were only to pretend to treat him?

Nothing could have been easier, but Kersten's respect for his calling, all his sense of professional ethics, forbade him even to consider such a course. A patient, whatever his role in life, was only a patient to his doctor and was entitled to all his skill and all his devotion.

The state of anxiety and confusion in which Kersten was living was betrayed in a chance remark which surprised even him.

On July 20, 1940, Count Ciano, who was Mussolini's son-in-law and Italian minister of foreign affairs and had come to Berlin on diplomatic business, asked Kersten to examine him, as the doctor had done regularly before the war. The two men were very good friends and so spoke freely.

"Are you really Himmler's doctor?" asked Ciano.

"I'm afraid so," sighed Kersten.

"But how is it possible!" exclaimed Ciano, and his voice contained all the scorn of a handsome, fashionable, proud and brilliant aristocrat for one who performs the lowest, most sordid jobs.

To his own surprise Kersten found himself saying, "Well, what do you expect, sometimes a man can sink pretty low in his profession. I have gone from bad to worse."

He immediately regretted this confession, which escaped him before he even knew what he was saying. Ciano burst out laughing and said, "So I see."

Kersten's eyebrows shot together, and the line in his forehead deepened. His relationship with Himmler was nobody's concern but his own. It was no one's business to pass judgment on it, least of all one of Hitler's allies.

"Why did you enter the war?" he asked. "Have you not always assured me that it would be stupid and criminal?"

Ciano had stopped laughing. "I have not changed my mind," he said. "But it is my father-in-law who makes the decisions."

He made a gesture as if to dismiss unpleasant thoughts and continued, "You must come to Rome."

"I am a prisoner here," said Kersten.

"Oh, I can take care of that," said Ciano loftily.

That evening he told Kersten, "It's all settled. You can come."

Then he described the scene. "I had lunch with Himmler," he said, "and I asked him: 'Let me have Kersten for a month or two, I need him for my stomach trouble.' Himmler gave me a black look; he hates me as much as I despise him. He answered, 'We need Kersten here.' I then gave him such a look that he got frightened, for he knows how important good relations with Italy are for Germany just now. He knows how much influence my father-in-law has with Hitler. He pulled himself together and said, 'We shall see . . . but please note that I have no authority over Kersten. He is a Finn.' The old hypocrite! To which I replied, 'We are on good terms with the Finns. I will speak to their ambassador.' What could he do? So as not to lose face, he hastened to say, 'Oh! Do not trouble yourself. The doctor may go with you.' "

Kersten shook his head. "Thank you, but my wife is expecting a baby, and I cannot leave her alone."

"Don't let that stop you! Bring your wife!" cried Ciano. "Your child will be Roman."

"No, really," said Kersten, "there are too many problems."

Was this the real reason for his refusal, or did he feel some vague scruple which forbade him, in these terrible times, to enjoy himself under the peaceful Roman sky?

3

In early August Irmgard Kersten gave birth to a son; it was a very smooth delivery. After spending two weeks with her at Hartzwalde, the doctor returned to his work in Berlin.

He had a visit from Rosterg, the great industrialist to whom he owed his estate and because of whom he now had Himmler as a patient.

Rosterg told him, "I am going to ask you a favor which only you can do. I once had working in my kitchen a fine old foreman, honest, conscientious, and peace-loving, but a Social Democrat. For this crime, he was put in a concentration camp. I know you have Himmler's confidence and friendship. Have the poor man freed."

"But what can I do? Himmler won't even listen to me!" cried Kersten. He was being completely sincere; the notion that he might be able to do anything of the kind had never occurred to him. The very idea of intervening with Himmler frightened him.

But Rosterg was both persistent and convincing. "You'll see," he said. "In any event, here is a memorandum of all the facts in the case."

"I will be happy to read it, but I can promise nothing, because I have no influence," said Kersten.

He buried Rosterg's note in the bottom of his portfolio and, to tell the truth, completely forgot about it.

Two weeks passed.

On the twenty-sixth of August, Himmler had an excruciating attack of cramps. Kersten rushed to the Chancellery and, as usual, quickly relieved his patient of his pain. But the attack had been so violent that even after it was over Himmler remained lying down, half naked, on his couch.

From the depths of his blessed relief, he regarded Kersten with boundless gratitude.

"Dear Dr. Kersten," he said, his feeble voice trembling with emotion, "what would I do without you? I will never be able to express my gratitude, all the more because I have a very guilty conscience about you."

"What do you mean?" asked Kersten, with an astonishment not unmixed with uneasiness.

The answer was reassuring. "You take such good care of me," said Himmler, "and I still have not paid you anything."

"But you know very well, Reichsführer, that I do not charge by the visit, but by the completed cure," said Kersten.

"I know, I know," said Himmler. "But that doesn't keep me from feeling guilty. You have to live, and one can't live without money. You must tell me how much I owe you."

At this moment Kersten had one of those flashes of intuition which determine the course of one's life. He knew that if he agreed to let Himmler pay him, he would become in his eyes an ordinary doctor, nothing but a salaried person in his employ, and that Himmler would feel released from any sense of obligation toward his doctor in exact proportion to what he paid him for the treatment. For Himmler, as Kersten knew, had only a very modest personal income. His single-minded fanaticism made him the only honest dignitary—and for that reason, all the more unapproachable—among the Nazi higher-ups. He appropriated nothing for his own use from the secret funds at his disposal, and contented himself with his official salary, which amounted to little more than two thousand marks a month. With this sum he had to support not only his lawful wife and his daughter, but also an ailing mistress who had two sons by him.

Kersten put on his most playful expression and said amiably and ingenuously, "Reichsführer, I do not want anything from you. I am much richer than you are. You know perfectly well that I have a smart clientele and that they pay me very high fees."

"It is true," said Himmler, "I am not as rich as Rosterg, for example. Compared to him, I am even a pauper. But that doesn't matter, it is my duty to make you some compensation."

Kersten waved his hand good-naturedly, and replied, "I take nothing from poor people. It's one of my principles. I make the rich pay for them. Someday when you are better off, rest assured, I shall be merciless. Meanwhile, let's leave things as they are."

Half-dressed, his legs dangling, Himmler was sitting up on the couch. Never had the doctor seen him so moved. He exclaimed, "Dear, dear Dr. Kersten, how will I ever thank you?"

By what hidden spring of memory, by what tuning of mind and instinct did Kersten suddenly remember Rosterg's request? Was it because he had heard Himmler pronounce the industrialist's name a few moments before? Because he sensed, as one inspired, that this was the moment—now or never—to try his luck?

Kersten himself could not tell us, but he took his portfolio, and hardly knowing what he was doing, he took out the note concerning the old Socialist foreman. With an innocent, expansive smile, he handed it to Himmler, saying:

"Here is my bill, Reichsführer: this man's freedom."

Himmler gave a start which made his slack skin and muscles quiver slightly, then read the note, and said:

"Because it is you who asks me, naturally I agree."

He shouted, "Brandt!" His private secretary came in.

"Take this memorandum and have this man released, our good doctor wishes it."

"At once, Reichsführer," said Brandt. He stood still for a moment, but he gave Kersten a brief look of approval. It was then that Kersten knew for sure that in Brandt he had a friend, a trustworthy ally against the Gestapo and the death camps. The look on Brandt's face also brought home to him the incredible truth: he had extracted a life from Himmler.

He stammered his gratitude.

4

Three days later the Reichsführer, completely recovered, asked Kersten dryly, "Is it true, as my agents in Holland tell me, that you have maintained your house in The Hague?"

Himmler seized with both hands the frames of his steel-rimmed spectacles and began to push them up and down on his forehead. It was a sure sign that he was angry. He continued with some heat:

"This must stop. It is out of the question for you to have a home in The Hague. I have warned you more than once that the Nazi party in Holland is gunning for you because of the connections which you continue to have there."

The seesaw motion of the spectacles on Himmler's forehead accelerated. "Do you suppose we know nothing about the letters you receive, and from whom? I cannot cover for you any longer. You must liquidate this house."

Kersten saw at once that all discussion would be futile and even dangerous. By now he was thoroughly familiar with his patient's behavior. Once restored to health, Himmler no longer let himself be influenced by Kersten and became even with his doctor-magician just as fanatical and intractable as he was with everyone else.

This time Kersten had to give in.

He had mixed feelings about what he had to do. He experienced a profound grief at the thought of leaving the house which had seen his happiest years, in a country to which he was bound by the strongest and sweetest ties. On the other hand, the necessity of performing this melancholy duty provided him with the only possible excuse for revisiting a place which was "off limits" for him.

"I will do as you wish," he told Himmler. "However, it is absolutely necessary that I manage the removal myself."

"Very well," growled Himmler. "But I give you ten days, no more. And you must leave immediately."

By the first of September Kersten, armed with the necessary papers, was at The Hague. His emotion on returning to the city which he loved so much was even stronger than he had expected. Every street, every turn brought back some strong memory. Work, honors, friendships, love affairs, everything had gone well for him here, everything still smiled on him from a past which was not yet distant. But his happiness was short-lived. Kersten had to go directly from the station to the headquarters of the head of the Gestapo in Holland. This was an Austrian by the name of Rauter, who was both boorish and cunning at the same time. He received Kersten with a curtness that bordered on incivility. The doctor shuddered to think that the life and liberty of millions of people depended on his whim.

Kersten was obliged to report to Rauter's office daily, following Himmler's orders. "A matter of courtesy," he had told the doctor, but in a tone which did not try to conceal the fact that he was placing Kersten under strict surveillance. The prospect of having to see this person every day cast a shadow over Kersten's visit before it had even begun.

However, as yet he knew nothing about the way in which Rauter exercised his power. This he learned as soon as he got home and made a few phone calls. Friends flocked to him, and each one had a more horrible story to tell about the desperate state to which the country had been reduced by the German occupation, through the intermediary of the Gestapo. Arrests, hunger, deportations, torture, summary executions—a nightmare panorama unfolded before Kersten's eyes. He listened to all of it without saying a word.

No one in Holland knew about his connection with the head of the S.S. and the Gestapo; he had to be cautious. But after most of his visitors had left and he found himself in the presence of a few men of whom he was absolutely sure, Kersten talked without reserve.

"I believe I have come to have a certain amount of influence over

Himmler," he said. "You must, therefore, write me regularly and tell me everything you can find out: imprisonments for no reason, thefts, plundering, unfair punishments."

"But how can we send such compromising letters through the mail without terrible risks for both of us?" his friends wanted to know.

"You have only to send them," said Kersten, "to Military Postal Sector No. 35360."

A voice rose, fearful and unbelieving: "And the secret will be . . ."

"Absolutely safe, I will guarantee it personally," said Kersten.

His tone prohibited further questions and yet left no room for doubt. In a little while his friends went away.

Kersten was not taking chances when he had assured his friends that their correspondence would be safe. The postal number he had given them was, as a matter of fact, Himmler's. This unusual privilege had been obtained very easily, as is so often true of the most unlikely successes.

Before leaving Berlin, Kersten, who foresaw how useful it would be to him to have his correspondence outside the control of censors and spies, had told Rudolf Brandt, as if he were confessing something rather reluctantly, that he was planning to see in Holland several women with whom he had had amorous relations. He was sure these women would want to write to him. And he was sure that Brandt would understand how it pained him to think that his love letters would be read by the censors. And above all, he added, no one was above an occasional indiscretion, and there was always the danger of his wife getting wind of these liaisons.

Whereupon Brandt, who no longer bothered to conceal his liking for the doctor, had told him, "Then use Himmler's postal sector. I am the one who sorts his mail, and I will give you your letters." And when Kersten asked whether this method was really safe, Brandt had answered, "It is the only safe number in Germany."

But would Himmler agree to it? "I have good reason to think he will," Brandt had said with a smile.

He was counting on a weakness of the Reichsführer which was well known to his associates and often an object of ridicule to the high-ranking S.S. officers. For Himmler—the puny, sickly pedant, as undernourished physically as he was morally, and whose life was strictly regulated between his paperwork, his diet, his wife, and his mistress, all equally insignificant—dreamed of being the embodiment of the superman who was his ideal for Germany: athletic, warlike, great eater and drinker, tireless studhorse for the reproduction of the chosen race.

Sometimes he tried to live this dream. He called his staff together for gymnastic exercises in which he took part. The weakness of his muscles, his awkwardness, and his stiffness made him a ridiculous and clownish figure, a sort of "Sandpiper of the S.S." His movements were a caricature of those being executed around him by the strong, supple bodies, trained and hardened to any ordeal.

The contrast was so obvious that in the end the Reichsführer noticed it himself and returned with redoubled zeal to his work, his secret reports, the interminable lists of his victims, to the sense of his terrible power.

But the image of the great lover, which he was so painfully aware he was not, continued to people his mind with exalted dreams.

This chronic sexual frustration served Kersten's purposes ideally.

The excuse which the doctor had trumped up to assure the privacy of his correspondence—secret love affairs—delighted Himmler. As soon as Brandt had mentioned it to him, he spoke of it to Kersten with approval and enthusiasm. It gave their relationship a whole new dimension. It was no longer just doctor to patient, but man to man, male to male, accomplices in their virility—just like two cavaliers of old Germany.

To beguile a dream which he could not realize, Himmler, the most suspicious man alive, was happy to grant Kersten the forbidden protection of his postal sector.

This extraordinary privilege enabled Kersten to organize, in a few days, a veritable private information service in Holland. He had spies everywhere; then he chose the most cautious, the best informed, as his correspondents.

Kersten had been at The Hague five days, or half the time Himmler had given him, when early one morning when he was still in bed a friend rang his bell and stammered breathlessly:

"Doctor, Doctor, the police have been at Bignell's house since dawn. They are searching it and threatening to arrest him."

Bignell was an antiquarian and auctioneer. It was through him that Kersten had purchased his best Flemish paintings, and he was extremely fond of the old gentleman.

Kersten got up, dressed, seized his cane, took the first tramway he could find, and arrived at the antiquarian's house. The police had completely surrounded it and did not let Kersten go inside. He took another tramway and went to the general headquarters of the Gestapo in Holland, straight to the office of Rauter, the head man.

The latter was not surprised to see the doctor: Kersten had to report to him every day.

Ordinarily, Kersten cut the obnoxious formality of his visit as short as possible. He came in and as soon as he had received the grunt which served as Rauter's greeting, went away. This time he did not leave so quickly. After having observed the usual ritual, he said in a neutral tone:

"I tried to visit my friend Bignell this morning, but the police were searching his house and I was not permitted to enter it."

"They were acting on orders," said Rauter, fixing on Kersten his inflexible gaze. "My orders. Bignell is a traitor in communication with London. After the investigation he will go to prison where I"— Rauter smiled icily—"will interrogate him."

Kersten had promised himself when he had arrived at the office of the Gestapo that he would not lose his self-control. But the thought of what was in store for his friend, a man of advanced years and precarious health, made him shudder. On a sudden impulse, he said, "I guarantee his innocence. He has done nothing against Germany; free him."

A look of disbelief passed over Rauter's face. What! A foreigner, a suspect, under daily surveillance, was giving him advice, practically ordering him! He banged his fist on the table and started to shout:

"Free the swine? Under no circumstances, least of all because you say so. And here is some advice: mind your own business, or else!"

Anger breeds anger. Kersten, ordinarily so calm, was suddenly furious. No one could talk to him that way. He had to put this brute in his place, no matter how!

In his rage, an idea came to him which at any other time he would have dismissed as insane. But his anger gave him the necessary impetus to carry it out. He asked coldly:

"You have a telephone?"

Rauter was taken aback. He had expected anything but this.

"Obviously," he said.

"Very good," said Kersten. "Get me Himmler in Berlin."

Rauter leaped from his chair. He shouted, "But that is impossible. Im-pos-si-ble. Even for me. When I want to talk to Himmler, I have to go through Heydrich, the head of all the services, as you know, and you, you are nothing but a civilian with no title, no position."

"Try it anyway, we shall see," said Kersten.

"Very well," said Rauter.

They would indeed see, he would get just what he deserved for violating the strictest regulations, this fat doctor who was so infatuated with himself. Rauter picked up the telephone, transmitted Kersten's request, and then pretended to be engrossed in the papers on his desk.

Five minutes had not passed before the telephone rang. Rauter took the receiver with an ominous grin. They would see, indeed. . . .

A look of terrified amazement came over his face. He thrust the mechanism at the doctor. Himmler was on the wire.

If Kersten had been able, he would have retracted his request. The wait had given him a chance to reflect. He knew Himmler and his blind determination to protect the heads of his various services. The course he had embarked on had not the slightest chance of success; but retreat was no longer possible.

Then Kersten remembered Bignell and the torture that was destined for him. His anger returned. He seized the telephone and said, almost violently, "One of my best friends has just been arrested. I guarantee his innocence. Do me a favor, Reichsführer: let his case drop."

Himmler seemed not to have heard the doctor. He asked in a mournful, feverish voice, "When are you coming back? I need you desperately."

Kersten almost fainted with relief. The fates were with him. Himmler in pain, Himmler calling his healer to the rescue, was no longer for Kersten the fanatical bureaucrat and lord of torture and extermination. It was that other Himmler, that pitiful piece of human dough which he could knead into any shape, the addict prepared to do anything for his drug.

"My time here is not up until next week," said Kersten, "and if my friend is arrested I will return to Berlin in no condition to help anyone."

"Where are you calling from?" asked Himmler.

"From Rauter's office," said Kersten.

"Put him on, quickly!" ordered Himmler.

The head of the Gestapo in the Netherlands took the receiver: at attention, heels together, head and shoulders rigid, face frozen. He maintained this attitude throughout the conversation, and all Kersten heard was, "Very good, Reichsführer! At once, Reichsführer!"

Then Rauter handed the telephone back to Kersten, and Himmler said to the doctor, "I trust you. Your friend will be freed; but come back, come back as soon as possible."

Kersten promised he would and thanked him from the bottom of his heart; then the connection was broken. There followed a long silence, during which the two men looked at each other vacantly, both the victims of an astonishment which seemed to have suspended the workings of their senses. But while Rauter's stupor was simply that of humiliation and frustration, Kersten's was quite another thing.

To be sure, he had already had the experience of depriving Himmler of one of his victims: Rosterg's old foreman. But that had been a rather unique situation. He had, in effect, exchanged his whole medical fee for the liberty of a single man. Moreover, this had happened in Germany, and the poor wretch had been guilty merely of belonging to the Social Democrat party. What a difference here! Bignell had been accused of high treason, and by whom? By Rauter himself, the commander in chief of the Gestapo forces throughout the Netherlands. And a word from Kersten had been enough to defeat him.

The doctor passed his hand slowly over his deeply lined forehead; he felt slightly dizzy.

Finally Rauter broke the silence. "Himmler has ordered me to release Bignell," he said. "I know that Bignell is a traitor, but an order is an order. I will give you a car and one of my men. You may go and fetch him yourself."

Rauter had spoken in his customary surly manner. He must have remembered the favor Kersten enjoyed with Himmler, because he forced his features into a grimace of amiability, and asked, "Does this please you?"

"Very much, and I thank you very much for it, too," said Kersten.

Kersten had not been frightened by Rauter's rudeness or by his anger, but the forced smile in which his cold eyes took no part made him profoundly uneasy. This man would never forgive him.

After he returned home, having freed Bignell, Kersten made his movers work without a moment's rest. In twenty-four hours everything was packed. Nevertheless, when he took the train for Berlin, Kersten took nothing with him and left his house in The Hague open, against Himmler's orders. He wanted to leave himself an excuse to return.

Himmler soon heard about it from Rauter, but apparently he needed Kersten too much at the moment to be suspicious at his disobedience. In any case, he did not mention it to him.

GESTAPO

1

Brandt, who, as Himmler's private secretary, was in a position to know a great deal, congratulated Kersten on his success in the Bignell case. At the same time he warned the doctor that Rauter had the full support of Heydrich, who was head of all the Gestapo agencies in Germany and elsewhere. And Heydrich would never forget that Kersten had humiliated his authority and that of his man in Holland in going over his head to Himmler.

"Be careful," Brandt finished.

Kersten repeated this conversation to Elizabeth Lube, who was keeping house for him in Berlin. He told her everything; it was a habit he had formed twenty years ago when, a lonely, struggling young man, he had found in her an older sister.

As for his wife, on the other hand, who scarcely left the house any more at Hartzwalde, some protective instinct told him to keep her in complete ignorance of the side of his life which was beginning to be dangerous.

Elizabeth Lube listened to the doctor in silence, shook her head, and said, "Whatever happens, you were right. Something has to be done about this vampire, Himmler."

The latter, now fully recovered from his attack, talked of nothing but the forthcoming German victory. Hitler had promised it once again.

It was the time of the bombing of Britain. According to Himmler, the Luftwaffe was going to bring the British people to reason. They would get rid of that Jew, Churchill, and would beg for peace.

But the English pilots were holding their own, and from Holland letters began to arrive for Kersten at the only postal number that was safe in all of Germany.

Brandt would hand him with a knowing wink, all innocently, the envelopes he thought were filled with fond protestations. Kersten would give him a wink of the same kind in return and hurry off with his messages.

At first he was afraid. He felt as if each letter he received at S.S. headquarters was burning him right through his clothes. But once safely at home, when he had finished reading it, he promptly forgot the risk he had run. Now the letter was nothing but a long cry of anguish, a desperate appeal.

Naturally, it was impossible for Kersten to intervene in every case of injustice and suffering his friends told him about, or even in the majority of them. In the dreadful list the doctor selected the individual cases which moved him the most and the general measures which he found the most inhuman, and at the propitious moment during the treatment he mentioned them to Himmler.

Gradually he evolved a whole technique for his petitions. When Himmler's illness was in its acute phase and only Kersten's hands had the power to relieve him, the doctor addressed himself, as he had done the first time, to the Reichsführer's feelings of gratitude and friendship for him. Then it was in his own name, for his personal satisfaction, that he requested a pardon, a release from prison, the cancellation or postponement of a decree.

But the opportunities for using this method were very rare. Once the crisis was over, Himmler forgot about it. Then Kersten had to appeal to the Reichsführer's vanity, which was almost legendary.

The ex-schoolmaster worshiped the Germany of the high Middle Ages. He had found his heroes, his *beaux ideals,* in the emperors and princes of that epoch, such as Frederick Barbarossa and, in the tenth century, Henry I, the Fowler. The glory of this latter, above all, excited him to the point of ecstasy. So great was his desire to identify himself with this man that at times he believed himself to be his reincarnation in this century.

Kersten, to whom Himmler had confided these dreams more than once, turned them to his own use. At first he advanced cautiously, for fear he would go too far. But he soon saw that Himmler, while he protested for form's sake, enjoyed listening to him. Step by step, by means of imperceptible attacks on the Reichsführer's vanity, Kersten would end up telling him, in that persuasive tone which psychiatrists use with madmen:

"In the centuries to come you will be called the greatest leader of the German people, a hero of Germany, the equal of the old chevaliers, the equal of Henry the Fowler. But remember that these men did not owe their fame to force and courage alone. They owed it also to their justice and their generosity. For truly to resemble these valiant men, these paladins, you must be as magnanimous as they were. I say this, Reichsführer, because I am thinking of your reputation in centuries to come."

And Himmler, who had complete confidence in Kersten's hands because they had the power to find and cure his physical pain, now believed his flattering words, because they both probed and soothed his mental torment.

"My dear Dr. Kersten," he would say, "you are my only friend, my Buddha, the only one who both understands and helps me."

And he would summon Brandt and order him to draw up a list of the names designated by Kersten, and would sign the decree of their liberation. And often, when there was still some space on the paper between the last name and the signature, Brandt, who was wholeheartedly on Kersten's side, out of friendship, but also and above all because deep down he felt an ever greater shame and horror at having to prepare in ever increasing quantity the documents which brought misery to his fellow men, Brandt would, unbeknownst to Himmler and with Kersten's advice, add two or three more names to the list. And those so added found, thanks to the seal and signature of the Reichsführer, liberty instead of torture, and life instead of the gallows.

These rescues made Kersten very happy but at the same time they were a source of profound anxiety. For the Gestapo chiefs, the inquisitors, the man-hunters, the starvers of men, the executioners, could hardly fail to wonder what was causing Himmler to free and pardon all these people. They were not accustomed to leniency from such a quarter. He had always asked, and continued to ask of them, an implacable, unrelenting fury in persecution and terror. Why the change?

Sooner or later, Kersten thought, the idea was bound to occur to Rauter or Heydrich to assign the responsibility to the man who had snatched Bignell, the antiquarian, from his dungeon.

But weeks passed, and the Gestapo left him alone.

2

In November, 1940, Kersten accompanied Himmler to Salzburg. There was to be a big conference there at which Hitler and Mussolini, Ribbentrop and Ciano were to meet.

Kersten was very busy. He continued, of course, to treat Himmler. He looked after his old friend, Ciano. And finally Ribbentrop asked Kersten to take him as a patient.

Ciano took advantage of this meeting with Himmler to renew his request that Kersten be permitted to come to Rome. He was supported by Ribbentrop, who had further business in the Italian capital.

Before the two ministers of foreign affairs of the Axis, Himmler had to give way.

Kersten spent two weeks in Rome. During his visit, Ciano gave a huge dinner in his honor at which he bestowed on him, in the name of the king, the rank of commander in the Order of Maurice and Lazarus, one of the most coveted in all Italy, because it is as old as the *Toison d'or*.

Not one of the Germans in Ribbentrop's following was considered worthy of it. The honors they received were of much less importance. They did not look kindly on this preference shown to a civilian, a neutral person, over them, the allies, the military, the Nazis.

When Kersten returned to Berlin, Himmler's first words on seeing him were about his decoration.

"You have made yourself new enemies by this," he said brusquely. "As if you did not have enough already!"

And Kersten, who among the pleasures of Rome had forgotten the Rauters and the Heydrichs, returned with a jolt to the sinister world he had managed to escape for a few days.

It was the end of December. He left to celebrate Christmas and New Year's at Hartzwalde.

3

In a country at war, this estate had become a sort of pastoral world unto itself. One lived there for the land and the animals. Irmgard Kersten, under the guidance of her father-in-law, the old farmer who, at ninety, still had the spirit and energy of youth, thought of nothing else. The land was cultivated, and the cows, pigs, chickens, ducks, and geese multiplied.

Kersten sighed with relief to be back here. In spite of the assurances of Himmler, who continued to predict victory for the following month, the war threatened to be long, and food restrictions were getting worse and worse. At least they would never want for milk, butter, eggs, poultry, or ham; this was very important to the doctor.

He returned to Berlin at the beginning of the new year, 1941, well fed, rested, and refreshed. In his large car, driven by a chauffeur who had been with him for fifteen years, he hummed all the way from his property to the capital, a trip of some sixty kilometers. Once there, he was happy to get back to his familiar and spacious apartment in the Wilmersdorf section, at the edge of a big park.

The first day back he saw several patients and met a few friends. He did not have to see Himmler until the following day.

However, the next morning at six o'clock the buzzer in his apartment rang violently. The January dawn was still dark, and the servants were asleep. Kersten went to the door himself.

Someone must be in a bad way, he thought as he walked through the large rooms. On the landing, he found two men in the uniform of the Gestapo. For a moment he remained paralyzed with surprise. They faced each other: the soldiers, rigid in their tunics, and he, groggy, still half-asleep, clad only in his pajamas.

"We wish to speak with you," said one of the officers curtly.

"At your service," answered Kersten.

As he led the two men into his study, his mind worked anxiously. At last Heydrich was getting his revenge. But on what grounds? For what crime? Had one of his friends in Holland betrayed him, or simply confessed under torture that he had been sending the doctor information, and what postal number he had used? Had they discovered that Brandt had been adding names to the lists of those pardoned, at his instigation, and without Himmler's knowledge? In both cases, the men would be coming from Himmler himself, and Kersten was done for. And he could think of no other reason for their visit.

Once in his study, the doctor was about to ask the two men to be seated but he did not have a chance. The one who had already spoken asked in a surly tone, "Have you ever had any Jewish patients?"

"Of course," said Kersten without a moment's hesitation. After what he had been dreading, he was much relieved.

"You do not realize, then, that it is forbidden, absolutely forbidden?" shrilled the police officer.

"No," answered Kersten. He studied first one, then the other of the two men, and went on, "And furthermore, it does not concern me."

The policemen both spoke at once.

"You place yourself outside the law of the German people," said the first.

"You do not behave as a German doctor should," said the second.

Once more Kersten's eyes went from one to the other. "I am not a German doctor," he answered politely. "I am Finnish."

"So you say; show us that precious passport of yours."

"With pleasure," said Kersten.

When they were shown undeniable proof that the doctor had been a citizen of Finland for more than twenty years, the policemen suddenly looked very sheepish, and the one who had been the more aggressive of the two was now the more cringingly apologetic.

"Forgive us, Dr. Kersten," he said, "it is not our fault, we have been misinformed. We were given absolute assurances that you were a German doctor."

"I have a German degree as well," said Kersten, "but first and foremost I am a Finn and even, in my country, *Medizinalrat*. Would you like to see that document too?"

"Oh no, please do not trouble yourself," cried the officer, as if overwhelmed by the title. "We have no further business here. Again, a thousand apologies."

Kersten went to wake up Elizabeth Lube and ask her to make him some strong coffee. While he drank it—heavily sweetened, as usual—with buttered bread, he went over with his old friend all possible hypotheses suggested by the visit from the Gestapo. Had the leaders who had sent the two agents really thought that the doctor was not Finnish? It was true that in his youth he had changed his citizenship three times in as many years, and during the war of 1914, before enlisting in the Finnish Army, he had been a German citizen. But if he had remained one, he would have been drafted into the Wehrmacht. And then, the Gestapo had only to go to the Finnish Embassy to get the information. No, it didn't hold water.

What then—warning? Intimidation? Blackmail?

"The main thing," said Elizabeth Lube at the end of their conversation, "is to find out whether Himmler knew about it and agreed to it."

At noon, the regular time, Kersten walked into Himmler's office at the Chancellery. Before even taking off his coat, he said jokingly to the Reichsführer, "When you want to find out something about me, you don't have to bother sending the Gestapo. You have only to ask me yourself."

Himmler, who had not seen the doctor since the Christmas holidays and who was coming toward him with outstretched hands, stopped cold, as if he had been hit in the solar plexus.

"You had a visit from the Gestapo?" he exclaimed. "But that is impossible."

He seized the telephone and demanded immediate information. When he heard what had happened, he let the receiver dangle at the end of the cord and said, without looking at Kersten, in the voice of one who is very much annoyed, "It seems that you were to be arrested for treating Jews."

Abruptly, Himmler took the receiver again and, his face pale with anger, shouted, "I forbid anyone to interfere with Dr. Kersten, for any reason whatsoever. This is an order. The doctor is responsible to me and me alone." He slammed down the receiver, struggled to catch his breath, and began pushing his spectacles up and down, up and down, on his forehead. Kersten could tell from this mannerism that his anger had not died down and was now turning against him.

"You cannot be my doctor and treat Jews," exclaimed Himmler.

"And how am I supposed to know my patients' religion?" asked Kersten. "You know I never ask them that. Jews or non-Jews, they are my patients."

This was not the first time Himmler and Kersten had spoken of the Jewish question, and Himmler knew very well that, for the doctor, there was not the slightest difference between other men and those which the National Socialist party deemed unworthy to live. But these conversations had been purely theoretical, and Himmler had either conducted them with a superior, ironic smile or broken them off with a shrug of the shoulders. Now it was quite another matter. Kersten's opposition had passed from the realm of ideas into the arena of daily life, where it became contempt of the law, active rebellion, a crime against Hitlerian doctrine—in short, everything which it was Himmler's job to track down, punish, weed out, and annihilate.

And he could not afford to lose his healer.

In his anger, the Reichsführer's voice rose several notes. He screamed, "The Jews are our enemies! You cannot treat a Jew! The German people are engaged in a war to the death against the Jew-infested democracies."

Kersten said quietly, "Do not forget that I am a Finn. In Finland, there is no Jewish problem. I will wait for my government to prescribe a line of conduct for me."

"That is a stupid way to argue!" cried Himmler. "You know very well what I mean. Do me a favor and leave the Jews alone."

Kersten had gone too far. If he yielded now, if only outwardly, he would deny everything he stood for. He said in a half-voice, "I cannot. The Jews are men like everyone else."

"No," squeaked Himmler. "No! No! Hitler has said so. There are three categories of creatures: men, animals, and Jews. And the last must be exterminated so that the other two can exist."

The gray face of the Reichsführer suddenly took on a greenish tinge, his brow broke out in perspiration, and his hands clutched his stomach. "Here it comes again," he groaned.

"How many times have I warned you not to let yourself go this way," said Kersten, as if he were talking to a foolish child. "It is very bad for your cramps. Come now, take off your clothes."

Himmler hastened to obey.

4

Heydrich, head of all the Gestapo agencies in Germany and occupied countries, knew Kersten very well. The two men often ran into each other in the huge building on the Prinz Albert Strasse: in the halls of the S.S. headquarters, in the offices of the Chancellery, in the mess hall of the general staff. It even happened—and this was an indication of his authority—that Heydrich, when his business was particularly urgent, came into Himmler's office when the doctor was treating him.

On all these occasions, Heydrich had been all affability and courtesy to Kersten. This manner corresponded with his physical appearance: he was tall and slender, elegant. He had a handsome, fair-skinned face, and carried none of the marks, none of the scars that the life of a police officer can leave on a man who leads it with a religious zeal. Of a keen and quick intelligence, he excelled equally in tests of strength and cunning. He practiced fencing and pistol-shooting every day. He had a relish for danger in its extreme form. An amateur pilot, he had not been able to rest until Goering let him go on hunting expeditions, where sixty missions had earned him the Cross of Iron, First Class.

Nevertheless, this handsome, clever, courageous, and fascinating man had not a single friend, not even an acquaintance. Nor were Heydrich's duties and the sort of sinister aura which they gave him sufficient to explain this phenomenon. Other high Gestapo officials, specialists in the most horrible tasks (such as Müller, for example, head of arrests and interrogations, known for what he was, a torturer) had companions with whom they shared their pleasures and their troubles. It was Heydrich himself who had chosen his solitude. People were important to him only insofar as they were useful to his career. After that, he rejected them coldly. With women, his relations were brief, brutal, cynical. He lived only for his own glory.

These characteristics of temperament and behavior frightened all who came into contact with Heydrich. And even Kersten, in spite of Himmler's protection and even though he took no part in the secret and bitter rivalries which consumed his colleagues, felt a certain uneasiness whenever he saw the tall, flawlessly uniformed figure of the Obergruppenführer of the S.S., the head of the Gestapo, Reinhardt Heydrich, with his sharp profile, his tawny blond hair, and his ice-blue eyes.

This man, thought Kersten, could not stand for any influence on Himmler over which he had no control.

Shortly after the early morning visit of the Gestapo, Rudolph Brandt warned the doctor to be more than ever on his guard. Heydrich had told his colleagues that he suspected Kersten of being an enemy agent, or at least an active ally of the nations at war with Germany, and of using his power over Himmler in their behalf. Heydrich had assured them that he would soon be able to furnish proof.

One day in late February, 1941, as Kersten was leaving the office where he had just been treating Himmler, he found himself face to face with Heydrich, who said with his usual civility, "I would like very much to have a little chat with you, Doctor."

"Whenever you like," answered Kersten as amiably as possible. "Today, if that is convenient for you."

The hour was set for that evening in the section of the building set aside for the offices of the head of the Gestapo.

One of the first things Heydrich did, after Kersten had entered his office, was to press a concealed button under his desk. The movement had been so swift and unnoticeable and the click that followed so muffled, that a man who had not been warned in advance would have noticed nothing. But Kersten had been told by Brandt that Heydrich made considerable use and misuse of the microphone. He said pleasantly, "My dear Mr. Heydrich, if you really want us to speak without reserve, it would be better if you were my guest, at Hartzwalde."

"But why?" asked Heydrich. "We can talk just as well here."

"Yes, but there it would be I who would push the button," Kersten answered cheerfully.

The head of the Gestapo proved equal to the game. He stopped the mechanism and said, smiling, "You seem to be very well informed about the ways and means of eavesdropping, Doctor, and a skillful politician."

"Anyone who frequents this building must be prepared for the use of the microphone," Kersten said mildly. "But as for politics, to tell the truth I have very little experience in that line."

"That would be very unfortunate, if it were true, which I do not believe," said Heydrich. All at once his face and eyes became cold.

He went on, "You have been very successful in treating the Reichs-führer. Now, it sometimes happens that great men begin to look upon the doctor who relieves their suffering as a savior, and to lend a favorable ear to all his ideas. For this reason, I would like to be able to think of you as very well informed. You would then be in a position to select the opinions which you share with the Reichsführer with full knowledge of what you were doing."

Without answering, Kersten crossed his hands on his stomach and waited for what would follow.

Heydrich was coming to the point. "I think you would find it interesting to study the original texts—instructions, reports, etc.—which define the spirit of the S.S. and set forth their successes."

"In that area, I have all the information I need," said Kersten. "My reading and my conversations with Himmler have given me a very clear picture in my own mind."

"Then we are further along than I had thought," remarked Heydrich. "But I am sure that you would like to read the reports I have received on the situation in Holland and Finland, and to see exactly what our policies are in those countries."

Immediately, Kersten thought, He knows that I am getting information from my friends in Holland and Finland, and that the changes Himmler has made in certain of his plans are due to my intervention.

There was nothing in Heydrich's manner to justify such a fear. His voice had been perfectly natural, almost friendly, and his eyes of frosty blue betrayed no emotion whatever. But Kersten's sudden certainty sprang from an instinct which had heretofore never deceived him in critical moments. He answered without hesitation, "I will be very happy to read these reports. Holland and Finland are the two countries which are dearest to me. Whatever concerns them, concerns me."

"Perfect, perfect," said Heydrich.

He squinted slightly, as if to see more clearly what road to follow. Then he said, "Do you know, Doctor, that we could really be very useful to you? When people come to you to ask you to intervene for them with the Reichsführer, it is your duty, is it not, before going to

him, to form an objective opinion of these people: their social and
political status, their character, their resources, etc. It is always tire-
some to have to change one's mind after the fact when one has been
mistaken. I should imagine that up to now it has been very trouble-
some for you to collect the information you need. We would be only
too happy to take care of this research for you, to make it our responsibility. And please note that you would be entirely free to make
up your own mind as to the veracity of our information and to use it
just as you saw fit. All that I ask is that when you do make use of our
sources, you tell the Reichsführer that I was of some assistance to
you. This way, he will know that I am co-operating with a man whom
he respects so highly."

Beneath his surface calm, Kersten listened to this speech with the
keenest possible attention. In it, Heydrich at last revealed his true
purpose. And whatever else he felt, the doctor could not help admir-
ing the maneuver. How sincere, how spontaneous the offer seemed!
And how believable was the final argument for anyone who was familiar with Heydrich's consuming ambition and his constant desire
to further himself in Himmler's good graces! Actually, all this had
but one purpose: to get Kersten to reveal to the Gestapo the names
of his correspondents in Holland and Finland.

Never, never, thought the doctor. However, he, too, said with an
air of absolute sincerity, "I am very grateful for your suggestion.
It is possible that I may be able to make use of it."

Heydrich appeared to be satisfied with his answer.

The doctor repeated this conversation to Brandt.

"Please, I beseech you, redouble your precautions," said Himmler's private secretary.

"Don't worry, I have already decided to do so," said Kersten.

A few days later, he was forced to abandon all caution.

A NATION TO SAVE

1

On the first of March, 1941, Felix Kersten got out of his car at the general headquarters of the S.S. It was noon, the hour when according to a long-established custom the doctor came to give Himmler his treatment.

The sentries in their heavy helmets let him pass without showing his permit or saying a word. The officer on guard did likewise. Dr. Kersten had become a familiar figure in this world of soldiers and policemen, with his civilian clothing, his big cane, his corpulence, and his good humor.

He went up to the floor where Himmler's personal services and private office were located. While climbing the huge marble staircase, Kersten reflected that two years had already gone by since he had first set foot in this place, and he sighed. How good, how beautiful life had been before! Nothing had threatened his status as a free man! While now . . .

But Kersten's optimistic philosophy soon told him that he had nothing to complain about. The war had spared his own person, his property, his family. He still had his wife and two sons, his father, Elizabeth Lube. He had considerable material advantages. And even the Gestapo, after the reprimand that Himmler had given them and the conversation he had had with Heydrich, were leaving him alone.

Kersten deposited his cane, hat, and coat in the cloakroom and walked into Brandt's office so that the latter could announce his arrival to Himmler. The private secretary told the doctor there would be about a half hour's wait; the Reichsführer was holding an important conference which was running overtime.

"Good," said Kersten, "let me know when it's over."

He did not need to say where he could be found. It often happened that he had to amuse himself until such time as Himmler finished his business, and on these occasions he always went to the general staff mess hall.

It was a very large room, because the general staff numbered around two hundred officers. In addition, Himmler had a much bigger personal guard than any of the other Nazi leaders. He had to be surrounded, protected at all times, for he was in constant fear of attempts on his life. The man who dreamed of being Henry the Fowler lived in a state of panic during air raids; he literally shook from head to foot.

As Kersten crossed the crowded room, it buzzed, as usual, with unfriendly voices. Not one head was raised as he went by. The hostility against him was still alive, but his well-established position as Himmler's protégé imposed silence.

Kersten found a corner seat. The manager of the mess hall, a noncommissioned officer in Himmler's private guard, soon rushed over to him. The Reichsführer had ordered him to give the doctor the best possible service. He knew Kersten's tastes and brought him a very strong cup of coffee, heavily sweetened, and the richest, most cream-filled cakes he could find.

The doctor was happily indulging his *gourmandise,* which was increasing with the years, when he became aware of a commotion around him. He stopped eating long enough to see two men cross the room. He recognized the short and stocky one as Rauter, and the slender and elegant one as Heydrich. It was the entrance of the latter which had created all the agitation. The officers got to their feet, saluted, and hastened to make a place for him. In the hierarchy of terror, only Himmler was above Heydrich.

The two men, however, paid no attention to these marks of respect. Lost in conversation, the head of the Gestapo in Holland and the head of the Gestapo in all occupied nations advanced to the foot of the large room, to the side where Kersten was devouring his pastry.

Are they coming for me? the doctor could not help wondering, for he still got regular reports from Holland at Himmler's postal box number. But even though they sat down at a table very near his, neither Rauter nor Heydrich noticed him, so absorbed were they in their conversation.

Kersten hid his face and shoulders as well as he could and returned to his cakes. Then all at once, it was all he could do not to turn around and look at them. The voices at the neighboring table had risen, and Rauter's, which Kersten remembered only too well, said with great excitement:

"What a surprise those Dutch pigs are in for, what a panic it's going to be! At last they'll get what's coming to them. Only this week, in a riot, they stoned two of my men. Filthy swine!"

"It's cold enough in Poland to cool them off," said Heydrich with a slightly metallic laugh.

Kersten bent even further over his cakes and coffee, but he felt as if his ears were standing at right angles to his head in his effort to hear the voices behind him.

"I have just received my general directives for the deportation," Heydrich went on. "You will have the working plans shortly, and then there won't be a day to lose."

"What is the date?" asked Rauter eagerly.

At this point, Heydrich lowered his voice, and Kersten could make out nothing more. But what he had heard was enough: a new ordeal, and apparently an even more sinister one than all those which had threatened Holland up to now.

"Keep calm, keep calm," he told himself. "Act as if you had heard nothing, as if they were not there."

Although each beat of his heart urged him to dash out in search of more information to verify what he had heard, he managed to finish his plate of cakes a mouthful at a time, to empty his coffee in slow gulps, and to leave the mess hall with his usual dignified manner, as if nothing had happened.

Once outside, he rushed to Brandt's office, but Brandt was not there. Kersten was about to look for him, when an aide-de-camp informed him that the Reichsführer was now free and was awaiting him.

2

"I am very glad to see you, my dear Dr. Kersten," said Himmler.

"Are you in pain?" Kersten asked mechanically.

"No, but I am exhausted. We have been working all morning on a very important project, something very pressing."

The Reichsführer took off his tunic and shirt and stretched out on the couch. Kersten sat down near by. Everything proceeded as usual, and yet everything was unreal, impossible.

For the project which had brought on Himmler's fatigue, the fatigue of which Kersten would relieve him, must be (Had not Heydrich just come from the conference? And had not Rauter been called to Berlin for this reason?) the doom which was about to overtake the people of Holland. But what could Kersten do, what could he even say? He had overheard a state secret; he had no right even to refer to it.

The doctor's hands, of themselves and without his really being aware of what they were doing, followed their usual course and kneaded the nerve groups just beneath the skin. Every once in a while Himmler would give a little cry, or sigh with relief. Everything was going according to the daily routine.

Nevertheless, there was a flaw in the mechanism. In the rest periods

Kersten, who was ordinarily so alert and talkative, only half listened and said nothing.

At last Himmler said affectionately, "You're a thousand miles away. It's those letters from Holland, I'll bet. Brandt tells me that your lovely friends write you very faithfully. Ah, women!"

And Himmler gave Kersten a light, conspiratorial pat on the shoulder, man to man, male to male. "But that has not prevented you," he went on, "from doing wonders for me. I shall work like a god. Goodby, until tomorrow. . . ."

3

When Kersten got home, Elizabeth Lube knew from the look on his face that something terrible had happened.

When the doctor told her what he had overheard, she shared his alarm. However, for the past twenty years she had made it her job to help and encourage him when things were difficult. She pointed out that perhaps he was upsetting himself over nothing. The words he had overheard were only fragmentary. And, too, was he sure he had interpreted them correctly? Before giving in to despair, he had to have more information.

She succeeded in getting Kersten to eat lunch, but after the meal he realized that he would not be able to endure very much longer not knowing the answers to the awful questions that were preying on his mind.

He telephoned Brandt and asked if he could see him alone. Brandt agreed to meet that evening at six o'clock in his office.

With Brandt Kersten did not beat around the bush; he came straight to the point. He repeated exactly what he had heard Heydrich say to Rauter in the mess hall.

As Brandt listened, his fine, sensitive features fell, and his eyes avoided Kersten's. At last he said in a low voice, "You know, then . . ."

"Then it's true? You knew about it? What's going on?" His questions were like cries of pain.

Brandt hesitated for a moment; then he looked at the doctor's face, the only one among all those which surrounded him night and day which corresponded with his image of a human being. Brandt could not resist what he saw on that face. He went over and locked the door and, still with lowered voice, told Kersten, "If someone should come in, I will say that you are giving me a treatment."

Then he went over to one of the tables which were covered with papers arranged in neat, precise piles. From one pile he drew an envelope which bore in capital letters the words TOP SECRET, and placed it on top of the pile. Having done this, he came close enough to Kersten to touch him and whispered, "Don't forget that I have told you nothing, that I have seen nothing. For God's sake, don't forget!"

Then he turned his back and walked over to the window, where he glued his forehead to the glass. Below, in the Prinz Albert Strasse, a fine, late winter rain made passers-by hurry through the deepening twilight. But Brandt scarcely saw them.

Kersten remained standing for a few moments, the large envelope in his hands, not daring to open it. Finally he sank into an armchair and began to read.

Then it was that he saw unfold, in black and white, in full detail, point by point, down to the last comma, the condemnation of an entire people. The document he had before him was formal and precise. The Dutch, it said, of all occupied nations, deserved the worst punishment; they were guilty not only of resistance, but of treason. The people of Holland were actually of pure Germanic blood, and they should have been infinitely grateful to Germany for delivering them from a Jewish queen and a Jewish government. Instead of which they had turned against their liberators and joined forces with the English. They had failed in their duty of gratitude and, capital offense, they had betrayed their race.

Only recently, in Amsterdam, rioters had inflicted losses on officers of the Gestapo. The measure was full; it was time to put these traitors where they could do no further harm.

Therefore Adolf Hitler, Führer of Great Germany, had authorized Heinrich Himmler, Reichsführer of the S.S., to carry out the mass deportation of the Dutch people to Poland, to the province of Lublin.

And Himmler, in turn, had outlined the procedure as follows: Three million men would be sent on foot to the territory which had been assigned to them. Their families—wives, children, and old people—would be put on ships at the ports of the Netherlands bound for the city of Königsberg, and from there they would be sent by rail to Lublin.

This plan would be put into effect as of April 20, the date of Hitler's birthday, as a birthday present to him.

Kersten had finished his reading, but he sat with the pages in his hands, which he could not keep from trembling slightly. From these pages there rose a vision which was like a panorama of hell.

Torn from the mild, peaceful shores of the Zuider Zee, millions of men advanced toward the frozen lands of the east. They had all of Europe to cross, under the whips and gun-butts of their guards. They marched in endless columns along endless roads, starving, their shoes and clothing in rags, drenched by rain and bitten by the wind. Here and there in the thick of this waking nightmare, certain faces stood out from the ranks of the exodus: they were Kersten's dearest friends.

And he saw the women, the children, the old people, packed into the bottom of the hold to the point of suffocation, or penned up in freight cars, dying of thirst, asphyxiated by the lack of air and their own wastes. . . .

Kersten dropped the papers onto the table, took a notebook out of his pocket, tore out a page, and on this scrap of paper summarized the contents of the ghastly document. His hand shook.

It was the evening of the first of March. In a few short weeks Himmler would present Hitler with his birthday present.

Kersten put the papers back in the envelope and returned the envelope to its pile. Brandt turned around and met the doctor's eyes.

"How do you like this project?" asked Kersten.

"It's horrible," said Brandt, "a whole nation sent into captivity, into slavery."

He covered his face with his hands as if he could not bear the shame of participating in this monstrous business. Then he murmured in a voice in which self-loathing struggled with fear of punishment, "Please remember, my dear Kersten, never, never tell anyone that I let you read this document."

4

The big, comfortable car he liked so much, the chauffeur who had served him faithfully for fifteen years, his apartment, which ordinarily it was such a pleasure to return to: furniture, books, paintings, even Elizabeth Lube herself, wonderful companion through thick and thin, his support, his confidante—tonight it was as if he had never seen them before.

He wandered from one room to another, distracted, dull. It seemed to him that there was a clock inside his head, and with each tick he heard: *Deportation, Holland . . . Holland, deportation. . . .*

As soon as she opened the door, Elizabeth Lube saw that the disaster exceeded their worst suspicions. She tried to get Kersten to talk, but he said nothing all evening.

He, who so loved to eat, could not swallow a mouthful. He, who so loved to sleep, could not find a moment's rest. Elizabeth Lube spent the night at his bedside.

Kersten, prostrate, almost delirious, listened all night to the clock beating in his head: *Deportation, Holland . . . Holland, deportation. . . .* He felt as if he were about to suffocate.

When at last daylight appeared, he felt something inside him snap. He could no longer carry alone the burden which was weighing him down. He showed Elizabeth Lube the scrap of paper on which he had scrawled the main points of the document which Brandt had let him read. Then, walking back and forth, wiping his brow, or standing stock still, staring at his friend with vacant eyes, he let it all out at last, for hours, the vision which was haunting him: that endless procession, driven across all of Europe, in which he recognized—stumbling, weakened, urged along with whip blows—his companions, his dearest friends.

He finished, almost in tears, "What can I do to stop this thing?"

"Try to talk to Himmler about it," said Elizabeth Lube.

"But that's impossible," cried Kersten, "that is the worst thing about it: I must not know about it, you see. I cannot know about it. God forbid he should suspect that I might be in on it. There is nothing to do . . . nothing."

He started to pace the room again, but Elizabeth Lube stopped him. "Listen to me," she said. "You are going to sit calmly in this chair and you are going to pull yourself together. You must, for the sake of those you want so much to help."

At the end of his rope, Kersten obeyed like a child. Elizabeth Lube went to make him some strong coffee. Then she prepared an ample and delicious lunch, which she forced him to eat.

Then she said, "It is almost noon. It is time to get dressed and go to the Chancellery."

At the thought of having to care for the man who was to organize and direct the deportation, Kersten had a moment's angry rebellion.

"I will not go!" he cried. "No matter what happens, I will not, I cannot associate any longer with these monsters."

But his old friend was shrewd and stubborn. She knew just how to appeal to the doctor's reason and emotions. She found the right words to persuade him. His only chance, however slim, to help the nation so close to his heart, was to stay with Himmler.

As the doctor drove to the Prinz Albert Strasse, he made up his mind to attempt the impossible. But how?

5

Once more we find Kersten in Himmler's office, which is now so familiar to him that he could find his way around it blindfolded. And once more we find the Reichsführer stretched out on his couch, half naked, confidently surrendering his wretched body to the strong and skillful hands whose power he knows so well. And once more they perform their familiar miracle. And the Reichsführer shuts his eyes with bliss, and his breathing becomes easy and peaceful, as if from the effects of a benevolent drug.

And as for Kersten, he now sees before him the herd of slaves, of the damned, friends he knows and those he doesn't know, about to undertake their journey to the end of hell.

And all of a sudden, without forethought or even volition, he is seized by an inner impulse which admits of neither doubt nor hesitation. He presses gently on the nerve center which he knows to be the most vulnerable in Himmler's body, and asks in a normal voice, "What is the exact date that you plan to start the deportation of the Dutch?"

His hands are now at rest. In the nerves of his patient, the pain is beginning to recede and, by the operation of a mechanism which has almost the force of a reflex, Himmler answers, in the most natural voice in the world, "We start on the twentieth of April. On Hitler's birthday. These Dutch are always rebelling. When one is a traitor, one must expect to be punished."

Whether it was the intensity of the silence which fell over the room at this point, or whether the torpor which had caused Himmler to answer like one who is hypnotized, passed away of its own accord, he suddenly got up, thrust his face into Kersten's and demanded in a very low voice, "How and where did you get this information?"

Above the Mongoloid cheekbones, the dull gray eyes, framed by their steel-rimmed spectacles, bored into Kersten with a suspicious sharpness, an icy cruelty which the doctor had never seen in them before.

"Yesterday, while waiting for you," said Kersten, "I had coffee and cake in the staff mess hall. Heydrich and Rauter sat down not far from me. They discussed the deportation so loudly that I could hear them. Naturally, I was interested in what they said, and I resolved to speak to you about it."

"The idiots!" screamed Himmler, but at the same time his face showed how relieved he was to find his doctor innocent. "They babble in public about something that is absolutely confidential and about which they are only half informed. I have given them neither all the details, nor all the documents. And they dare . . . right in the mess hall? It is very important that I know how indiscreet they are. Thank you for telling me about it."

Himmler sank back down on the couch again. Kersten's hands resumed their work. Now they seemed charged with a whole new vitality.

He had passed the moment of mortal danger. Himmler had accepted the fact that he knew a major state secret and even that he talked of it. It was an enormous step forward. For Kersten it meant a possibility, however slender, a hope, however imaginary, of saving the Dutch people.

He knew only too well that his plan was ambitious to the point of madness. There was little comparison between the fact of having succeeded in obtaining a few isolated pardons, and the idea of stopping a sovereign decree of the head of the Third Reich, who was already putting in motion all the inexorable machinery of an immense police force. But it was precisely each step, each success in obtaining each one of these pardons which had enabled Kersten to study Himmler's psychology and had given him more and more power over the man who was in full charge of the monstrous exodus, the man who was now half naked and once again, for the moment, putty in his hands.

His massive body leaning forward, his heavy lids closed beneath the high, deeply lined forehead, his powerful stomach resting on the couch, bending over Himmler in the attitude and with the gestures of a baker kneading dough, Kersten said with great force and gravity, "This deportation is the greatest mistake of your career."

"What are you talking about?" exclaimed Himmler. "It is absolutely necessary, and the Führer's plan is sheer genius."

"Calm yourself, Reichsführer, I beg of you," said Kersten. "Or else I will have to stop the treatment. You know how bad it is for your nerves when you become angry."

"But all the same, when one knows nothing whatever about politics, like yourself!" cried Himmler.

"Exactly, I am not interested in politics, and you know it," Kersten interrupted in the tone of the doctor who is annoyed by his patient's disobedience. "It is your health that concerns me."

"Oh! That is why you are talking to me like this," said Himmler. His face wore an expression of almost childish gratitude, and his voice was apologetic. "I should have guessed it," he went on. "You don't know, my dear Dr. Kersten, how your concern touches me! But I dare not think about my health. My work comes before everything, at least until our victory."

Kersten shook his head obstinately, like a man who is sure of himself.

"Your reasoning is false," he said. "When I protect your health, I am protecting your work as well. One depends on the other. You have got to be able to hold together until the victory, if you want to administer properly the tasks entrusted to you."

Himmler started to speak. Kersten prevented him by increasing his pressure on one of the nerve groups. "Let me finish," he said.

It was one of those moments during the treatment when a breathing spell was indicated. Kersten marshaled all his powers of persuasion and went on, "Do you remember that several days ago you asked me to increase the treatments? You told me yourself that, aside from your regular duties, overwhelming in themselves, Hitler had charged you with a mission which was enough to kill a man: you must bring the number of the S.S. up to a million before summer, when they are scarcely a hundred thousand today. In other words, you have three months to select, dress, arm, organize, and train nine hundred thousand soldiers. Have you forgotten about this?"

"How could I!" cried Himmler. "It is my most important job."

"And do you propose," cried Kersten, in his turn, "do you propose to add to this enormous work load the task of the Dutch deportation?"

"I have no choice," said Himmler with determination. "It is a personal order from the Führer."

"In that case," said Kersten, "I must warn you that I am incapable of giving you sufficient strength to carry out these two missions at once."

"But I believe that I am capable of doing it," said Himmler.

"You are wrong," said Kersten in a serious, almost solemn tone. "There are limits to what the human body will endure, and once these are exceeded, I can do nothing."

"But I must, I must carry out the plan," cried Himmler in a shrill ascending tone.

Then, half raising himself, he talked with mounting excitement, as if he were trying, by means of the picture he unfolded before Kersten, to forget the doctor's warning.

"Listen, listen to how brilliant it is," he cried. "We have taken Poland, but the Poles hate us. We need real Germanic blood there. The Dutch are of Germanic origin; in spite of their treason, this is undeniable. In Poland they will learn to change their attitude toward us. The Poles will treat them as enemies, because we are going to give their land to the Dutch. So, lost among the Slavs, pursued by their hatred, the Dutch will have to be loyal to us, their protectors. Thus we will have in eastern Europe an entire Germanic population allied to us by necessity. And as for Holland, we will fill it with good young German peasants. And the English will lose their best landing field. Admit it, admit it, only the Führer could find such a perfect solution. Is it not sheer genius?"

Kersten felt his pulse quicken. There actually was in the plan the kind of terrible perfection which characterizes the logic of madmen.

"Possibly," he said drily. "I am thinking only of your health. You must choose between your two assignments."

The time of the rest period was up. Kersten's fingers once more kneaded the exhausted nerves of Himmler's body.

"I am going to ask you to answer me frankly," said Kersten, "as patient to doctor. Of the two orders which you have been given, which is the most important, the most urgent? Raising the S.S. forces to a million, or deporting the Dutch?"

"The S.S.," said Himmler. "Without the slightest doubt."

"Then you must, in the name of your health, postpone the deportation until the victory. What difference will that make? Have you not assured me yourself that you will have won the war in six months?"

"Impossible," said Himmler. "The deportation cannot be put off. Hitler wishes it now."

The treatment was over. Himmler got up and dressed. Once again he was invulnerable. But Kersten had not thought for a moment that he could defeat him in one round. The main thing was that the battle had begun in a completely natural way and on the only terrain where

Kersten was entirely free to pursue his enemy without arousing suspicion. All was not yet lost.

Suddenly, a terrible thought struck him. If, by some miracle, Himmler gave up the deportation of the Dutch, would not the job be given to Heydrich or some other high official over whom Kersten would have no influence?

As he was leaving the Reichsführer, he asked him anxiously, "Are you the only man capable of organizing the deportation? Why not look for someone else?"

Himmler brought his palm down on the table and cried, "For a mission of this importance, the Führer trusts only me! No one else could do it, no one else will be permitted!"

The inflamed, insatiable vanity which Himmler's face expressed at this moment reassured Kersten. If he should ever have to abandon his horrible duty, Himmler would go to any lengths to prevent anyone's replacing him.

When Kersten returned home, he was an altogether different person from the tired, defeated man who had left the same place an hour before.

"I will have him yet!" he told Elizabeth Lube. And he rubbed his hands together, not as a sign of rejoicing, but as one who polishes his weapons for a long battle.

"I still have time!" he cried. And the space of time which the night before had seemed to mock him, now seemed to him more than adequate.

6

Kersten's confidence, all the greater for the depth of his initial despair, was short-lived: Himmler did not yield an inch.

In vain the doctor used all the methods which had been so successful up to now: the request in the name of friendship, the threat of serious consequences to Himmler's health, the appeal to his patient's gratitude, flattery. Though his timing was perfect, nothing worked.

"The deportation will take place on the appointed day," repeated Himmler.

This time, shielding him from Kersten's influence, was another and greater authority: that of Hitler, his master, his god.

Kersten had an almost physical sense of this presence standing between himself and his patient. It canceled out all his efforts. Every morning, day after day, he renewed his reasoning, warnings, entreaties, all in vain. He had the feeling that he was doing battle not with Himmler, but with the shadow that enveloped him.

And time was running out. It was almost the end of March. The possibility of escape was growing steadily slimmer, like the walls of some horrible prison which contracted a little every day. Kersten knew that the wheels and springs of the machine that was to tear the Dutch people from their country and send them forth on that dread journey were already being put in order. Soon the infernal device would be ready, and all would be lost.

And then, a strange thing happened. For the first time in two years, Kersten's treatments stopped working. The miraculous hands whose very touch had been enough to banish Himmler's pain were suddenly incapable even of assuaging it.

Did Kersten do it deliberately? Or was it rather, as he affirms, that the obsession, the anxiety in which he continually lived, unhinged his own nerves to the point of paralyzing his skill and rendering his care ineffectual? Whatever it was, conscious or not, Kersten's hands deserted Himmler.

And since the reorganization of the S.S. and the preparations for the Dutch deportation demanded an enormous, ever increasing effort, Himmler was soon in agony. The pain grew worse from one day to the next.

Every morning, more waxen and hollow-eyed, drenched with sweat, he stretched out on his couch and offered his tormented body to Kersten's hands with an avid, feverish hope. They had helped him so often in the past that he could not believe that they had suddenly lost their magic power. The keen frustration of waiting doubled his anguish. And Kersten's hands went to the same spots as always and went through the same motions, executed the same pressures, the same twists. Himmler's nerves shrank more and more, cried out for the miracle . . . it was coming, it had to come. Arched with pain, the wretched body prayed, begged for relief. In vain: the doctor's hands could no longer save him.

"I warned you," said Kersten. "You cannot carry simultaneously these two overwhelming burdens: to increase the number of the S.S. tenfold, and to organize the deportation of an entire population. It is too great an ordeal for your nervous system; it no longer obeys me. Renounce the lesser of the two missions, and I guarantee I can cure your pain."

"Impossible," Himmler almost sobbed, "impossible, it is an order from my Führer."

A moment later, he begged, "Try, try again . . ."

"I will try," said Kersten. "But I am sure it will be useless."

And so it was.

7

In early April, 1941, the German troops attacked Yugoslavia. Their tremendous superiority in numbers, arms, and knowledge of war assured the Wehrmacht a new victory in the war of destruction. To be in on the kill, Hitler set up his headquarters on the boundary between Austria and the invaded country.

As usual, Himmler had to accompany him. His private train was stationed at Bruck an der Mur, on the same frontier.

The departure had cost Himmler a terrific physical effort. The trip itself almost killed him.

At Bruck he never left his bunk in the private train except to see Hitler, whose headquarters were set up some twenty kilometers away.

Kersten virtually lived in the Reichsführer's compartment. He was on call night and day.

"Do something, I can't stand it any longer," Himmler would whine.

"But I have already given you several treatments since this morning," Kersten would answer. "They have had no result; another will not help."

"Try, try anyway, the pain is too great."

And Kersten would try again, in vain.

Each session—and there were now ten a day—was a new contest, a new battle for the same object.

Beyond the railroad tracks, outside the windows of the motionless train, spring was coming to the hills and woods, but Himmler and Kersten, each the prisoner of a torment of a different nature, but of equal force, were unaware of it.

"You are mad, Reichsführer," Kersten said over and over. "You see for yourself the state to which you are reduced. You see for yourself that you cannot do everything at once. Postpone the deportation until the end of the war, and I promise you that my treatment will be as effective as it was before."

Himmler was contorted, ravaged by his suffering. On his pinched and waxen face, which looked like that of a dying man, streamed a cold sweat, mingled with tears of pain which he could not hold back.

Nevertheless, he would not give in.

"I cannot, it is an order from the Führer."

"I cannot, the Führer trusts only me."

"I cannot, I owe everything to my Führer."

It was now only a week before the deportation was scheduled to begin.

If Kersten still fought, it was now only from a sense of duty and because he could not do otherwise. He had given up hope. He knew that there was nothing organically wrong with Himmler and that he could direct and put into motion the monstrous plan from his bunk, if necessary, provided he could bear the pain. And the Reichsführer found the necessary courage in the fear and idolatry inspired in him by Hitler.

However, Himmler was in such agony that he could no longer stand the discomfort of his bunk in the train. He took rooms in a small hotel in the neighborhood. Kersten, naturally, went with him.

At two o'clock in the morning, when the doctor was asleep, the telephone rang in his room. Kersten's mind was always clear and alert from the moment he woke up. Nevertheless, the doctor hardly recognized Himmler's voice. It was no more than a gasp, indistinct and broken with sobs.

"Come, come quickly, dear Kersten. I can no longer get my breath."

Kersten, accustomed as he was to seeing Himmler suffer, was amazed at the violence of his agony. Himmler had thrown off all the bedclothes, unable to bear their contact, and stripped bare, motionless, every muscle contracted, his arms stretched out flat, he lay as if crucified.

"Help me, do something!" he panted.

It did not occur to Kersten at that moment that the torture Himmler was suffering might be some sort of inherent justice, or that the man who had authorized, directed, and organized so much torment deserved to suffer. For the doctor, Himmler was a patient whom he had been treating for two years, and his professional conscience, which was so deeply ingrained, made it his absolute duty to give him the best and quickest relief he could. Besides, after living in such close contact with Himmler, and studying all his reactions and reflexes, Kersten no longer saw in him only the police officer and the executioner, but also the human being.

At the sight of this contorted body Kersten felt with all their force both the physician's imperative and common pity for a man, whoever he was, who suffered to such an extent. He felt that he was on the verge of weakening. His hands instinctively reached out toward Himmler.

Then they fell back. The other duty, which had been overshadowed for a moment, gained control again: that of saving an entire nation from the most frightful fate in its history.

And Kersten realized that in spite of the sense of duty which urged him to help Himmler and the pity which he felt for him, he would be unable to do anything as long as he was obsessed by the horror of the impending deportation. There was nothing he could do about it: it was a sort of inner paralysis. But were Himmler to give up the accursed project, oh, how joyfully, how confidently he would rescue him!

Kersten took a chair, brought it to Himmler's bedside, sat down, and bent over the sick man until their faces were almost touching. This time he did not argue, he did not reason, he did not fight. In a tone that was humble, affectionate, and almost imploring, he said, "Reichsführer, I am your friend. I want to help you. But listen to me, I beg of you: put off this Dutch thing until later, and you will soon be better, I promise, I swear to you. You are not a doctor, but a child could understand this. Your suffering is of nervous origin. I can keep your nerves under control, except when too great and too constant an anxiety eats into them like an acid. For you, the acid is the anxiety caused by your obsession with this matter of the Dutch. Free your mind of this anxiety, and I will be able to control your nerves again, and you will have no more pain. Remember how effective the treatments were before this matter came up? It will be like that again, if only you will go to Hitler and ask him to postpone the deportation until the victory."

Himmler listened hungrily to this almost tender voice, these words which were so easy to understand, and watched as if hypnotized the palms and fingers which even now were offering to put an end to his hellish torment. In his eyes, bright with unshed tears, the image of Hitler became blurred, obliterated.

Convulsively, Himmler seized one of the doctor's hands and sighed, "Yes, yes, dear Kersten, I really believe you are right. But what am I going to say to the Führer? I am in such pain that I cannot even collect my thoughts."

At that moment it was all Kersten could do to conceal his joy. "It is very simple," he answered in the neutral tone of a man unmoved by political problems. "Very simple. You tell him that you cannot meet both responsibilities at once. Mention the lack of ships, the crowded roads, point out that this superhuman work load threatens your health and that, if it continues, you cannot guarantee the completion of your first duty, which is the reorganization of the S.S."

"It's true! You are right!" cried Himmler. "But how am I going to talk to Hitler? I can't move."

Kersten asked rather hoarsely, "Then you have made up your mind? You are sure? Really sure? Because if you haven't, I repeat, I will not be able to help you."

"You have my word, the word of a German officer," groaned Himmler. "Only give me the strength."

So great was Kersten's secret joy that he found himself thinking, Relax, my friend, in half an hour you will be perfectly capable of going to him.

Never had he been so confident of success. Never had he felt this warm flow of blood from wrists to finger tips, this inspired elation. And Himmler, who had thought he was destined to suffer forever, once again found solace in the hands of Kersten. Terrified to make a movement which might undo their good, he began to relax, to breathe again. From time to time, he murmured, incredulous, "I think . . . yes, I believe the pain is going away."

Then he would say nothing, as if overwhelmed by happiness. Kersten worked in silence. When he was done, Himmler, moving slowly and cautiously, got up, breathed deeply, and cried, "I am better . . . the pain is gone."

"Only because you have decided to talk to Hitler," said Kersten. "You must do so at once; one never knows when the cramps will return."

"I am going, at once!" cried Himmler. He snatched his clothes and dressed hurriedly.

Just then the telephone rang. "Yes," said Himmler into the instrument, "speaking."

He listened without saying a word, then hung up, turned to Kersten and said, "Yugoslavia is ours. The Führer has just left for Berlin and orders me to follow." He put on his jacket hastily and added, "Pack your bag. Our train is already warming up."

Already Himmler had recovered his voice and attitude of authority. And Kersten, who knew how the Reichsführer's whole personality changed and became unmanageable when he was feeling better, could not help thinking, I cured him too fast; he will think it over and forget his promise, and return to his fanatical determination to tear the Dutch from their home on the appointed day.

But the fates were with Kersten that night. During the trip Himmler's cramps returned in full force. And while the private train rolled through the darkness, Kersten had to treat him once again. The treatment was successful. He managed, however, to prolong it in such a manner that Himmler was helpless right up until the time that the convoy arrived at the station in Berlin.

"You see," the doctor told his patient, "you see how much longer it takes. You still have that deportation business on the brain. You must free yourself of it, or everything will start up again."

"Oh, rest assured, dear Kersten! I understand," said Himmler.

He drove to Hitler right from the station. Two hours later he telephoned Kersten.

"The Führer is as generous as he is brilliant. He is sympathetic to my poor health. The deportation is postponed. I have it in writing; I will show it to you."

Elizabeth Lube was with Kersten when he heard the incredible news. He repeated it to her, word for word. Afterwards, they sat side by side for a long time, speechless.

8

Exhausted by all his emotions, Kersten went home to Hartzwalde for a rest. He said nothing to his wife about his experiences of the last few weeks, but he picked flowers in his garden and placed them before the signed portraits of Wilhelmina, Queen of Holland, and her husband, Prince Hendrik, which he kept on his bureau in spite of the implacable hatred borne them by the Nazis.

GENOCIDE

1

During the whole discussion of the deportation of the Dutch, Himmler never suspected Kersten's motives as being other than those of a doctor and friend. Hitler accepted Himmler's reasons for postponing the exodus. Himmler had spoken of his health and of the impossibility of doing so many important things all at the same time. How could Hitler have imagined that his oldest, most zealous and submissive hatchet man could have been influenced by anyone else?

But there was a less credulous man. Heydrich, chief of the Gestapo—his job was to be suspicious—immediately thought of Dr. Kersten. He could not do anything yet. He waited.

2

Among the men high in the regime, Himmler was the only one who retained Kersten as his permanent private doctor. Some of the others went to Kersten occasionally.

Ribbentrop was the first to come. Kersten hated the minister of foreign affairs. He was conceited, boastful, and arrogant. Kersten was dismayed to see such a stupid man holding such an office. He charged the minister such high fees that he stopped coming.

Rudolph Hess was next. Kersten was not so hostile to Hess. Hess's instability was obvious, but compared to the other megalomaniacs, sadists, and racists who ruled the Third Reich, he was harmless. Hess lived in a state of childish exaltation. He was crazy about the novels of Jules Verne and Fenimore Cooper, especially those about the Indians on the plains. When he saw a soldier and a girl arm in arm on the street, he would sigh: "What a combination of purity and virility."

Hess was an unbridled mystic. He deplored the ravages of the war and had vowed to retire to the desert to live as an ascetic when it was over. While he waited, he talked incessantly about doing a great deed—a deed which would make his name live, which would be of service to Germany, to the world, to war, to peace. He never stopped imagining what it would do. He was also unhappy about not being able to fight. He was an excellent pilot. Hitler, who liked him very much, had expressly forbidden him to go into combat.

Kersten treated Hess for cramps of the stomach and the sympathetic nerves. However, Hess sought the aid of many doctors. He also consulted astrologers, fortunetellers, and faith healers.

At the beginning of May, 1941, he told Kersten, "I've made up my mind. I'm going to do something big enough to shake the universe."

On the twelfth of May he secretly flew his private plane to England. He was sure he could persuade England to make peace with Germany. Hitler wanted to be free to conquer the rest of Europe. Hess landed in Scotland. He was arrested and then interned. His deed did not shake the world, but it did shake the Nazi party. Hess had been Hitler's favorite and secretary general of the party.

The second day after Hess's flight, Kersten was told to be in Heydrich's office at three-thirty in the afternoon. The order upset the doctor. Hitler had ordered the arrest of all the doctors, whether quacks or not, who had seen Hess in the days before his flight. He feared that Hess might have told them things about the party and government.

Before going to Heydrich, Kersten went to see Himmler. He had left unexpectedly for Munich. Brandt was with him. Kersten told the S.S. officer on duty: "I request that you inform the Reichsführer by telephone that in a few moments I have to be in Heydrich's office. It is important. Do it without fail." The officer promised to let Himmler know.

At exactly three o'clock Kersten was led into one of Heydrich's staff offices. The room was empty. A half hour passed. No one came, no one asked for Kersten. He wanted to find out what was happening. The doors of the office were locked from the outside.

Kersten had a lot of patience and composure. He forced himself to dominate his nerves. Finally, Heydrich appeared; he was very elegant, well groomed, and courteous, as usual.

"Excuse me for being late," he said, "but right now I have a great deal of work." Then he asked, "Did Hess tell you anything concerning the government?"

"Nothing," Kersten answered.

Heydrich watched him with his clear, cold eyes, smiled and offered him a cigarette.

"Thanks, I don't smoke," Kersten said.

He remembered that Himmler had told him about the drugged cigarettes which were given to people when they were being questioned and added, "Anyhow, I wouldn't want to smoke tobacco that does things."

Heydrich's smile became even more friendly.

"It's not that kind of tobacco. I see you know how we operate."

Without changing his tone or his smile, he went on, "I am sorry, but I have to arrest you. I don't believe a word you say. I am sure it is you who influenced Himmler in the Dutch deportation business."

Kersten thought, So we've come to this—but he has no proof.

"That's really giving me too much importance. You flatter me," he said.

Heydrich leaned back slightly, passed his well-kept hand through his sleek blond hair, and said, "No one will be able to convince me that a doctor who practiced at the Dutch court is a friend of ours. I would like to know who sent you to Germany."

"Himmler can answer you better than I," Kersten said.

Heydrich's eyes had become fixed, and his smile froze.

"The day will soon come when you will have to answer me."

"Do you think you have that kind of power?" Kersten asked.

He spoke calmly because he did not want to seem guilty. He also did not want to give Heydrich any kind of hold over him. Now he began to be afraid. How far did Hitler's orders go? Had Himmler been reached in Munich? His liberty, his life depended on that.

In a neighboring office, the telephone rang. Heydrich went to answer. Left alone, Kersten consulted his watch. He had been in the room for hours. He listened. Was it Himmler calling finally? He could not hear anything.

Heydrich came back, sat down again, lit a cigarette and smiled. "Where were we—Oh, yes—Holland," he said. "I am amazed that you know so much about what's going on there."

Kersten's fear came alive. If they had found out about his correspondence with his friends in the Netherlands, he was liable for the severest punishment. Himmler's postal number was supposed to be completely confidential. But how could one be sure?

"Don't you want to tell me about your sources of information?" Heydrich asked.

Kersten hid his fear in laughter.

"Maybe I'm clairvoyant," he said.

"Perhaps I am, too," Heydrich said. "I am even beginning to guess who you are. Soon I shall prove it."

His eyes fixed on the doctor, showing merciless determination. Kersten thought of the interrogations by torture which the Gestapo carried on in its cellars.

Heydrich got up and said, "You are free. Himmler just called me. He is ready to answer for your loyalty to the Führer himself. I am forced to let you go. I have been explicitly ordered to do so. But be ready to come back here. Don't worry, we will see each other again." *

3

When Himmler returned from Munich, he immediately asked for Kersten. He was smoking a cigar when Kersten arrived. That meant he was well and had not called for a treatment. He was also moving his eyeglasses up and down his forehead, which meant he was in an aggressive mood. He did not refer to Heydrich's interrogation. He felt Kersten was above being suspected and did not like openly to disown his subordinates.

"I have here," he said irritably, slapping some papers in front of him, "a report from The Hague that informs me that you still have your apartment and furniture in that city. Is that true?"

"It is," Kersten said.

"Yet I sent you down there, practically a year ago, with precise instructions to liquidate everything," Himmler shrieked.

Kersten knew that it was very dangerous, even for him, to give the Reichsführer the idea that his orders were not being taken seriously. Heydrich had lost no time, but Kersten had been ready for this question for a long time.

"You remember," Kersten said, "that I had to interrupt my stay in Holland suddenly to come back and take care of you. You were very sick. I left everything the way it was in order to obey your summons."

Himmler calmed down immediately. It was always painful for him to have to suspect his healer and his only friend.

* See Appendix, Note 4.

"You are right," he said. "But this time, I request you to get it over with. You will have all the necessary trucks." And as if in apology, he added, "You understand, I can't appear to lack authority in front of my staff."

"I promise," the doctor said. "I'll take my wife with me so that I may get things done more quickly."

By the sixth of June all the doctor's Dutch possessions—the antique furniture, the beautiful books, and the old masters—were at Hartzwalde.

4

Two weeks later, on the twenty-first of June, 1941, Hitler threw all his forces against Russia. He had taken the ultimate gamble. Some remarks of Himmler's, and especially his frenzied haste to raise the Waffen S.S. to the strength of one million men, had led Kersten to expect it. Preparations of such breadth could only mean a new big war. On the same day, June 21, Himmler's private train started for the eastern border. The Reichsführer required that Kersten be on it. He felt like a prisoner when he left.

Finland had also declared war on Russia. She had given up her neutrality to ally herself with the Third Reich, in a war which was lost even before it was started. Kersten felt his liberty shrink even more.

The place chosen for Himmler's mobile headquarters was in East Prussia. It was in a half-cleared wood, cut up by railroad tracks. As soon as the train was parked on one of these sidings, Himmler's men went to work; spying, making arrests, setting up concentration camps, punishments, and summary executions.

Around the private train numerous barracks were built for the staff and for the soldiers who guarded the train. One of these barracks even had a movie theater which could seat five hundred people. A half dozen concrete shelters were camouflaged under the trees. Himmler saw Hitler every night at his headquarters which were never very far away. He came back late. When he awoke, Kersten treated him. The doctor had nothing to do for the rest of the day. The meals were very hard on him since he took them in the dining car which served as mess for Himmler's staff.

The first successes against the Russians intoxicated the Nazi officers. They were sure that they would achieve an overwhelming victory. They already saw the great Reich reaching the Ural Mountains. Repeating assurances they had from Himmler, who in turn had them from Hitler, they already divided the spoils of the huge country. "Each German soldier," they declared, "will have property in Russia. It will be Germany's paradise."

"I want a factory," one said.

"I shall have a mansion," another shouted.

In order to escape these discussions and rid himself of his boredom, Kersten contrived petty daily tasks. While the fate of the world was being decided in enormous battles on a front that stretched from the White to the Black Sea, Kersten looked for mushrooms in the woods, dried them in a bread oven, and sent them to Hartzwalde. He picked wild strawberries, walked a great deal, and entered more and more notes in his journal. In the evening he went to the movies where there was always a different film; captured American, English, and Russian films, in addition to the current German movies. These showings were reserved for Himmler and his principal officers. Kersten could go, but the seats of this country movie theater were too primitive and narrow for Kersten's great bulk. He could not bear them and complained to Himmler. The Reichsführer had a leather armchair, wide enough for the doctor, put in for his exclusive use.

Every once in a while there was another nighttime distraction, the roar of Russian airplanes above. Even if the alert lasted only for a few minutes, the Reichsführer took off for his shelter, his long nightshirt flapping against his thin calves.

This was all there was to Kersten's life for two endless months. The rapid German advance gave Himmler more work every day, and he was in too much pain to let Kersten go. Finally, toward the middle of October, Himmler felt better, and Kersten was able to return to Berlin.

5

An early and terribly harsh winter stopped operations in Russia. The German Army was immobilized in its frozen foxholes. For the first time since 1940, triumph did not crown the hurling lightning. Despite severe losses of men as well as territory, the Russians held on. They had weather and space on their side. In the west, England, more tenacious than ever, prepared for future battles. America was soon to enter the war. The two arms of the pincers were still very far from each other, but already one could distinguish the shape and the future fate of the Third Reich.

Kersten, who at the bottom of his heart had never believed—even when everything seemed lost—that the Nazis would succeed in imposing their law on the world, now saw real reason to justify his instinctive doubt.

Himmler returned to Berlin, and the doctor resumed his treatments. One morning he found the Reichsführer in a peculiarly melancholy mood. Himmler sighed continually and there was a kind of despair in his eyes.

"Are you suffering?" Kersten asked him.

"It's not a question of me," Himmler answered without looking at him.

"What is the matter, then?" the doctor asked.

"My dear Dr. Kersten," Himmler said, "I am terribly distressed. I cannot tell you more."

"All that bothers you bothers me," the doctor said, "because it affects your nerves. Perhaps you can talk about what you are anxious about. I may be able to help a little."

"No one can help me," Himmler mumbled. He looked up at the round, florid, reassuring face, at the good and wise eyes and said, "I will tell you everything. You are my only friend. You are the only person I can talk to." And Himmler talked.

"After the collapse of France," he said, "Hitler made several offers of peace to England. But the Jews who run that country rejected his offers. Nothing worse could happen to the world than a war between

England and Germany. The Führer knows that the Jews will go all
the way in the war. There will be no peace on earth as long as they
are in power—that's to say, as long as they exist."

The Reichsführer's nails were mechanically scratching the table
top. Kersten thought: Hitler sees that he is beginning to lose. But his
madness cannot accept it. He needs a reason for his losses, which
will explain and excuse everything. Again, it is the Jews.

The doctor asked, "So?"

"So," Himmler said, "the Führer has ordered me to liquidate all
the Jews in our power."

His hands, which were long, thin, and dry, were still, as if frozen.

"Liquidate . . . what do you mean by that?" Kersten exclaimed.

"I mean that this race has to be killed off," Himmler said.

"But you can't," Kersten cried. "Think of the horror that this
means, of the suffering. What will the world think of Germany?"

Usually, when Himmler talked with the doctor, he was lively, even
intense, but now his face remained impassive, and his voice was dull.

"The great have to step over corpses. That is their 'tragedy,' " he
answered. Then he let his chin drop to his narrow chest and remained silent. He seemed overwhelmed.

Then Kersten said, "You see that at heart you cannot accept this
atrocity, otherwise you wouldn't be so upset."

Himmler suddenly straightened up to look at Kersten. He was surprised.

"But that's not it at all," he said. "It's on account of the Führer."
He shook his head as if he could not stand what he remembered.
"Yes," he continued, "I acted like an imbecile. When Hitler explained to me what he wanted, I answered without thinking, from
simple egotism. 'My Führer,' I said, 'I and my S.S. are ready to die
for you, but please do not give me this mission.' "

Himmler, breathing hard, told what had happened after he had
said that. Hitler had been carried away by one of his insane tan-
trums. He could not stand the slightest opposition. He had jumped
on Himmler, seized him by the neck and shouted, "I've made you

into everything you are. And now you refuse to obey me. You are acting like a traitor."

Himmler had reacted with terror and despair.

"My Führer," he had begged, "forgive me. I will do everything, absolutely everything you order me to do, and even more. Never, never say that I am a traitor."

But Hitler had not calmed down. He had shouted again, stamping his feet and foaming at the mouth. "The war will soon be over, and I have given the world my word that at the end of it there will not be one Jew left on earth. We must move quickly and vigorously. I am not sure you are capable of it."

When he had finished his account, Himmler looked at Kersten. He looked like a beaten dog.

"You understand now?" he asked.

Kersten understood all too well. Himmler did not care about destroying millions of Jews. He was worried because Hitler did not have complete confidence in him. Kersten shuddered when he thought of the murderous zeal Himmler was going to show in order to restore Hitler's confidence in his abilities.

He felt that there was nothing to do against such a perversion of human values. But, nevertheless, he tried to stir up Himmler's conceit and his love of glory.

"Do you have a written order?" he asked.

"No, only oral," Himmler answered.

"In this way Hitler makes *you* responsible; your name will be a disgrace to the German people for centuries."

"That doesn't matter."

All the rest of the day Kersten forced himself to concentrate on his patients and the other things he had to do. It took a great deal of effort. That night he could only think of one thing. The rumors he had heard were true. Millions of innocent human beings were going to be rounded up, penned in, and coldly and methodically slaughtered. It was to be done by mass production. This was more than savagery: it made one ashamed to be a human being.

Kersten thought of Hitler: the madman was beginning to rage; he was demanding rivers of blood.

The doctor trembled with horror and impotence before the things he imagined. He had succeeded in stopping the deportation of the Dutch. But miracles don't repeat themselves. Even if he again started to play upon Himmler's pain, and even if Himmler was incapable of accomplishing the monstrous job, it would not matter. The ruling madman would give it to another of his merciless hatchet men.

Kersten vowed he would take every opportunity to save as many individuals as he could. It was the only thing he could do and it was his duty to do it. But this was small comfort. What did it matter, compared to this gigantic massacre, this holocaust of millions of Jewish men, women, and children, which Himmler was getting ready to offer up to his idol?

THE JEHOVAH'S
WITNESSES

1

Meanwhile, the seasons passed, and life went on as usual. Kersten went to Hartzwalde for his third Christmas of the war.

In the beginning of 1942 Kersten suffered a great personal loss. His father, Frederic Kersten, at the age of ninety-one, was still vigorous and remarkably active. In the winter he could not work the land as much as his muscles demanded, so he would walk for four or five hours on the estate to loosen them. One morning he crossed a brook on a narrow flimsy bridge made of branches. The old man slipped and fell into the freezing water, which was less than waist deep. He pulled himself out immediately on the other side of the brook and, despite the cold, continued his walk. When he got back to the house, soaked to the skin, everyone was alarmed.

"It's absolutely nothing. The upper part of my body is dry," he said.

Two days later he had severe pains in the stomach. Kersten took his father to the nearest hospital. There, an emergency operation for an intestinal occlusion was performed on the old man. He did not recover.

For a while Hartzwalde seemed terribly empty without the old farmer. But some singular guests were soon to arrive.

2

The Jehovah's Witnesses had about two thousand followers in Germany. Because they were against the war and thought that God was above Hitler, they were seized and thrown into concentration camps, where they were treated in a particularly inhuman manner. Kersten found out about this and decided to help them.

With war consuming more and more human lives, it had become common practice to use the people in concentration camps to work in factories and on farms. Inspectors, and even dogs trained to make them work as quickly as possible, came along with them.

One day Kersten told Himmler that he lacked hands at Hartzwalde. He asked him if he could get some from the concentration camps.

"What kind of prisoners do you want?" Himmler asked.

"You have many Jehovah's Witnesses," Kersten said. "These are honest and good people."

"See here," Himmler cried, "they are against the war and the Führer."

"Let's not get into an intellectual discussion. I have a practical problem. Do me a favor, give me some women from this sect. They are real hard-working farmers."

"Very well," Himmler said.

"But without guards and dogs," Kersten continued. "That would make me feel like a prisoner. I promise you I'll keep an eye on them myself."

"Agreed," Himmler said.

Sometime later, ten women in rags and with their skeletons showing through their skins, arrived at Hartzwalde. But they did not ask
for bread or clothes; first they wanted a Bible. They had been deprived of theirs while they were in the camps. To them no hunger
or torture could compare with not having a Bible. However, since
it was a capital crime for them to possess a Bible, the doctor wrote
his name in capital letters in the one that he gave to them. After
this they were ready to die for him if necessary.

The Jehovah's Witnesses loved to work. They were descendants of
many generations of farmers and had a need to cultivate the earth.
Irmgard Kersten had been in complete charge of the estate after the
death of her father-in-law and found them very helpful.

They were more than enough to take care of the estate; before the
war there had never been more than a half dozen people working
there. Yet the doctor asked Himmler for more Jehovah's Witnesses
for Hartzwalde. He got thirty in all, including some men.

These ragged and emaciated people covered with sores and striped
with whip scars, clutched at the Bible and bread. They worked with
a kind of mystic ardor. They worshiped Kersten. He was a messenger
from the angels who had pulled them out of hell. "You know," they
would say, "we pray to God for you each day, and each time we see
a golden throne waiting for you near the Lord."

"Thanks, my friends," Kersten would answer, "but I'm not in a
hurry."

What impressed Kersten the most was their devotion to him, and
their innate hostility to the Nazis. He could have absolute trust in
them and could speak freely with his family and friends without
fearing that his remarks would be reported. They listened to the German language broadcasts with him, and together they prayed for
Hitler's defeat.

The Witnesses' friendship and complicity helped Kersten and his
family with other, more petty problems which, however, were becoming increasingly irksome in those difficult times. As the war continued, Germany enforced strict rationing. Severe rules limited the
amount of poultry and livestock allowed to each person. Kersten

owned many more cows, pigs, chickens, ducks, and geese than he was allowed. Every day inspections became more frequent and more strict.

But with the Jehovah's Witnesses the doctor had nothing to fear. They were constantly on the lookout for the inspectors and sighted them when they were still far away. If they were coming to check on the fowl, the barnyard would be thinned out instantly, as if by magic. Of 120 fowl there would never be more than nine. Since Kersten was allowed ten, he was under the limit. The fowl were tied up in sacks and scattered among the nearby bushes and woods. If the inspectors came to check on the livestock, the methods were different, but the results were the same.

When high-ranking officers of the S.S. dropped in for a meal or for tea, the Witnesses made much of the drivers, orderlies, and policemen of the party. They stuffed them full of food and drink. Even though the sect is extremely prudish, the prettiest girls were not stingy with their smiles. The visitors did not get much of a chance to snoop around.

3

The Jehovah's Witnesses did not forget their time spent in the concentration camps. They were the first to give Kersten detailed accounts of the atrocities carried on there. Kersten had heard of what went on, but, like most Germans, only in vague and unverifiable accounts. The Jehovah's Witnesses gave him a clear picture. They talked about it even though they had signed a statement that made them liable for the death penalty for speaking about the camps. They passed whole nights recounting the terror. There seemed to be no end to the tortures that they recalled. At dawn, when they took leave of the doctor, they would say, "It is written in the Bible that when one is in great trouble an angel will descend to help. We have this angel before us."

They would go away filled with this triumphant belief.

Their accounts obsessed Kersten. At the same time he was troubled by their continual exaltation. These people who saw him as a heavenly creature, wouldn't they also see the fires of hell on earth? He resolved to put his mind at rest. But this was not easy: he had to verify what the Witnesses said without revealing his source. The least slip would send them to their death. They had even been made to agree to the penalty in advance. Thus Kersten had to wait for an occasion when it would be impossible to establish a connection between his information about the concentration camps and the Witnesses.

He waited a long time. At last, in the Ukraine, he found it.

4

"Pack your bags for a trip to Russia. We're leaving in a couple of hours," Himmler told Kersten on the third of July. A month before, the Wehrmacht had launched its second offensive against the Soviet Army. They had started from the territories conquered the year before and were aiming for the Volga and the Caucasus. It was a tough proposition. Hitler was using all his forces and counted on bringing Russia to her knees.

In the first battles he had taken several provinces. Himmler, as usual, was leaving to "organize" them. Hitler's headquarters were at Vinnitsa in the Ukraine. Himmler's were at Zhitomir, sixty kilometers away.

On July fifth the Reichsführer got off his train and went to the group of buildings where he was to work and live with his staff. It was an old Russian barracks, surrounded by a wall and spikes. Himmler lived in a little house which had been inhabited by a high-ranking Soviet officer before the invasion. Kersten was lodged not far from him in a similar house.

For all practical purposes, Kersten was a prisoner. He could walk only within the limits of the dismal camp. Outside the walls and spikes, everything was barricaded and mined. When the doctor wanted to go into town, he had to get permission and a pass. Two armed soldiers accompanied him in the car to see that he did not get out.

"We are in enemy territory," Himmler said. "And I don't want you to take any chances." He himself constantly feared an attack by Russian partisans and never moved without a large escort. In an atmosphere so different from Hartzwalde, Himmler would not be likely to remember the Jehovah's Witnesses. The doctor finally broached the question which had been on his mind for so long.

"Is it true," he asked one evening, "that in your concentration camps men and women are systematically tortured to death? Up to now I did not want to mention it to you, but in Berlin, just before our departure, I was told such things that I cannot help asking."

Himmler laughed heartily, at least he seemed to.

"Come now, my dear Kersten," he exclaimed, "you are falling into the traps of Allied propaganda. It is part of their kind of war to spread rumors."

"It is not a question of Allied or any other propaganda," Kersten said quietly, "but of facts which I would like to discuss with you because I have them from a reliable source."

"What source?" Himmler asked eagerly.

Then Kersten told him the story he had carefully prepared to keep all suspicion from the Jehovah's Witnesses.

"I met two Swiss journalists on their way to Sweden, at the Finnish Embassy in Berlin," he said.

"So?" Himmler asked.

At this point Kersten took a chance. In the Reichsführer's mess he had heard that the S.S. guards had been ordered to photograph and film all the tortures they indulged in. He had found it difficult to believe that they had done such a crazy and ugly thing, but he spoke as if he were certain.

"These journalists," he said, "bought photographs from some S.S. guards near the camps. They were photographs of torture."

Himmler started up from his cot at this. Kersten realized that the incredible rumors were true.

"Are these journalists still in Germany?" Himmler asked abruptly.

"No, they are in Sweden now, perhaps already in Switzerland," Kersten replied.

"Do you know how I could buy back those photographs at any price?" Himmler exclaimed.

"I don't," Kersten said. He shook his head reproachfully and continued, "Wouldn't it be better if you spoke to me openly? Don't you think I deserve the truth?"

Himmler looked away. He was at a loss.

"You saw the photographs yourself?" he asked.

"Of course," Kersten said without hesitation.

Only then did Himmler make up his mind.

"All right," he said. "I must admit that things happen in the concentration camps that you, with your Finnish mentality and the intellectual habits acquired in the democracy of Holland, cannot understand. You have not been taught by the Nazis."

Without realizing it, the Reichsführer had begun to preach.

"It does not surprise me, therefore, that you disapprove of some of our methods. But it is right to make traitors and enemies of the Führer suffer, as long and as cruelly as possible. We are punishing them legitimately and making examples of them for others. The future will show that we are right."

His voice grew even more dogmatic.

"Do you," he said, "know why the S.S. guards were ordered to photograph all the tortures inflicted in the camps? It is so that a thousand years from now people will know how the real Germans fought the accursed Jewish race and the enemies of the German Führer. And future generations will admire these pictures of the century of Adolf Hitler. They will be grateful to him for all eternity."

Kersten wanted to hear no more. He felt the acrid taste of nausea in his mouth. Never had the feeling of living among madmen been so strong: the bloody madman and the half-mad fanatic, the two of them haunted him.

"So this is what the honor of the S.S. amounts to. They are nothing but executioners," he said, forcing himself to be calm. He knew very well he was touching a sore spot.

"It is not true. You cannot say that," Himmler cried. "My S.S. are soldiers. Those in the camps are the rejects from our army. Everything is well organized."

Himmler was accustomed to speaking without restraint to Kersten when he was being treated by the doctor, so now, impelled by his professional conceit, he again took up his tone of infallible pedantry. "This is how things are worked out," he said. "Say a soldier of the S.S. or a noncommissioned officer breaks a rule, he disobeys a superior, he is late in returning from leave, he is absent without authorization, or commits some other offense. He is brought before a disciplinary committee. There he is given a choice; he can either be punished and have this punishment on his record (and thus lose all chance of promotion), or he can go to a concentration camp and serve as a guard with the prerogative of doing what he wants with the prisoners. Let's say he chooses to go. Soon after he has arrived at the camp, his superior asks him—notice, he is not ordered, only asked—to torture and then to execute one of the prisoners. Usually the new arrival is shocked and refuses. Then the superior gives him a choice; he can return to his outfit and undergo a severer disciplinary punishment, or he must go through with his task in the camp. Usually the soldier prefers to stay. The first time he is reluctant to make a man suffer. He kills him reluctantly. The second time it is easier. After a while he gets a taste for it and starts to boast about his work. Then, because it is still too early to make these things public, he in turn is liquidated and replaced by another."

The two men were silent for quite a while—Himmler to savor his pride in the ingenious system, Kersten to regain his composure.

"You devised this system?" Kersten asked.

"Not me," Himmler said, glowing with his deepest faith. "Not me. It was the Führer himself. His genius extends even to the minutest details."

"Did he also prescribe the tortures?" Kersten asked.

Again Himmler's narrow body started with indignation.

"Do you think that anything can be done without Hitler's orders? When the greatest mind that has ever lived on earth orders such things, who am I to criticize him?" He looked into Kersten's eyes and mumbled, "You know very well that I cannot hurt anyone with my own hands."

It was true. No one knew as well as Kersten how fainthearted and feeble his patient's nerves were. The chief executioner, the master of tortures could not stand the sight of suffering or of blood.

"And if the greatest mind on earth ordered you to kill your wife and daughter?"

"I would do it without thinking," Himmler answered, carried away. "Because the Führer would have a reason to give such an order."

Kersten got up suddenly from his chair. The treatment was finished.

"That will not stop you from going down in history as the greatest murderer of all time."

Now Himmler got up and, to the doctor's astonishment, burst out laughing.

"No, dear Kersten, no. I will not be responsible to history."

The Reichsführer took a wallet from his pants pocket, took a paper from it, and handed it to Kersten.

"Read it," he urged cheerfully.

At the top of the paper Hitler's name was engraved in gold. At the bottom was his signature. It stated that Hitler took complete responsibility for all orders relating to the torture and extermination of the Jews and other prisoners of the camps. It absolved the Reichsführer of all responsibility.

"You see!" Himmler exclaimed triumphantly. He started to put on his shirt and tunic. Seeing that the doctor was not convinced and wanted to prolong the discussion, he ended it by saying, "It's absurd to talk about this. No one will have the chance to hold me responsible. Germany will win the war before autumn."

In fact, in the months of the summer of 1942, the armored cars bearing the swastika had reached out to the Volga, and Von Paulus' victorious army was approaching Stalingrad.

HITLER'S DISEASE

1

The summer of 1942 passed and autumn came without bringing Hitler his victory. Wave after wave of desperate and ferocious assaults by the Third Reich's best troops broke upon the ruins of Stalingrad. The German tide had reached its ebb.

After a trip to Finland,* Himmler returned to Berlin. It was winter, the second winter of the war against Russia, and in spite of Hitler's hysterical and frantic orders, Stalingrad still held. In the snow-covered steppes, reddened by German blood, Von Paulus' army awaited its doom.

Since November the Allies had been in North Africa.

* See Appendix, Note 5.

On the twelfth of November Kersten found Himmler extremely nervous. He was restless and could not follow a conversation. He was obviously eaten up by some anxiety. Kersten asked him what it was.

"Could you successfully treat a man who suffers from severe headaches, dizziness, and insomnia?"

"Certainly," Kersten answered. "But before committing myself, I'd have to see him. Everything depends on what is causing these symptoms."

Himmler took a deep breath, as if he were suddenly winded. He gritted his teeth, and his cheekbones became more pronounced, more Asiatic. He spoke in a choking voice.

"I will tell you the name of the sick man, but you must give me your word of honor that you will never repeat it to anyone. You must swear to keep what I am going to tell you absolutely secret."

"Reichsführer, it is not the first time that I will have to keep medical facts confidential. It is a rule of my professional life."

"Excuse me, Kersten, but if you knew . . . ," Himmler said.

He went to his safe, took out a black portfolio, and took some papers from it.

"Here," he said, handing them to Kersten with a gesture that cost him visible effort. "Read it. You are holding a secret report on the Führer's illness."

Later Kersten often wondered why Himmler had shown him the report. What anxieties had pushed him to it? Had Hitler's mental faculties suddenly given way? Had his rage been worse than usual? It was the moment when the fortunes of war were turning brutally against Germany. Perhaps this had spurred Himmler to get an opinion on Hitler's health from a man he trusted completely. Kersten was never to find out why.

The report was twenty-six pages long and was a compendium of all Hitler's medical reports since the time he had been treated for serious eye trouble at the hospital in Pasewalk. The following facts were established: In his youth, Hitler had contracted syphilis. He had left Pasewalk apparently cured, but in 1937 symptoms appeared that showed beyond all possible doubt that the disease was still active. Finally, at the beginning of 1942, the current year, there had been manifestations which made it evident that the Führer was suffering from progressive syphilitic paralysis. Kersten finished reading the report. Without saying a word he gave it back to Himmler. The implications of the document made it difficult for the doctor to think for a few minutes.

"Well?" Himmler asked.

"Unhappily, I can do nothing for such a case," Kersten answered. "I am a specialist in manual therapy, not in mental illness."

"According to you, what can be done?" Himmler asked.

"Is he under treatment?" Kersten asked.

"Certainly," Himmler said. "Dr. Morell gives him injections which he assures him will stop the progress of the disease, and in any case will preserve his capacity for work."

"What guarantee do you have that this is true?" Kersten asked. "In modern medicine there is no recognized cure for progressive syphilitic paralysis."

"I have thought of that myself," Himmler said.

Suddenly he started to walk across the room, the report in his hands, talking at the same time. As he talked, his speech became more rapid, nervous, and intense. The Reichsführer was thinking out loud. He was really trying to convince himself.

He said that it was not a question of just any sick man, but of the leader of the great German Reich. He could not be examined in a clinic for mental illness. It would be impossible to keep the secret. The Allied intelligence services would find out. The enemy would broadcast it to the German Army and people. The most disastrous defeat would follow. That was why he had decided to let Morell do what he wanted. For Morell had promised to preserve Hitler's capacity for normal activity and his genius while the regular doctors would surely offer no hope. He would certainly watch him constantly to make sure that nothing irreparable happened. But it was essential that Morell sustain Hitler until the victory. After that he would see. Hitler could then retire to a well-earned rest.

"You see what anxieties I have," Himmler said. "The world considers Adolf Hitler a giant. I want him to remain that for history. He is the greatest genius who ever lived. Without him the great German Reich, stretching from the Urals to the North Sea, is impossible. What does it matter if he is sick now that his work is practically finished?"

Himmler put the report back into the portfolio and returned it to the safe, turning the combination.

2

When Kersten left, he was in a fog, but there were glimmers of light here and there. He was beginning to understand many things that had been incomprehensible before. Above all, he wanted to know how many people were familiar with the medical report. For this reason he went to Brandt's office and with his usual caution asked him if he knew about a secret document, drawn up by hand on blue paper, which was about twenty-six pages long. Himmler's private secretary turned pale.

"Did the Reichsführer really speak about it to you? Don't you know what danger you are in now? You, a foreigner, have knowledge of our most important state secret. Outside of Himmler, only Bormann * and maybe Goering have this information."

"Who wrote it?" Kersten asked.

"I won't tell you, not for the whole world," Brandt said. "All you have to know is that the author of it has a deep sense of responsibility. His integrity is indisputable. He felt it his duty to warn the Reichs-führer. He had a long conversation with him several weeks ago at his headquarters. Himmler asked him for a written report. Now, after much thought and anguish, Himmler does not dare doubt the facts. For God's sake, never refer to it, even to Himmler. You risk your life if you do," Brandt told Kersten.

Kersten followed his advice. The following week he saw Himmler each morning, but in their conversations there was not one word about Hitler's health. It was as if the report did not exist. But there was hardly a moment during those days when the doctor was not haunted by what he had learned.

* Secretary general of the National Socialist party, who had succeeded Rudolph Hess.

A syphilitic ruled Germany and the countries she had conquered. A man whose body and spirit had for years suffered from the ravages of a growing paralysis, controlled her still terrible power. The fate of the whole world depended upon a brain diseased to its core. Kersten could not get it out of his mind.

Since June, 1940, when Kersten had learned that Himmler was in charge of drawing up the bible of the Third Reich, the doctor had felt he was living among madmen. What he had seen since, among the Nazi leaders, confirmed his uneasiness. Up to that time it had been based on his impressions, his own inferences, and various hints. But now the doctor had read a report which gave the plain medical facts. He could *see* Hitler's sickness. And thinking of the power of this madman, he was terrified, not for himself but for all mankind. The king of madmen, instead of wearing a strait jacket, fed his fancies on the blood of whole peoples.

And yet, it was still nothing compared to what would happen in the future, for the disease had not yet reached its height.

3

This was Kersten's train of thought when, on the nineteenth of December, Himmler himself brought up the tabooed subject. He asked the doctor if, during the past week, he had thought of a way of treating Hitler effectively.

Suddenly the dam broke. All the fears and visions pent up in the doctor burst forth in a flood of words. Neither caution, nor the desire to manipulate the situation, restrained him.

First, he gave Himmler a medical picture of the incurable disease which was destroying Hitler: his judgment was affected, his critical faculties were unbalanced. The headaches, the insomnia, the weakness of the muscles, the trembling of the hands, the fumbling with words, the convulsions, the paralysis of the limbs would increase relentlessly. The ecstatic illusions, the megalomania would have no check.

Since this was the case, Kersten did not understand why Himmler had chosen to leave Hitler in Morell's hands. The Reichsführer was taking a terrible chance. He was allowing decisions which determined the fates of millions of men to be obeyed as if they were conceived by a normal brain, when in fact they came from a man suffering from a terrible mental illness. Who could say whether these decisions were made in an interval of lucidity or of madness?

The Reichsführer did not speak. Kersten, surprised at his own boldness, spoke even more explicitly.

Only a man in complete possession of his faculties had the right to rule. From the moment when this was no longer the case, Himmler did not have the right to recognize Hitler as his Führer.

Finally Himmler spoke, but not to threaten Kersten with punishment for sacrilege, not even to tell him to stop.

"I have thought of all that," he mumbled, bowing his head. "Logically, you are right. But here logic loses its hold. It is impossible to change horses halfway down the hill."

In spite of his familiarity with Himmler, Kersten never imagined that he could ever have entertained the idea of rejecting his idol. After this admission, Kersten felt that he could abandon all reserve.

"Everything is in your hands, Reichsführer," Kersten said. "You still have the S.S. If you call together the most important generals and show them that, for the sake of the nation, Hitler must resign, they will see that you are a statesman of the greatest initiative. They will follow you. But it's up to you to make the first move."

Himmler shook his head again, to show that he had already thought of this solution.

Then he answered, "But it is precisely this that is impossible. I cannot make a move against the Führer. I am commander of the S.S. whose motto is, 'Honor is Loyalty.' How could I do it? The whole world will think I am acting from a personal desire to gain power. To be sure, I could justify my actions with medical reports, but everybody knows how easy it is to get them. Appearances are against me. If the Führer was examined openly by specialists, no one would doubt the reality of his illness. But such an examination would only be possible after we had acted, and then people would be suspicious. It's a vicious circle."

Himmler suddenly straightened his neck and shoulders. He had gone as far as he could in facing the situation honestly; he could not stand it any longer.

"And then imagine," he said with a dull voice, full of hope, "imagine what would happen if the diagnosis of specialists showed that the report we have read was wrong. I would have overthrown a genius capable of the greatest ideas because some doctors had a hunch he was ill."

"It is more than a hunch," Kersten said.

"Possibly," Himmler said, "but nature has been known to behave in miraculous ways that completely refute medical science. And the Führer is a superman."

"All right," Kersten said. "Then you're going to let things go on this way. You're going to let Hitler go from bad to worse. You're willing to leave the destiny of the German people in the hands of a paralytic?"

Himmler thought for a while, brow furrowed, before answering. Finally he said, "The risks are not yet such that I am forced to act. There will still be time to act when the facts leave no room for doubt."

With these words the conversation ended.

4

Four days later Himmler made an unusually generous response to the doctor's tireless efforts on behalf of a small group of Swedes who had been brought to his attention six months before by Kivimoki, the Finnish ambassador, and Richart, the Swedish ambassador. Was this to encourage Kersten to forget their conversation, or was it a manifestation of renewed friendship? The Swedes were engineers and industrialists who had been arrested in Poland and convicted of espionage.

Two of the less important ones were immediately set free. The others, who had been condemned to death according to martial law, had their sentences commuted to life imprisonment. Himmler promised to free them eventually.

Kersten informed the two embassies and left to spend New Year's at Hartzwalde.

5

The estate continued to exist apart from the world's troubles. The enchanted calm of trees and of fruitful earth, of the family hearth and the devotion of the Jehovah's Witnesses reigned at Hartzwalde. Kersten's two sons were growing; they were now strong and lively. Irmgard, even though she was pregnant with her third child, was her usual gay, friendly, and active self. She ran the house and catered to her husband's love of good food.

Kersten, with his feet on the andirons beside the roaring fire in the big fireplace, or all muffled up driving his cart through the woods and fields looking at the magical drawings of the frost, savored each day with all his strong and enduring capacity for happiness. But his knowledge of terrible secrets, his involvement with tragedies, and his dealings with their most sinister participants, had completely broken the shell in which he had been able to shelter himself.

He could not lose himself in the beauties and the activities of his estate. Instead, by contrast, they made him feel the miseries and suffering of Europe more acutely. He was more acquainted with them than most of his contemporaries. There, in that quiet safety, he thought of all those who were each moment being arrested, being tortured by the Gestapo, and then surrendered up to the S.S. executioners.

At meals the abundance of the food reminded him that famine was wasting away whole nations, even threatening their very existence. He was sure of one terrible thing: Himmler had put into execution a plan of organized famine to depopulate Holland, Belgium, and France.

The doctor had been hearing of this project since 1941, but only in very vague terms. It was only in August, 1942, six months before, that Kersten had learned of its extent and monstrosity from random information he had pumped out of Brandt.

Besides the requisitions and confiscations of conquest, the goal of the plan was to starve the countries in a subtle manner. Nothing could have been easier or simpler. The occupation armies, commanded by Himmler, were to get the citizens of the occupied countries to buy up all the food on the black market. It was then to be shipped to Germany.

To be sure this was true, Kersten asked Himmler directly. So as not to be suspected, he had spoken only of Holland. The Reichsführer knew how deeply he cared about that country.

"Is it true," Kersten had asked, "that you are draining the Netherlands of all their food?"

"Not only the Netherlands, but also Belgium and France," Himmler had answered.

"Why?"

"For two reasons," Himmler said with satisfaction. "First, to complement our own supplies. Second, we will be very glad to see these people die of hunger. It will be their fault. Thus a large number of Frenchmen (they are our real enemies) will disappear. The fewer there are, the better it will be for Germany."

"It's diabolical," Kersten had exclaimed. "Humaneness aside, think of the spiritual level of the peoples you are secretly exterminating, of their culture and of what they have given to the world."

Himmler had smiled and answered, "Dear Kersten, you are too much of a humanitarian and a humanist. In a war to the death, all means are legitimate. Why did these people want to fight us? All they had to do was to join us."

Afterwards, Himmler had half dozed off, his eyes closed, in the comfort which the hands of the doctor had given him.

Then Kersten tried once more to get Himmler to make a gesture of clemency. He had pleaded for France, because she was the principal objective of the plan. Kersten thought that the day that the Reichsführer stopped systematically starving France, Holland and Belgium would also benefit.

Each morning the doctor had spoken of the great painters and writers of France, of the great kings, of the knights and barons. Far from giving in to Kersten, Himmler had shown himself to be very proud of his demoniac plan.

He had said, "The farmers will always survive. We need a purely agricultural France, a milk cow for Germany. The city people, the workers, and the intellectuals will perish. We've figured it all out. About twelve million will die."

He continued, "I am sure it will work. If the French hesitate to accept paper money, we will give our agents silver money which we have gathered throughout Europe. If silver is not enough, we will give gold. The French will not be able to resist gold."

Finally Himmler had said, "In all this, Germany will not be involved. The death of millions of Frenchmen will be the fault of the black-market men, who will be pure-blooded Frenchmen. We will keep our hands clean."

Kersten had left for Hartzwalde without being able to get the least mitigation of this perfect crime. Just before he left, Brandt had told him distressing news about the food situation in France. The black-market men, with their inexhaustible sums of money from Germany's treasury fat with the spoils of war, were already sucking the vital substance of the nation like leeches. Food was growing scarce, morals were crumbling, and tuberculosis was spreading rapidly. When he saw his sons who had been brought up on the richest milk, the freshest eggs, and the most wholesome meat, the doctor could not forget the undernourished children who hardly had a crust of filthy bread. He was pursued by a vision of all the men and women who were feeble with hunger, while Irmgard, thanks to the clandestine slaughter of their animals, stuffed him with the tenderest fowl, veal, and pigs.

6

But after his vacation, during the beginning of 1943, the opportunity that Kersten had so eagerly awaited finally came. In the first days of February, Himmler made an urgent call for the doctor from his headquarters in East Prussia. Kersten found Himmler in the midst of an attack and deeply depressed. This time physical suffering was not the only cause. It was accompanied by anguish and melancholy which, strange as it may seem for a Reichsführer of the S.S., stemmed from the worst kind of German sentimentality.

The landscape of the railway tracks, the freezing fog, the narrow compartment in the train which served as headquarters, his isolation among a staff (each officer of which he suspected of betrayal), all contributed to this depression. There was also the disaster of Stalingrad and the Allied invasion of Sicily. The handwriting of destiny was on the wall. All this rendered Himmler as susceptible to the advice of a friend as an adolescent of Werther's time.

Kersten knew his patient's disposition too well not to sense his inner mood. After having relieved him of his pain, he sat at the head of the bed and spoke to him in the softest, saddest, dreamiest, most romantic tone of voice.

"Have you ever thought, Reichsführer, how painful it must be for a French mother to see her child's body contorted by hunger cramps when she has nothing to give him to eat? Perhaps you do not realize it, but hunger cramps, like yours, are caused by the sympathetic nerves. And those poor people do not have a doctor to cure them. Think of what I do for you, and be in turn a Dr. Kersten to the unfortunate French. In a thousand years history will still speak of Reichsführer Heinrich Himmler and celebrate your generosity."

With Himmler in such a state, each word spoken by Kersten touched either his sentimentality or his conceit. He gave way to a philosophical sadness and took pity on men. Touched by his own goodness he cried, which made him feel better.

"My dear and good Kersten," he exclaimed, "my magician, my Buddha, you are undoubtedly right. I am going to see the Führer. I will do everything in the world to persuade him."

Himmler kept his word. During his daily conference with Hitler he told him that if they continued to starve the French, the Resistance would gain that many more recruits and thus give the Wehrmacht even more trouble. Hitler had no reason to suspect that his "faithful Heinrich" had been influenced by someone else. He let himself be easily convinced. Himmler ordered his supply services as well as the occupation army to stop all purchases on the black market. The order was in the Führer's name. As Kersten expected, this order was automatically extended to Belgium and Holland.

7

During the next three months nothing special happened. Kersten spent the weekdays in Berlin and the week ends at Hartzwalde. He treated

Himmler each morning when he was in the capital. If Himmler suffered from a sudden attack when he was away, Kersten traveled to his field headquarters. In his journal there are many notes from this period. Kersten does not now remember the specific incidents they refer to, since they were so frequent and so much a part of the daily routine. Here are some examples of these notes:

"Today I obtained pardon for forty-two Dutchmen condemned to death."

"I have been lucky today. I succeeded in saving fourteen Dutchmen who were condemned to death. Himmler is suffering a great deal and is weak. He is ready to give anything I ask."

"Yesterday I succeeded in getting three Estonians, two Letts, six Dutchmen, and five Belgians out of concentration camps." *

The doctor continued to live like this until May, when his wife gave birth to a third son. He spent two happy weeks at Hartzwalde. He had expected to stay longer, but the vacation was cut short on the eighteenth of May when he received a telephone call from Brandt:

"Take your car and go to Berlin. An airplane is waiting for you to take you to Munich. At the Munich airport you will find a military car which will take you to Berchtesgaden. Himmler is in terrible pain," Brandt said.

Himmler's private plane was an old Junker 52, slow but solid and tried. Himmler preferred safety to speed. In this, Kersten was like him.

Kersten had been in the air for about an hour, flying southwest, when on his left and above him he saw some small shining spots moving toward the plane. There were more of them. They rapidly turned into fighter planes.

"Now, who could they be?" Kersten asked himself, almost like a tourist.

A loud, broken hammering against the part of the fuselage behind him was his answer. The old Junker dove instantly.

* The high proportion of Dutch among the saved victims was due to the fact that through Himmler's personal postal number, Kersten continued to receive a flood of information. In order to ask for pardon or freedom Kersten had to know the names of the people who were to be saved and some simple details about them.

God, the English. We are finished, thought Kersten.

The heavy Junker, not made for acrobatics, was diving vertically. At the same time, Kersten had swift, clear thoughts. They seemed to come in groups like the bursting of the machine gun which accompanied them.

It's over. Interesting, in this moment the brain still works. How can I let my wife know I am dead? In any case my life is at an end. . . .

The airplane was shaken by a violent shock, so that it shuddered from propeller to tail as if it were shattering.

I am dead, Kersten thought. For a moment he believed it.

The plane stopped shaking, and the pilot came out of the cockpit. "Doctor, Doctor," he shouted. "We've had great luck. I succeeded in shaking them off by buzzing the treetops. Look!"

The pilot was showing him the holes of the English bullets in the fuselage. His finger stopped at two rows of holes which framed the spot where Kersten had leaned his head against a porthole. They were the marks of two bursts. The gunner had shot as in practice, with the regulation pause of one second between pulls of the trigger. That second had saved Kersten's life. The doctor understood the meaning of those little holes surrounding the place where he had leaned his head. He felt suddenly very hot.

The pilot took a flask of cognac from the pocket of his coveralls and drank eagerly. Kersten reached for the flask and had the first and only drink of his life. It tasted wonderful.

The pilot examined the plane and found that nothing essential had been hit. They had landed in a large meadow and could take off. They reached Munich not much later than planned.

8

When he learned of the danger Kersten had come through, the Reichsführer was much concerned.

"It's your lucky day, dear Kersten. Here in Berchtesgaden you have just escaped another danger, different, but just as serious. The Führer questioned me about you. You had been denounced to him—I do not know by whom, but don't worry, I'll find out—as an enemy of Germany, as a double agent placed next to me. Of course, I answered for your loyalty, and of course that was sufficient."

Kersten thanked Himmler, who was obviously uncomfortable about something he still had to say.

"Hitler asked me if I thought your treatment could help him." Himmler coughed loudly.

"Well?" Kersten asked.

"I answered that you were a specialist in rheumatism," Himmler said very quickly. "You understand, if the Führer knew how sick I am, he would not have the same confidence in me."

This was not surprising, because Himmler was very secretive about his illness. No one knew about it except Brandt. "You can be sure that all those low *arrivistes,* Bormann, Goering, Ribbentrop, and Goebbels, would use my illness against me."

"That's true," Kersten said.

"And you can be equally sure," Himmler went on, "that Morell and the Führer's other doctors would ruin you if you treated him. I hope you do not hold it against me."

"Oh, no," Kersten exclaimed from the bottom of his heart.*

"Above all, since you yourself told me you could do nothing . . ."

He didn't finish the sentence but his meaning was clear. Himmler was thinking of the report he had shown the doctor that day in December.

"You understand?" he asked.

"I understand," Kersten said.

And the subject was dropped—for the time being.

* See Appendix, Note 6.

THE GREAT PLAN

1

During the beginning of September, 1943, the government of Finland asked Kersten to come to Helsinki and make a general report. Kivimoki, the Finnish ambassador to Germany, made the request. Since Kersten was both *Medizinalrat* and a Finnish officer, Himmler could not easily oppose the trip; he even pretended to approve of it.

"Maybe you can find out why your government hasn't handed over its Jews to us," he said.

As Kersten was getting ready to leave, he received another, more important invitation. Richart, the Swedish ambassador, let the doctor know that if he stopped in Stockholm on his way to Helsinki he would be welcome. He should plan to stay for a while because the Swedish ministers wanted to have several confidential interviews with him.

The offer affected Kersten as liquor does someone not used to it: his head swam. He could not even imagine what it would be like to spend a few weeks free, in a free capital. How could he force Himmler to let him go?

At first he thought it would be impossible, but with his friend Kivimoki, he found a good excuse. In his childhood he had often heard the Russian proverb, "Misery breeds guile." He thought about the excuse so much that he began to convince himself it was actually true.

"I have received serious news from the embassy. I am going to be drafted in Finland and will not be able to return here."

It was not true, but since Kersten had often spoken of it, Himmler believed him and was panic-stricken.

"For nothing in the world! I do not want to lose you. I cannot."

"Since it is official, I do not see how I can refuse," Kersten said.

"It must be avoided," Himmler cried.

"There is a way. I figured it out with the ambassador," Kersten said thoughtfully.

"How?"

"There are five or six thousand wounded Finns in Sweden. They are crippled or incurable and permanently out of the fighting. Finland lacks the personnel and medical supplies to take care of them properly." (This was true.)

"Then what?" Himmler asked feverishly.

"I could be deferred for a long time, if you gave me two months to treat the wounded Finns in Sweden," Kersten lied.

"Two months. That's a long time," Himmler said.

"Do you prefer to have me drafted until the end of the war?" Kersten asked.

Himmler did not answer. As the silence continued, Kersten recalled a very difficult moment.

He asked quietly, "Do you remember, Reichsführer, that in May of 1940, when you were getting ready to invade Holland, you forbade me to leave Hartzwalde? I spoke then of getting in touch with my government. You laughed at the idea and answered, 'Finland will not declare war on us on account of you.' "

"I might have said that," Himmler answered, without looking at Kersten.

The doctor continued, even more gently, "Today, it is my turn to say to you, 'If you want to save me from the orders of my government, declare war on Finland.' "

Like most of their crucial conversations, this one took place during a treatment. Kersten saw Himmler's puny shoulders drop.

"War on Finland?" Himmler murmured. "Not now. Our situation has become too difficult."

Himmler was silent. Didn't they have enough to handle? Rommel's African army was finished, Von Paulus was defeated on the frozen steppes of Stalingrad, the Soviet Army was beginning to advance like a ground swell, hundreds of Allied planes bombed the German cities daily. In short, in three years Hitler's plans had been completely overturned. Himmler's few words told the whole story.

Kersten put on his good-natured tone.

"Since it is not appropriate to use force against Finland, let us use diplomacy. Believe me, it is better. Agree to let me go to Sweden for two months to treat my countrymen."

"All right. Go." Himmler sighed.

Suddenly he seized Kersten's hand. "You will come back for sure? There is no question of your return? If not . . ." he said in a changed voice; it was hard and hoarse.

The doctor pulled his hand away carefully but firmly.

"Why do you speak to me like that?" he asked. "Have I done anything to deserve such suspicion?"

Once again there was genuine regret on Himmler's face.

"I beg you, from the bottom of my heart, dear Kersten, to forgive me. You know my life has made me suspicious by second nature. But not toward you. You are the only man in the world in whose sincerity and good will I believe."

Intuition served Kersten as much as reason in his dealings with Himmler. He was quick to take advantage of his momentary humility.

"I intend to bring my wife and my youngest son—who is still being nursed—and the nurse, to Sweden. My son is only three months old," Kersten said casually.

Himmler scratched the leather of the sofa he was stretched out on. He looked at Kersten out of the corner of his eye, with his usual sharp and fearful look. But his voice remained the same.

Then he asked, "Are the other two boys going also?"

Kersten almost said yes, but when he opened his mouth to speak, he heard himself answer, "No, of course not. They do not have to be with their mother all the time. They will stay at Hartzwalde with Elizabeth Lube, my sister. You know her."

The intuition which led him to change his answer at the last moment was correct. Himmler's face lit up immediately. He was full of good will and trust.

He said, with the smile of a family man, "You are right. The country is so much better for children than the city, even if the city is Stockholm."

Kersten answered with a similar smile.

"That's just what I think. The milk is excellent on my property."

2

To understand Kersten's feverish happiness, one must remember or try to imagine what it was like in Hitler's Germany. There was a shortage of food, clothing, and heat. There were interminable lines for the most essential supplies. Many cities were without light at night. This was the normal life of millions and millions of men. Everybody was afraid. They feared for those on the front and for those in the camps. They trembled during the terrible night raids, and those who survived feared the dawn sound of policemen's fists banging on their doors.

Kersten suffered much less from the shortages than most people. But he risked the death penalty for secretly raising and slaughtering livestock. The little war against the inspectors, the tricks of the Jehovah's Witnesses, all this now seems like an amusing anecdote, but then it wore them out with worry. Above all, Kersten had for a long time been unable to ignore the suffering that surrounded him everywhere. The shortages, the cold, the anguish families went through for their relatives, the fear of being reported, the fear of saying one word too many, all increasingly weighed him down. As for the police terror, he lived in the middle of it. From where he was it spread its tentacles throughout practically all of Europe.

One simple detail shows the almost childlike joy Kersten felt at being able to spend two months in a free country. He chose the thirtieth of September, his birthday, to fly to Stockholm. This was his way of saying that there was no greater gift he could receive from life and from himself.

Kersten, who was traveling as a diplomatic courier, had nothing to fear from the customs or police inspectors. In his luggage there was one suitcase, stuffed with compromising papers, including his journal. He had kept it for three years and filled it with accounts of his conversations with Himmler. Even the conversations on the most dangerous subjects, such as Hitler's syphilis, were recorded there. In this suitcase were also numerous copies of secret documents which, thanks to Brandt, Kersten had been able to take from the Reichsführer's Chancellery.

Irmgard Kersten, who still knew nothing about this side of Kersten's life, was surprised by the unfamiliar suitcase.

"I guess," the doctor told her laughingly, "that I have overestimated the cold Swedish weather. I have taken enough warm clothes for a regiment."

Kersten's big car brought him to Tempelhof. The airplane took off. But it was only when the pale green moving sea spread out under it that Kersten thrilled with freedom. Delwig, an old Baltic friend, one of whose ancestors had been Pushkin's tutor, met him at the airport. He accompanied Kersten to a comfortable and modest pension, just what Kersten had asked the Swedes to find for him. As soon as the luggage was brought there, Kersten asked his friend if he knew a place where he could safely leave a very valuable suitcase. Delwig advised him to rent a safe at a bank and suggested doing it right away. But in spite of his impatience to have his documents safely tucked away, Kersten had an even more pressing desire.

"Let's wait until tomorrow," he said to Delwig. "Now let's get to the pastries. There's nothing like them in Germany."

The next day Kersten brought his documents to a bank. He did not have to rent a safe. They told him that sealing the suitcase would make it completely secure. So the suitcase was tied up and sealed with lead, imprinted with the doctor's ring which carried the coat of arms that Charles V had given to his ancestor, Andreas Kersten. Then his journal and secret documents were put in a corner of the cellar.*

Two days after the doctor's arrival, an underling from the Ministry of Foreign Affairs came to tell Kersten that Gunther, the minister of foreign affairs, wanted to see him, but in his own house, informally, practically in secret.

By a strange coincidence, Gunther's apartment was just around the corner from the pension which the Swedish authorities had rented for Kersten. It was there that the two men met and held a conversation crucial to the fate of thousands of men.

The minister began by thanking Kersten for the commutation of sentences which he had secured for the Swedes who had been arrested by the Gestapo in Poland.

"I expect to be able to get them released one day," the doctor said.

"That's more than we can hope for," Gunther said. "I am sure you know that that is not the reason for our invitation to you. I want to talk to you about a matter of much greater importance. Every day the Allies put more pressure on us to enter the war against Germany, which is contrary to our traditions of neutrality and to all our interests. The day after we declare war, German airplanes would turn Stockholm into another Rotterdam. Instead, I have thought of a great humanitarian plan which would be very valuable to the Allies. The idea is to save as many of the people in the concentration camps as possible. Will you go along with us?"

"Of course," Kersten said. "For two years, as you know, I have been trying to help the prisoners and those condemned to death. It doesn't matter what nationality they are, Dutch or Finnish, Belgian

* They were to remain there until the end of the war when Kersten reclaimed them.

or French, Norwegian or Swedish. I have tried to aid all the unfortunates about whom I could get precise details. I am ready with all the means at my disposal to help people who are suffering."

"Then let us try to think big," Gunther said.

From that day on Kersten often saw the minister of foreign affairs. The two men devised a plan whose vastness made it sometimes seem like a fantasy. They wanted to wrest thousands of prisoners from the camps and bring them to Sweden. The Swedish government would have to convince the Germans that it would be responsible for giving the prisoners asylum and transporting them. The Red Cross, represented by Count Bernadotte, would serve as intermediary. Kersten's role was the most important and the most difficult. He would have to convince Himmler to allow the prisoners to leave.

3

On the fifteenth of October, 1943, Kersten left Stockholm for Helsinki. An official car waiting for him at the airport took him to Mr. Ramsey, the Finnish minister of foreign affairs. Kersten made an extensive report on the German situation and concluded by saying that Germany could not hold out for more than a year or a year and a half. In his opinion, Hitler had lost the war. The minister said that his government also felt that way, and his one desire was to make peace with Russia. Since he could not approach Moscow directly, he instructed Kersten to try to negotiate through some American representatives in Stockholm. The doctor, who had never been involved in politics, thus became a secret messenger for international diplomacy.

Back in Sweden Kersten got in touch with the Americans. The Finnish overture was communicated to Washington. Roosevelt made it known that the Finnish government should approach Russia directly. Nothing else was done.

Meanwhile Kersten had made another attempt at peace. He had kept the Finnish move a secret from Himmler but had suggested that he sound out the Americans for terms to end hostilities.

Himmler had not opposed the suggestion; on the contrary, he sent his head of espionage and counterespionage, Walter Schellenberg, to

Stockholm in the greatest secrecy. But the negotiations came to nothing, and Schellenberg returned to Berlin.

At the end of November Kersten himself had to face going back to Germany. He had no choice. There was another difficult problem: his son, who was a few months old, and his wife. Was he going to bring them back to a country at war, where the situation got worse from day to day, and where he was going to be in greater and greater danger? In Stockholm they were safe, while in Germany . . .

Kersten thought of Himmler's reaction. He knew that even if he returned alone he would be welcome; the Reichsführer needed him too much. But at the same time Kersten knew instinctively that if he wanted to have Himmler's complete blind trust, if he wanted everything to be in his favor in the game he was about to play with the Reichsführer, he would have to bring his wife and son back to Germany. They would be proof of his trustworthiness.

In the middle of the night, seated in his armchair with his hands resting together over his belly, the doctor brooded anxiously. Before his conversations with Gunther he would not have hesitated to leave his son and wife in Stockholm. But since then he had a much larger view of his duty. Up to that time he had helped men more or less at random. He had not even been completely aware of what he was doing each time he saved someone. It was part of his daily routine, somewhat like an extra patient. Once he had done it, he 'forgot about it. It was only now that he understood the role that destiny had forced upon him. A boundless horizon opened up before him. He could help a whole segment of humanity given up to torture and despair. The task he had set himself with Gunther was extremely difficult, and the more precarious the situation in Germany became, the more dangerous it would become. Kersten had a vision: he saw the king of madmen at the moment of his downfall, and he was afraid for his wife and son.

"But on the other hand," he told himself, "just because the times ahead are going to be fearful, if I do not give Himmler complete proof of my loyalty and affection, my mission will be impossible. The only guarantee he will understand is the return of my wife and son."

The sleepless night was over. Sighing, Kersten got up from his armchair. The die was cast.

"Irmgard, we're going back," the doctor told his wife as lightly as he could. "I am sure you will be glad to see your sons again and to manage the property."

Irmgard Kersten, who loved Hartzwalde with its eight horses, its twenty-five cows, its twelve sows, its enormous boar, and the twenty fowl she took care of, was happy to return to her estate. She had no idea of the difficulties her husband would have to face in Germany.

Kersten boarded the plane for Berlin with a heavy heart, but he was certain that he had made the right decision. His life, and even his family, did not count so much when measured against the task he was about to undertake.

4

On the twenty-sixth of November, Kersten was back at Hartzwalde. He telephoned Himmler immediately.

"Come, come at once," Himmler said. "I am glad you are back."

There was a short silence, then Kersten heard the Reichsführer again.

"Of course you left your wife and son in Sweden?"

He spoke in a politely matter-of-fact tone of voice, as if he did not care. But Kersten was not fooled. He also answered matter-of-factly, for he, too, had learned how to assume this tone.

"No," he said, "they are with me."

Kersten could feel Himmler's joy through the phone.

"Really. I am very happy," he exclaimed. "Then you still believe in the German victory. Now I know you are a real friend. But I had thought . . .

"What?" asked Kersten.

"Oh, nothing—nothing, excuse me," he said hurriedly. "It's silly of me, but there are so many rumors about you. No. No, I was sure you would bring your family back. Come right away."

5

Kersten felt that his life had grown richer than ever. Before, he had had his family, his friends, his patients, Himmler, and the chance, occasionally, to save some unfortunates. But since his trip to Sweden, even though he continued to do the same things, he had a greater goal. To achieve it he had been willing to endanger his family.

When he and Gunther had formulated their plan in Sweden, it had seemed extremely difficult. But it was only when he got back to Germany that he saw how great the obstacles were. Freedom makes one quickly forget the somber, grim life of a police state. A few weeks in Stockholm, with its lights, its pastries, its free talk (one did not fear the police or informers), and its civilized ways, had dissipated the memory of Hitler's Germany. By contrast, everything in Berlin seemed heavier, more relentless and sinister.

It was December. The cold and fog penetrated into the badly heated houses. The starved faces of the people became green with the winter cold. Night came early into the unlighted streets. The Allied bombers had plenty of time to drop their cargoes of fire and steel. Every day more of them came, and more often. The news from the Russian front became steadily worse. Little by little the harassed people began to feel only fear, hunger, hate, and suspicion. The Gestapo doubled its severity, anticipating any dissatisfaction which might arise from the hard times. In such times, how could one hope for humanity from the leaders of a regime which was inhuman if it was anything? How could one conceive, even for a minute, of getting the men and women out of the concentration camps? To Hitler, Himmler, and the other Nazi leaders, these people were simply traitors, rebels, desecrators, and Jews. How could one wrest the victims from the callous and contemptuous S.S. who thought of them as corpses, even while they still breathed?

Yet this was what Kersten had vowed to Gunther, and above all to himself, to do. After he got back, he saw that he did not have enough power over Himmler. He needed allies and trustworthy friends. But outside of Brandt, there were none. He had at least to find people who would support him for personal reasons.

6

Searching his mind for likely supporters in his campaign on Himmler, Kersten thought of Colonel Walter Schellenberg and General Berger, both of whom worked closely with Himmler. However, they were not at all alike.

Schellenberg was young (thirty-four), blond, elegant, and well groomed. He had a wide cultural background and a ready and flexible intelligence. He came from a good Saar family. He had impeccable manners and could speak perfect English.

Godlob Berger was close to fifty. He had been a subordinate officer who had risen from the ranks during the First World War. He had all the physical and psychological traits of the professional soldier. He was very big, broad-shouldered, rigid, and rough. He had no taste for nor interest in politics. He loved only the army, its virtues and its discipline. He had had to wait a long time before Himmler had recognized his passion for military strictness and his exceptional administrative talents, and had given him the post of commander of the, Waffen S.S.

Schellenberg, on the other hand, had left the university to go into the special espionage services which were under Himmler. Heydrich was in charge at that time. He recognized the value of his new agent at their first meeting and gave him the most difficult and ticklish missions. Schellenberg performed his duties so well that he caught Himmler's attention. From then on he had an extraordinary career. By the time he was thirty, he was a colonel and directed the network of espionage and counterespionage for which Himmler was responsible. But his ambition knew no bounds. He wanted to be promoted again, and soon. He also wanted to be Himmler's favorite and to have the most influence over him. The kind of relationship Kersten had with each of these men was determined by their characters.

The general of the Waffen S.S. and the doctor knew each other by force of circumstances. They were both part of Himmler's entourage.

Berger was immediately and openly hostile to Kersten. He instinctively disliked this fat and gentle civilian who moved freely among the military elite. He was out of place; he didn't look right.

Kersten, who was rather amused by Berger's attitude, told him one day that he, also, had once been an officer in the Finnish Army.

"I won't believe it until I've seen your papers," the general said.

Kersten showed them to him, along with a photograph of himself from those long past times.

Berger then said, "Even in a picture, you don't look like a soldier."

"Well," Kersten answered gravely, "Himmler wants to make me a colonel in your army."

"I wouldn't have you as a corporal," Berger grumbled.

Himmler cared about his associates' health, that is, he wanted them to be as effective as possible. He categorically ordered Berger to go to Kersten for a physical examination.

"I can't stand this, and I don't believe in your blessed miracles," Berger told Kersten.

"Just the same, get undressed," Kersten said.

Grumbling and swearing, the commander obeyed. Kersten auscultated him with the tips of his fingers and started to enumerate his body's disturbances. Berger was amazed.

"How can you know? Himmler does not know about these discomforts. I've never told him." He spoke without a trace of harshness or scorn.

As his treatments continued, Berger began to trust Kersten; he even became grudgingly friendly. The doctor found that the general was concerned not only with the army's dress and discipline, but also with his honor. He was deeply disgusted by the Gestapo, the death camps, and racism. He saw nothing in common between the real soldiers of the Waffen S.S. and the S.S. executioners, and he did not allow his men to fraternize with them.*

Kersten's contacts with Schellenberg came later. The chief of the Reichsführer's espionage service traveled a great deal, and during his

---

* See Appendix, Note 7.

short stays at headquarters his relationship to Kersten was mainly one of impersonal courtesy. But they watched each over covertly.

Kersten and Schellenberg found themselves together for a fairly long time in the summer of 1942, when Himmler was back in his field headquarters in the old Russian barracks in Zhitomir, Ukraine. The Reichsführer insisted that his favorite be examined by Kersten. When Kersten was informed of this, he was astounded. Schellenberg was only thirty-two and seemed in perfect physical shape.

"To tell the truth, I do not think he needs your care," Himmler said. "During your examination you can study him and then give me your opinion of his character. He is very able. He is a man with a future. But his boundless ambition makes me uneasy."

Their first meeting took place under odd conditions. It was already night, and Kersten was in bed in his dismal little house within the walls of the old barracks. The door of the room opened without a sound, and Schellenberg entered. His slim, elegant shadow stood out on the room's gray walls, and the poor light made his blond hair paler. The young colonel took a chair and sat next to Kersten's bed. They spoke in whispers.

"Himmler sent me to you," Schellenberg said.

"He said he would," Kersten answered.

The two men looked at each other in silence. They both knew that the purpose of the visit was a medical examination, but neither one made a move in that direction. They studied, gauged each other.

"I am glad to meet you at last, Colonel," Kersten said slowly. "You have many enemies in Himmler's entourage. You succeeded too rapidly. But, as far as I am concerned, you have nothing to fear. On the contrary, I can help you a great deal if we become friends."

Schellenberg answered without hesitation.

"I know that, Herr *Medizinalrat*. I have come to ask for your friendship. I'll do what is necessary for it."

"Good," Kersten answered. He lay back against his pillows, crossed his hands on his belly, and continued: "From what I have heard, you want to be a general. People hold that against you. They say you are in too much of a hurry. I think it is a very natural desire in a man like you, and I think I can help you."

In the semidarkness, Schellenberg's clear eyes seemed to grow big. "You'll find me worthy of your trust," he said.

From that time, Schellenberg supported Kersten's undertakings, either openly or indirectly. He did it with consummate skill, never giving a hint of the deal they had made that night. Because he was chief of counterespionage, his influence was decisive in the case of the Swedish spies who were pardoned.

7

Before saying a word about his plan to Himmler, Kersten tried it out on Schellenberg and Berger. He found them more inclined toward it than he had dared to hope. Schellenberg was drawn to it for two reasons: he counted on Kersten's steadily growing influence over Himmler to help make him the youngest German general; and his alert eyes saw that Hitler was finished. A man used to playing several games at once, he saw that, when the Allies had won, it would then be to his advantage to have saved thousands of prisoners.

General Berger's motives were simpler. The old soldier was disgusted by the atrocities in the concentration camps. He could not stand knowing that men who had been under his orders, and who had worn the uniform of the Waffen S.S., were serving as guards and torturers in the camps. It hurt his pride.

Thus, from the start, Brandt, Himmler's private secretary, who was privy to all his secrets and saw him night and day, Godlob Berger, commander of the Reichsführer's army, and Walter Schellenberg, chief of Himmler's espionage services, all were on Kersten's side. Kersten's sworn enemies were Kaltenbrunner, chief of the Gestapo, his staff, and all his agents. These men were not only opposed to any acts of mercy which they saw as undermining their power, but they also hated Kersten personally. They were exasperated by his increasing favor with Himmler and by the long list of pardons he had been able to wangle from him.

Kaltenbrunner had succeeded Heydrich, even though he was not at all like him. He was not as intelligent, nor as well educated, and he was not as cold-blooded. He was melancholy, violent, and eager for tortures and executions. Every time Kersten succeeded in saving a life, Kaltenbrunner was furious. He obsessively hated the doctor's compassion for humanity.

"Watch that brute. He is capable of having you murdered," Brandt had told Kersten.

8

The doctor did not think that Kaltenbrunner would go that far. However, there was one continuing offense in Kersten's life which would allow the Gestapo to get at him if it were discovered. He was not worried about his correspondence with Holland. Himmler's postal number had proved to be inviolable. But he feared the discovery of his clandestine slaughter of livestock. This offense against food rationing laws carried the death penalty. He could depend on the tricks and the devotion of the Jehovah's Witnesses, but it was always possible that, one day, they would be taken by surprise. Now that he was attempting something which would arouse all the Gestapo's powerful opposition, he felt that he could not run such a risk. Himmler was mercilessly strict and unrelenting when it came to breaking rules and regulations. Without telling him the real reason for his uneasiness, Kersten said: "You know how much Kaltenbrunner and his men hate me. When I am not at Hartzwalde, I fear for my family."

"I have given orders," Himmler said.

"I know, and I am grateful. But the Gestapo has found indirect ways, legal pretexts to ruin the lives of those who cannot defend themselves. There is only one way that would really assure our safety."

"What's that?"

"Give my estate extraterritorial status."

"You are dreaming, my dear Kersten. Ribbentrop would never allow it," Himmler exclaimed.

Kersten asked again but could get nowhere. He could not convince Himmler.

Then something happened which threw stunning light on Himmler's character.

One morning, during the beginning of 1944, Kersten left Hartzwalde and appeared at the Prinz Albert Strasse Chancellery, carrying a large brief case crammed to the bursting point. After treating Himmler with special care and bringing him to a state of profound well-being, he reached into his brief case and pulled out a magnificent ham.

"Would you like to have some with me?" he asked.

Himmler was always ravenous after Kersten's hands had alleviated his pains, and he had a weakness for pork. He cut a slice of ham with his S.S. dagger and ate it. It was tender, savory, and just salty enough to make one want more. This was the way Kersten liked it himself.

Himmler took another slice and said, "This is so good that one can eat it without anything else."

He cut a third piece. "Kersten, how did you manage to get hold of enough ration coupons to buy such a ham?" he asked, relishing it.

"I didn't have any coupons," the doctor answered.

With a full mouth, Himmler said, "I don't understand. . . . But then how did you get it?"

"This ham comes from a pig which was slaughtered on my estate," Kersten answered, as if it were the most natural thing in the world.

Himmler straightened up like an automaton. He looked with terror first at Kersten, then at the slice of ham which he still held in his hand, and then at Kersten again.

"Do you know what the penalty for clandestine slaughter is?" he whispered.

"I know, hanging," Kersten said.

"Well, then?" Himmler murmured.

The doctor pointed at the piece of ham in Himmler's hand and said calmly, "The law is explicit. Anyone who benefits from clandestine slaughter is also to be hung."

"That's true. My God, that's true," Himmler said.

He threw the evidence of his crime into the wastepaper basket and wiped his fingers with his handkerchief.

"This is terrible," he said.

He walked nervously back and forth across his office, his head in his hands. Kersten kept a very grave expression on his face, but he was amused watching Himmler. He knew that Himmler was an absurd stickler when it came to obeying the laws, and at this moment Himmler, whose power elevated him above all laws, felt himself guilty of a major crime and liable to the death penalty. Everybody has some kind of conscience, Kersten thought as Himmler continued to pace up and down the room.

"Terrible. What can we do?" the Reichsführer groaned.

"I see a way of fixing things," Kersten said.

"How?" Himmler asked.

"Agree to give my estate extraterritorial status. Then the slaughter of pigs would be legal."

"It's impossible," Himmler shouted. "I have told you so a dozen times. Ribbentrop won't stand for it."

"Then there's no way out. We just have to resign ourselves to the worst. That's the law, isn't it? And you're responsible for carrying it out."

Himmler bowed his head.

"There are only two alternatives: extraterritoriality, or the gallows."

Two days later Himmler gave Kersten a document signed by himself and the minister of foreign affairs of the Third Reich. It gave Hartzwalde extraterritorial status.*

9

At the end of the same month, January, 1944, Himmler had to go to Holland, and since he was suffering from cramps, he asked Kersten to accompany him.

The doctor made the trip in Himmler's private plane. General Berger was also aboard.

Kersten, who had not seen his favorite country for three years, was very happy to be on his way to Holland. But sadness and bitterness spoiled his joy, just as they had on his first trip to The Hague. Since

* See Appendix, Note 8.

he had been forced to give up his house in The Hague, he had to accept a room in the S.S. guesthouse, which was, ironically enough, situated just behind the Peace Palace. From the very day of his arrival, the friends he met gave him a horrifying picture of life in the Netherlands. Every year the poverty was worse. The Gestapo was completely in power, and arrests, executions, and disappearances were increasing. Nobody could feel safe anywhere. Many of Kersten's friends lived in hiding, with assumed identities. The Dutch who worked for the German police were even more treacherous.

As he heard about these things, Kersten remembered what the Reichsführer had said. "I only need three thousand men to direct things in Holland and a little money and food to give to informers. Thanks to them, the Gestapo knows everything. I have native spies in every resistance group. It's the same in Belgium and in France."

Kersten knew his friends were right when they urged him to be extremely cautious.

The day after his arrival, he went to treat Himmler in a mansion built in the middle of a large park at Klingendal, just outside of The Hague. Seyss Inquart, Gauleiter of Holland, had requisitioned it for Himmler's visit.

"I have just received an invitation to a dinner in my honor. Mussert, the leader of the Dutch National Socialist party, is giving it. He is going to introduce me to leaders of his group. You should come. It will be nice. Mussert has just moved into a luxurious house," Himmler told Kersten. He reached for the fancily printed invitation which was lying on the table by his bed.

"The Thurkow house," he elaborated.

The doctor continued to work on Himmler's nerves as if the name meant nothing to him.

"Why should I go with you? The owner did not invite me," he answered.

"Wherever I go, you can go, too," Himmler said.

"No, I am sorry, but it is impossible for me to go with you to that house. It belongs to Thurkow, not to Mussert. Thurkow is one of my best friends, and now they've thrown him out of his home."

"I didn't know anything about it. But if Mussert did it, he had good reasons."

The treatment was just finished when Seyss Inquart asked to be allowed to pay his respects to the Reichsführer. It was the first time he had received his boss in Holland, and he was extremely servile. He named all the people who were to be at Mussert's dinner.

"Who owns the house where the reception is going to be held? Does it belong to the party?" Himmler asked.

"Not yet, Reichsführer," Seyss Inquart answered. "But it will soon. It belongs to someone who is suspect. He supports the Dutch government in exile in London. Our reports on him are worse every day. We are going to arrest him and several other important accomplices tomorrow. Thurkow also owns some very valuable old masters. We are going to confiscate them for the profit of the Reich. There are about a dozen of his friends, all bankers, big industrialists, and shipowners, who also own valuable pictures. We are going to arrest them all. You see, Reichsführer—"

"Good," Himmler said. "Good work. When the important men disappear, the little people have no leaders. Watch these traitors. I will tell you what to do with them later."

The Reichsführer finished dressing and went to his office next door. The Gauleiter followed. On the threshold, Himmler turned and asked Kersten if he would be going to Mussert's dinner.

"I'm sorry, but I have been invited to the home of one of my former patients," Kersten answered.

"Do what you like," Himmler said, shrugging his shoulders. "But be sure to come back tomorrow morning to treat me."

Kersten took a car from the S.S. garage and had the uniformed chauffeur drive to the suburb of Wassenaar, which is right at the edge of The Hague. His friend Thurkow was living there under house arrest.

The doctor spent the day with his friend. It was a strange mixture of bitterness and gentleness. Thurkow and Kersten had a deep regard for each other. They had not been together for three years. They knew that this would be the last time they would meet, but they did not speak about it. What was the use?

Visitors came furtively and stayed for a short time. One of them, Mr. de Beaufort, brought his wife, a Dutch woman of French stock. He was in the Resistance. He gave the doctor a brief but vivid picture of the hunted life he led. Then he asked Kersten if he could get some mail into Sweden for him. From there it would be sent to London. Beaufort was desperate because he had been cut off from all his usual contacts.

"I guarantee your package will get to Stockholm. The Germans won't find out about it either." Kersten then asked to whom it should be delivered.

"To Baron Van Nagel, who is the Stockholm representative of our refugee government," Beaufort answered.

Soon after this conversation, Beaufort left. The two friends were alone. Night came. Each minute was long and heavy. Somewhere in the house an old Dutch clock rang eleven. Kersten had more and more difficulty controlling his nerves. They usually make arrests at dawn, he thought. In six hours, at the latest, the Gestapo will come for Thurkow. He got up and took leave of his friend, promising to see him the next day. They both knew this could not be, but they went through the motions. What was the use of breaking down?

The S.S. car took Kersten away into the night. Deliberately, he thought of nothing. Suddenly, even though it was dark, he saw they were driving through Klingendal, where Himmler's mansion was located. He knew The Hague better than any other city in the world. Without giving it another thought, he told the chauffeur to drive to Himmler's.

They were stopped at the first police guardhouse, but when Kersten showed his special pass, signed by the Reichsführer, he was saluted respectfully. At the second guardhouse the same thing happened. The last guardhouse was at the mansion's entrance. There they asked the doctor what he wanted.

"I want to see the Reichsführer," Kersten said.

"It's all right," the head guard said. "He just came back ten minutes ago."

A Gestapo agent led Kersten to Himmler's room. Himmler was

taking his shoes off. Holding one shoe in his hand, he looked with surprised delight at Kersten.

"You must be a mind reader!" he said. "I was just thinking of you. I have cramps, but since they are not too bad, I didn't call you. I thought you'd be asleep."

"I felt it, and here I am," Kersten said, without batting an eye. "Get undressed. We'll get rid of those cramps in a few minutes."

"I don't doubt that by now," Himmler said.

The pains disappeared, and the Reichsführer smiled blissfully.

"I don't even have to call you when I am in pain. You know it," he said, his voice softened by his gratitude.

"I am going through something very trying myself," Kersten said, bowing his head, "and you are the only one who can help me."

"Woman trouble!" Himmler exclaimed joyfully.

"I'm sorry, but it's not a woman. This morning I heard Seyss Inquart tell you that twelve Dutchmen are going to be arrested tomorrow. My friend Thurkow is one of them. I have just had dinner with him. That's why I couldn't go to Mussert's reception. I am sure you understand how miserable I am about it. For the sake of my friendship, cancel these arrests."

"Do you know the others?" Himmler asked.

"Most of them are my friends."

The Reichsführer was moving his glasses up and down on his forehead without being aware of it.

Suddenly he screamed, "They are traitors! They are in touch with London. I can't revoke orders which come from Kaltenbrunner. He is my right hand in Berlin. Seyss Inquart, Rauter, and his men would be baffled, especially just now, when they are doing their best to keep the Dutch from knifing us in the back."

A long discussion ensued. Himmler attacked the doctor's logic, and Kersten appealed to Himmler's feelings. Himmler brought up reasons of war and politics. Kersten tirelessly answered with friendship. He knew the facts were against him, so he simply begged and pleaded; he appealed to Himmler's feeling for him.

"I counted on you so much. I had such great confidence in your friendship," Kersten kept saying.

The Reichsführer's glasses slowly stopped moving up and down on his forehead. Himmler sighed wearily and sank down on his columned bed. He gazed at his palatial room. He was warm. He had no stomach pains.

"Oh, all right. You know I am right. But after all, we are not going to quarrel over twelve men, are we? That would be silly. These men are traitors. Twelve more or twelve less, it doesn't much matter. I'll speak to Rauter tomorrow morning."

"Tomorrow will be too late. I would be eternally grateful to you if you talked to him right away," Kersten said very gently.

"Rauter's probably asleep," Himmler said.

"He'll wake up," Kersten answered.

Himmler shrugged his shoulders and grumbled, "You always have to have the last word. All right. Call Rauter."

The telephone was at some distance from Himmler's bed. Kersten asked for Rauter. When he heard his voice, he said, "Herr Obergruppenführer, the Reichsführer is on the line."

Himmler got up and went to the telephone. The sides of his long nightshirt flapped against his thin calves.

"All tomorrow's arrests are indefinitely postponed. I'll decide about them when I am back in Berlin."

"Ja wohl, ja wohl, Reichsführer," Kersten heard Rauter's voice answer.

General Berger was with the head of the Dutch Gestapo at this moment. When his conversation with Himmler was over, Rauter grumbled: "We've fallen pretty low when the Reichsführer takes his orders from a foreigner. Kersten is dangerous. I'd like to know who's behind him."

"You're not smart enough to find out," Berger calmly declared. He hated the Gestapo. "Kersten has a longer reach than you. Himmler will only see you after a formal request, and in uniform. Kersten is in his room right now, seeing him in his nightshirt."

And in that room, after Himmler had put down the receiver, he said to Kersten, "Well, your will is done." He touched his stomach. "I feel much better."

He went back to bed, stretched out, and yawned slightly. He felt good but slightly uneasy. This time he had let Kersten go too far.

"You know," he said, "I am sorry I did not deport this whole country in 1941 as we had planned. If I had, there wouldn't be all these problems."

"Remember how sick you were," Kersten said. "It was physically impossible for you."

"Maybe, maybe," Himmler murmured. He leaned his elbows on his pillows and looked at Kersten with his gloomy eyes.

"Sometimes I ask myself if you would have felt the same way had they been Hungarians or Turks instead of Dutch."

Kersten answered calmly, "My conscience is clear. Do you suspect me?"

"Oh no, I assure you, no," Himmler said. "I'm sorry. It's because I'm tired. It's late. It's only because I'm tired. You can see how grateful I am to you. I have just made you a present of twelve men."

"That's right, Reichsführer," Kersten said, bending toward him a little. "You can sleep in peace. Good night, Reichsführer."

"Good night, dear Kersten."

When the doctor reached the door, Himmler called him back to say, "Seyss Inquart gave me some fruit and some candy. Let's share them."

Without waiting to be asked again, Kersten took six apples and six chocolate bars.

10

The next day Kersten kept a promise he had thought he would never be able to keep. He went to see Thurkow at Wassenaar. Beaufort came a little later and gave the doctor three large sealed envelopes, stuffed with papers. Their destination was London via Stockholm.

Two days later, the fifth of February, he was sitting next to Himmler in the Reichsführer's private plane. They were flying to Berlin. In front of them were two identical suitcases filled with important papers.

Himmler's was full of Dutch Gestapo papers which were awaiting his decisions. Kersten's carried the mail from the Dutch Resistance, which was relentlessly hunted by the Gestapo.

The weather was beautiful with only a moderate wind, and the trip went off without a hitch.

Kersten kept Beaufort's papers in a drawer at Hartzwalde while he waited for a chance to take them to Sweden.

11

Kersten spent several more weeks getting his bearings. He wanted to be certain of the power of his allies and his enemies before he started on the project worked out by the Swedish foreign minister. He said nothing specific to Himmler about names, numbers, or plans. He only hinted that it would be very noble and great for a German leader to show pity toward the most wretched victims of the concentration camps.

Himmler's behavior was equally tentative. He neither objected nor agreed. He listened, shaking his head.

But at this point Kersten asked for nothing else. The door to negotiations was half open; the rest would follow.

Kersten asked for permission to go to Stockholm on the pretext of treating the Finnish wounded again. This time Himmler didn't even discuss it.

"All right," he said. "But don't forget to come back." But when he saw Kersten's disappointed and reproachful look, he didn't even give him a chance to speak, saying: "I'm sorry, dear Kersten. The people who surround me force me into bad habits. I spoke without thinking. If I could only trust everybody as much as I trust you."

"Now that we are talking like friends, let me reassure you completely. During this trip my three sons will remain at Hartzwalde with Miss Elizabeth Lube. I'm not worried about them now, thanks to you. The statute of extraterritoriality makes it impossible for Kaltenbrunner to send his agents there."

The doctor and his wife took the airplane to Stockholm on the first of April. One of Kersten's suitcases contained the mail of the Dutch

Resistance which Beaufort had given him in The Hague. With his diplomatic passport, Kersten got by the inspectors without difficulty. On the day of his arrival, Kersten gave the envelopes to Baron Van Nagel, the Dutch government-in-exile's ambassador to Sweden.

Kersten was in Stockholm for two months. He had to stay that long because Gunther, the minister of foreign affairs, wanted to keep their meetings absolutely secret. He wanted to organize the whole project alone. Even at the ministry nobody knew what the two men were up to. When Gunther had to consult a high official about a technical matter, he did it in such a roundabout, piecemeal way that it was impossible for anyone to guess the whole plan. This took time.

Finally, at the beginning of June, everything was set. Gunther had arranged everything and gotten all the necessary authorizations and concurrences.

After a final conference with Kersten, he said, "I only need a signal from you in order to begin."

"I will start to work on Himmler as soon as I get back," Kersten said. "I can count on Brandt completely, and to a great extent on Schellenberg and Berger. There's no getting around our worst enemy: Kaltenbrunner. But, in any case, Himmler is even more powerful than he."

"How can I help?" Gunther asked.

"I don't need anything in Germany. But I would like to have two things here. I would like recognition of my doctor's degree in Sweden so that I may practice here."

Gunther nodded his head to show he understood that Kersten was thinking about the future. The precariousness of the Third Reich and the risks of his mission forced him to do so.

"All right. And then what else do you want?" asked the minister of foreign affairs.

"Permission from your government to rent a little apartment I've looked at in Stockholm. The housing shortage makes a permit necessary."

"That will be done," Gunther promised. He kept his word.

"The whole family will come on the next trip," the doctor told his wife. "One day we will be able to live a normal life again. We've made a start here."

Irmgard Kersten bought two children's beds. Then she thought of sheets. Her husband had not brought enough money from Germany for cotten or linen sheets, so she had to settle for paper ones.

Kersten and Irmgard flew back to Berlin on the sixth of June, 1944. Just before they left Stockholm, news of the Normandy invasions was broadcast over the radio. Better paper sheets in Sweden than silk ones in Germany, Kersten thought.

12

Kersten and his wife went directly to Hartzwalde from the Tempelhof airport. Spring was at its height, and the meadows and the woods were fragrant. Elizabeth Lube, the children, and the Jehovah's Witnesses joyously welcomed the travelers. Even the animals in their stables and pens seemed glad to have them back.

How long will all this last? Kersten could not help thinking. He went for a long, thoughtful, and dreamy walk in the woods. It was as if he were asking advice of the great trees and the flowers in the glades. Then he telephoned Himmler's headquarters in East Prussia, at Hochwald.

"I am here, Reichsführer," he said.

"Your wife? I'd like very much to give her my regards," Himmler said abruptly. It was clear that his politeness was only a way of checking up. But, when Himmler recognized Irmgard Kersten's voice on the telephone, he literally shouted with joy.

"I am very happy to hear your voice. You'll never feel as well at Hartzwalde as you do in Germany. Give me your husband again, please."

Kersten took the telephone again. Himmler was now very friendly.

"Kaltenbrunner scared me. He is sure you rented an apartment in Stockholm."

"It is true," Kersten said. "An apartment is much cheaper than a hotel."

"Of course," Himmler exclaimed. "Your wife is here and I don't care what Kaltenbrunner says."

Two days later Kersten was called to Hochwald. Himmler was very ill.

When he had to be in East Prussia, Himmler lived in a primitive barracks near the railroad tracks. The surroundings were dismal. Even when the Reichsführer was in good health, the atmosphere of the place depressed him. If he had an attack, he was that much sicker.

Kersten decided to take advantage of these favorable conditions and at last put into execution the plan he had made with the Swedish minister of foreign affairs. He started the first morning of treatment. Himmler, wearing one of his long, white nightshirts, was lying on a hard, narrow bed which some soldiers had made out of rough wood. The ceiling of the room was dismal, and badly squared beams projected under it. The doctor sat at the head of the bed in a makeshift chair.

In this setting the fate of many lives was to be decided.

As the doctor kneaded the Reichsführer's sore nerves, he said casually, "The Allied landings make me think that the war will not end as you expected."

"Impossible," Himmler exclaimed.

"We'll soon see," Kersten said. "But, in any case, you must have thought of the number of noncombatants who have already died in your concentration camps. What good can that do you? You are also killing the last survivors of the Germanic races in these camps, I mean the Danes, the Norwegians, and the Dutch. You are destroying your own blood. You, yourselves, are reducing your numbers."

This argument came from Himmler's own doctrines. Kersten had decided to begin by talking about only one specific group of prisoners.

"That's true," Himmler said. "But these people are opposed to us."

"You are one of the great German leaders. You are also one of the most intelligent people in the world." Himmler blushed with conceit at this. "Make use of your power, show your intelligence. Free as many of the Dutch, Danish, and Norwegian prisoners as is possible. This way you will save what remains of your race."

"The idea is right," Himmler answered, "but how can I talk to Hitler about it? One word of it and he will be very angry."

"You're the most powerful man in Germany. Why do you always think about Hitler?" Kersten answered.

"Because he is the Führer."

Kersten brought his face close to Himmler's. He pressed harder on his stomach.

"One division of the Waffen S.S. at Berchtesgaden, and you would become Führer. You would be a far better Führer than Hitler."

Himmler did something he had never done before. He seized the doctor's wrists and stopped the treatment.

"Are you aware of what you are saying? Do you really think it?" he screamed. "Me? Go against my Führer! But he is everything to us Germans. You know what's engraved on my belt buckle: 'Loyalty is Honor.' "

"Change the buckle, and everything will be all right," Kersten answered.

"Dear Kersten, I am infinitely grateful to you. You are my only friend," Himmler said with feeling. "But never talk like that again. Loyalty is sacred. I teach that to my soldiers every day."

Kersten sat up again and settled his large body in the thinly padded chair.

"Loyalty is no longer loyalty when one serves a madman. You yourself had me read Hitler's medical file. He should be in an asylum. Your greatest error is to let him stay at large. History will hold it against you forever."

With each point Kersten's hands had pressed more heavily on his patient's stomach. The Reichsführer gasped for breath. He was panting.

"I . . . quite . . . understand . . . but I . . . can't . . . I . . . can't. . . ."

Kersten pressed harder with his fingers and palms. Twenty years of practice had made them formidably strong. Himmler's whole body twisted and convulsed.

"Listen to me," the doctor ordered.

Himmler murmured faintly, "What . . . what?"

"Give me the Norwegian, Danish, and Dutch prisoners," Kersten said.

Straining for breath, Himmler groaned, "Yes, yes. But give me some time."

"Act alone. Don't go to Hitler for anything. No one can check on you," Kersten ordered.

"Yes, yes," Himmler panted. "You're right. How can I doubt it?" The hands did not press on him any more. Himmler breathed easily and deeply. He got a hold of himself and whispered: "If Hitler heard this conversation, it would be awful."

Kersten softened the movements of his fingers even more. He laughed.

"You mean to tell me you can't handle spies? You, the only man in Germany whose conversations can't be broken in upon."

"It's true. But if Hitler ever heard one word of what we have said . . ."

"Forget it," Kersten said. He had started to treat Himmler again in the usual way. The sick man felt himself come alive. After he had treated him for a while, the doctor went on: "It would be easy to free them. When I was in Stockholm I frequently saw Gunther, the minister of foreign affairs. He often talked about the prisoners in the camps. He's prepared to help the northern prisoners in every way."

Kersten stopped talking and looked at Himmler. He realized he was taking a serious risk. He had revealed the whole plan he and Gunther had made. They had hatched it in a foreign country, and somehow it was like a conspiracy. How was Himmler going to react to it? Would he be angry, afraid, or suspicious?

But Himmler was concerned only with his own body. The only thing that mattered to him was to prolong his physical well-being.

"Yes, I see, I see," he said, without opening his eyes.

Kersten continued forcefully: "The Swedes do not understand and cannot countenance the tortures you inflict on the unfortunates in the concentration camps. Especially on the Norwegians and Danes who are their blood brothers." Kersten was carried away by his own words. "They might even declare war on you."

The Reichsführer opened his eyes and looked at Kersten. Maybe he had gone too far. However, Himmler was still in a state of euphoria. He burst out laughing.

"Oh, they won't do that, my dear friend. We're still strong enough to fix them."

Himmler shook himself and got up happily. The doctor had made him feel well, and now he had even given him a laugh.

"Are you personally interested in freeing these prisoners? That's important to me."

"Yes," Kersten answered.

"Then I'll think it over," Himmler said. "I owe you that, especially since this is something that means a lot to you personally. You don't want an answer right away?"

"No," Kersten said. "But I'd like to have one when I take my next trip to Sweden."

"Very well," Himmler said.

Kersten felt he had won.

THE AMBUSH

1

Himmler was supposed to stay at his headquarters in East Prussia for a fairly long time. Kersten knew that the feelings of loneliness and sadness which always came over Himmler at Hochwald increased his power over him. In hoping for a quick success he was counting on the atmosphere of the place.

But Hitler abruptly called Himmler to Berchtesgaden, his retreat in the Bavarian Alps. There the Reichsführer found his idol in his sanctuary. Kersten could not get anywhere with him. Himmler did not refuse him but simply avoided talking.

About the middle of July he went back to Hochwald with the doctor, stopping off in Berlin for a few days. Once free of Hitler's spell, Himmler seemed again to be swayed by Kersten's arguments. Schellenberg helped Kersten discreetly while he was in Berlin.

But it took East Prussia to put Himmler literally back into Kersten's hands. Even though he had spoken to Himmler constantly, he himself was surprised at the impact his plan had had on him.

"I think you are right. We must not kill the whole world. We must be generous toward the German race," Himmler said, completely of his own accord. It was the twentieth of July, 1944.

"Reichsführer," Kersten exclaimed, "I always knew you were a superhuman leader, like Henry the Fowler." His voice resounded solemnly and with feeling in the dismal room. He saw the thousands of Norwegians, Danes, and Dutchmen who would live, and it was not hard for him to speak that way.

Himmler smiled blissfully; this was the greatest praise he could hear.

"Yes, I must be generous toward the German race."

Then Kersten asked gently, "And the French, Reichsführer? There are a great many of them in your concentration camps. Don't you want to go down in history as the savior of a great people, a people of great and noble culture?"

Himmler didn't answer. Kersten didn't push him. His silence was in itself encouraging.

When Kersten left Himmler's room, he was sure of his success. He was already considering when he could go to Sweden to tell Gunther that Himmler had agreed.

2

Kersten celebrated his victory with a large meal at the headquarters' mess. After that, with the help of the July heat, he had an afternoon nap.

His deep sleep was broken by the arrival of Himmler's chauffeur. The S.S. soldier burst into his room like a madman and shouted: "Get up, get up! There has been a frightful attempt on the Führer's life, but he is still alive."

Half awake, Kersten could not understand what the chauffeur was talking about. He wanted to question him, but the chauffeur had already gone, leaving the front door wide open. Kersten yawned, put on his clothes and shoes, and went to Himmler's barracks. He found Himmler on his feet in front of his worktable, busily thumbing through files and papers.

"What's happened?" the doctor asked.

Himmler answered quickly, hardly opening his lips. "They tried to kill the Führer at his headquarters . . . a bomb."

Hitler's headquarters were forty kilometers away from Hochwald. That was why the explosion had not been heard, Kersten thought. The Reichsführer was hurriedly sorting documents.

"I have orders to arrest two thousand officers," he said.

"Are so many guilty?" Kersten exclaimed. "Do you know who all of them are?"

"No," Himmler said. "A colonel made the attempt. I have explicit orders to arrest two thousand officers. I intend to carry them out."

Himmler took some papers from a file he was going through, and went to the corner of the room where there was an odd machine which destroyed documents. He put the sheaf of papers in it and pushed a button. The machine started up.

"What are you doing?" Kersten asked.

"I am destroying our correspondence with Stockholm. . . . One never knows," the Reichsführer said.

When Kersten saw Himmler, in his fear, feeding the papers into the metal teeth of the machine, he realized that this also meant the end of all his efforts and hopes.

"It's too bad they didn't get him. We could go our way without any trouble, if they had," Kersten said.

Himmler turned as if stung to the quick, a bewildered expression on his face. His face quivered.

"Do you really think a successful attempt would have been to my advantage?" he asked breathlessly.

When he saw the doctor about to answer, he cried hysterically: "No, no, don't say a word. I don't have the right to think about it. I forbid you to think about it. It's awful to have such thoughts. I am more loyal than ever to my Führer. I will kill all his enemies."

"Then you will have to kill ninety per cent of the population.

You told me that yourself. You said that after Germany's military losses only twenty per cent of the German people were for Hitler."

Himmler did not speak. Then, as if to avenge his own despair, he said with icy violence: "I am taking my airplane to Berlin immediately. Kaltenbrunner and his whole team are already waiting for me at Tempelhof airport." He gritted his teeth so that his cheekbones protruded. "We'll get to work at once."

Himmler must have seen how his words horrified and disgusted Kersten. He added dryly, "As for you, take the train today and wait for my instructions at Hartzwalde."

3

Kersten spent ten days on his estate, where summer was now at its height. In the woods, along the streams, in the cool rooms, an incredible peace reigned. The three boys played in the sun. During the day the branches and grasses crackled with the heat; at night they rustled in the breeze.

Meanwhile Himmler, Kaltenbrunner, and their pack were ravaging Germany in their merciless manhunt. Conspirators had dared to try to kill Hitler, and innocent and guilty alike paid for this sacrilege by the hundreds. Torturers broke bones and limbs. Executioners used the ax and the gallows. Uniformed officers were hung on meat hooks in butcher shops.

It took all Kersten had learned about concentration from Dr. Ko to keep his mind off these things. He forced himself to take advantage of this opportunity to rest; soon he would need all his strength to get Himmler to agree again to free the concentration camp prisoners. The attempted assassination had renewed Himmler's fanatical loyalty to his master, who wanted to see the blood of sacrifice running everywhere.

4

Very early on the first of August Kersten received a telephone call from Hochwald. Himmler was back in his headquarters and was very sick as a result of the intense work he had just finished. He asked the doctor to take his private train from Berlin for East Prussia, that very afternoon.

Kersten had a leisurely lunch with his family. He had asked for his car at three o'clock. That gave him more than enough time, for the train left quite late in the afternoon. His chauffeur knew the way very well, for they had been over it many times. He knew every street and turn in Oranienburg, the only town of any size which they went through.

After he had eaten, and had his heavily sugared coffee, the doctor embraced his family and went to his car. The chauffeur had just opened the door for him when they saw an army motorcycle coming toward them at top speed. The S.S. soldier, covered with dust and sweat, stopped right at his feet. He leaped from his motorcycle and handed Kersten a letter. "From Colonel Schellenberg, it's very urgent, Herr Doctor," he said.

The doctor took the letter and sent the soldier to the kitchen for refreshments, as he always did. Then he opened the envelope calmly and without much interest. Schellenberg often wrote to Kersten reporting on his progress with Himmler.

In the envelope there was a letter written on ordinary paper, but inside this sheet there was another small letter, all folded up, which fell to the ground. The doctor did not notice it. He leaned against his car, rested on his cane, and started to read.

From the first words terror covered his face.

"Look out . . . Kaltenbrunner has made plans to assassinate you. Be extremely careful. The danger is imminent. Kaltenbrunner has decided to kill you in spite of Himmler."

That was all Schellenberg had written. Kersten breathed deeply and shook his head as if stunned by a blow. Then he saw the little folded slip of paper at his feet. He picked it up eagerly. "Don't take your usual route through Oranienburg. Take the other way, the one through Templin. You risk death if you go the way you always do."

Kersten's first move was to go to the house and take from the bottom of a drawer a revolver which Himmler had given him special permission to carry. He hid it in the pocket of his overcoat. Then he began to think. Should he taken Schellenberg's advice? Their relationship was excellent, but still he did not blindly trust the head of the espionage services of the Waffen S.S. The only true friend he had among those around Himmler was Brandt. Schellenberg was completely motivated by his ambition and acted only upon cold-blooded calculation. His advice might be a trick, a way of getting rid of Kersten. Why? To whose advantage? How could he tell what was going on in the underhanded intrigues which Himmler's lieutenants carried on for the sake of prestige?

The doctor wiped the sweat from his face with one hand. With the other he gripped the revolver in the pocket of his light overcoat. "Be calm. I must think," he told himself.

He went over everything he knew about Schellenberg's personality. Kaltenbrunner was his one sworn enemy, his only dangerous rival. This was just the moment when Kaltenbrunner might be able to take Schellenberg's place as Himmler's favorite, for they had just done a bloody piece of work together.

Schellenberg's position was seriously threatened. It was in his interest to render the doctor an unusual service so that Kersten would reciprocate and back him up. It was the best way Schellenberg had of balancing the situation.

Kersten heard the sound of a motor outside and went out just in time to see the S.S. motorcyclist disappear around the turn in the drive.

Kersten got into his car and told the chauffeur, "Let's go. But today we won't go through Oranienburg. I like the other way better, the one through Templin. Let's take it for a change."

They had no trouble on the trip. Kersten got to the station in time to take the private train for Himmler's headquarters.

Once in his compartment, Kersten carefully reread Schellenberg's two letters. It was now clear that they had not been bait for a trap. But how could he find out if the advice they gave had actually saved him? Perhaps Schellenberg had invented the whole thing in order to have Kersten in debt to him for having saved his life.

5

The next morning Kersten arrived at the railroad crossing for Hoch-wald. Himmler's private car was there to take him to his barracks. Kersten found Himmler stretched out on his uncomfortable bed, contorted with cramps.

Kersten treated him, and Himmler felt much better immediately. There was a pause in the treatment.

"How lucky I am to be able to see you when I need you," Himmler said.

"This time you just missed never seeing me again," the doctor announced coolly.

"What do you mean?" Himmler asked.

"I am pretty sure I escaped being murdered," Kersten said.

Himmler looked at Kersten. He was bewildered. "I don't understand," he said. "You're joking, or are you?"

Kersten raised his voice, trembling with feelings he could not master.

"I have reason to believe that Kaltenbrunner wants to have me killed."

Himmler exclaimed: "Come on. Nothing can happen in Germany unless I know about it."

"This was one time you did not know."

Himmler got up with a start and sat on the edge of the bed. He was feverishly pulling at the buttons of his nightshirt, without being aware of it.

"What don't I know about?" he asked.

Kersten took Schellenberg's two letters from his pocket and handed them to the Reichsführer.

"Read them, will you?"

Himmler grabbed the letters and read.

"My God!" he said. "It's impossible."

He reached for the bell on the head of his bed. An S.S. guard rushed in.

"Get Brandt immediately," Himmler ordered.

The secretary was there a moment later. Still sitting on the edge of the bed in his nightshirt, Himmler spoke quickly and in a low voice.

"Listen, Brandt. I am going to entrust you with a very important mission. You must carry it out with great discretion. Read these letters. . . . Now, can you go to Berlin and find out if it's true, without letting anyone know what you're up to?"

"Count on me, Reichsführer," Brandt answered.

6

The next day Brandt was back.

He did not explain how he had found out. It was not necessary. Secret services, like the jungle, have their own laws. Kaltenbrunner had his agents in Schellenberg's network, and Schellenberg had his in Kaltenbrunner's. Brandt had procured agents for Himmler in both; he paid them well and gave them protection. The entire business was carried on in an atmosphere of hatred, suspicion, and rivalry.

Brandt appeared at Hochwald when Himmler was being treated and gave his report in Kersten's presence. Schellenberg had told the truth. Kaltenbrunner had carefully prepared an ambush to kill Kersten, and he would have succeeded if the doctor had not been warned.

This is how it had been planned: After they had finished their job as executioners, Kaltenbrunner and Himmler had returned to Hochwald. On the evening of the thirty-first of July, Kaltenbrunner had learned that Himmler was going to summon Kersten to his headquarters. That meant that Kersten would have to take the private train from Berlin on the first of August.

Himmler's staff knew that Kersten always took the shortest route to Berlin, through Oranienburg. Twenty kilometers outside of this town there was a wood, which grew on both sides of the road. On the night of the thirty-first, Kaltenbrunner had ordered his associates to send twenty of the most trustworthy Gestapo agents, armed with submachine guns, to these woods. During the night they were to hide in the woods on both sides of the road. They were to wait for Kersten's car, which was familiar to everyone, and stop it in order to check its papers. When the car stopped, they were instructed to shoot both the doctor and his chauffeur. The car would have been turned into a sieve.

As soon as they were certain that Kersten and the chauffeur were dead, the leader of the group was to report to Kaltenbrunner. He was to say that a car had refused to stop when ordered, and that he had been forced to have his men fire upon it. He was also to say that there had been a terrible misfortune: Dr. Kersten had been in the car and was dead. All that would have been left for Kaltenbrunner to do was to go to see Himmler and to express his profoundest regrets. There the report ended.

"Then it's true," Himmler mumbled. He still could not believe it.

"And you could have had nothing against Kaltenbrunner and his men, Reichsführer," Brandt said. "They would have had a perfect excuse. You yourself, if you remember, issued an order that cars which did not stop when hailed should be fired upon immediately. That was when escaping prisoners of war were stealing cars to get to the frontiers quickly."

"Then it's true," Himmler repeated. But his voice was more shrill, and he was moving his glasses up and down on his forehead.

Kersten spoke slowly: "Then if Schellenberg had not . . ." He did not finish. The words stuck in his throat.

"Yes," Brandt said. "You are lucky that one of Kaltenbrunner's personal aides is in Schellenberg's pay. He warned him about the plot."

"It was just in time," Kersten mumbled. He remembered the motorcyclist who had reached him just as he was about to leave Hartzwalde. He pictured the familiar little wood outside of Oranienburg, and he and his chauffeur being shot, point blank.

Himmler dressed with angry speed. When he had his uniform on, he looked at his watch. It was two o'clock.

"We're going to eat," Himmler told Kersten. Then he said to Brandt, "Tell Kaltenbrunner I want him to join us."

7

A dining car attached to Himmler's private train served as mess. On that day five people ate there. Kaltenbrunner and Himmler sat on one side of the table for four; Kersten and General Berger were on the other side. Kersten was facing Kaltenbrunner. Humble and self-effacing, Rudolph Brandt sat at a table for two which was just across the passageway. The meal began in silence. Himmler and Kersten were too tense to begin the conversation. The general of the Waffen S.S. was not a talker. It was Kaltenbrunner who spoke first. He addressed Kersten with heavy-handed courtesy and even more heavy-handed irony.

"Well, Doctor, how are things going for you in your dear Sweden where you like to spend so much time?"

His features hardened. His cold, black eyes, his thick, cruel lips: everything about Kaltenbrunner exuded a morbid hatred of Kersten which he could not conceal. When Kersten seemed to hesitate in answering, the head of the Gestapo provoked him rudely.

"You must be doing very well in Stockholm; I hear you've rented an apartment there."

"No," Kersten said simply, looking Kaltenbrunner in the eye. "Not at all well. I have no work there."

Kaltenbrunner, surprised, leaned back in his seat.

"Do you mean you had work there?" Kaltenbrunner asked.

The Reichsführer was playing with his fork; his face showed annoyance. Kaltenbrunner looked at him and then at Berger's impassive face.

"What were you doing?" he asked Kersten.

"Don't tell me you don't know. For five years the British secret service has been paying me to kill Reichsführer Himmler. I haven't succeeded, so I lost my job," Kersten answered.

Kaltenbrunner could not conceal his confusion at such a crazy answer. Bewildered, he looked at Himmler and saw that he was beginning to finger the frames of his glasses.

"Worse still, because of your attentions the doctor almost lost his job here," Himmler told Kaltenbrunner. Himmler was now moving his glasses along the ridge of his nose, up his forehead and down. Kaltenbrunner knew better than anyone that this was a sure sign of anger, and his fear was obvious.

Himmler spoke with merciless harshness: "Listen to me, Kaltenbrunner: You would not have survived Kersten by an hour. Is that clear?"

"Entirely, Reichsführer," answered the chief of the Gestapo.

"I hope it is," Himmler continued in the same tone of voice. "I hope that you and Dr. Kersten will both lead long, healthy lives. I will not tolerate any accidents; you are both too important to me. Get this, dear Kaltenbrunner: if anything at all should happen to Dr. Kersten, it would be very, very bad for you."

The meal ended as it had begun, in silence. Kersten hadn't eaten much. Sitting across from the man who had almost succeeded in killing him had dulled his appetite. He didn't even wait for coffee but got up to go to his compartment. Usually he took a nap after lunch, but that day he had no more desire for sleep than he had had for food. He took his notebook out of his suitcase and wrote up the scene he had just been through.

Then he stretched out in his bunk and began to think. He thought of the luck to which he owed his life. He thought that he was now safe from Gestapo ambushes, because Kaltenbrunner had to answer for his safety with his life. But it had taken all of Himmler's power and his absolute dependence on the doctor to bring this about. How many people who did not enjoy this kind of protection were pursued by Kaltenbrunner and his men? They didn't have a chance. The danger he had just been through made him feel closer to these people than ever before.

IN THE NAME OF
HUMANITY

1

The attempted assassination served to reinforce Himmler's feelings of friendship toward Kersten. His doctor became all the more precious and indispensable because he had almost lost him. Kersten knew how to take advantage of this. When he left for his estate a week later, the Reichsführer was on the point of agreeing to Gunther's plan.

The day after Kersten arrived at Hartzwalde, Miss Hanna von Mattenheim came to visit him. She was a friend of Karl Venzel, a sixty-year-old man who was one of the greatest landowners in Germany and one of Kersten's oldest patients. The doctor respected Venzel and was grateful to him for spending much time and energy advising Kersten when he had bought Hartzwalde and later, when he was making improvements.

"Our friend Karl Venzel disappeared six days ago. It is rumored that he has been arrested, but nobody knows anything. Everybody who cares about him is very worried," Miss von Mattenheim told Kersten.

Kersten immediately called Brandt at Himmler's headquarters in East Prussia, but Brandt knew nothing about Venzel. All he could say was that thousands and thousands of people had been arrested after the attempt on Hitler's life. However, he promised that he would do everything he could to find out about Venzel. Kersten promised Miss von Mattenheim that if Venzel was in trouble he would do everything in his power to help him. She left, reassured.

Three days later, Kersten was visited by another of his friends, Mrs. Imfeld, a lady of German origin who was Swiss by marriage. She also came to ask for help, but of a very different kind.

"Switzerland is ready to take twenty thousand Jews if they can be gotten out of the concentration camps. This plan is the idea of some important German industrialists and the Red Cross. They have the consent of the Swiss government," she said.

Kersten took it upon himself to try to persuade Himmler to agree to the plan.

2

On the seventeenth of August, 1944, in response to Himmler's summons, Kersten again took the private train from Berlin to East Prussia.

The moment he arrived at Hochwald, he asked Brandt about Karl Venzel. Brandt had found the great landowner's file and showed it to Kersten.

The doctor saw that his worst fears were justified. The Gestapo had arrested Venzel on the thirty-first of July, at Halle. He was accused of taking part in the conspiracy against Hitler. Venzel was a friend of Dr. Gördeler, who had been one of the leaders of the twentieth-of-July conspiracy. Gördeler was to have taken the place of the Führer in the provisional government. The report said that Gördeler had named Venzel minister of agriculture.

"The document is top-secret. I am not permitted to show it to anyone, not even you. Behave as though you have not seen it and ask Himmler himself," Brandt said when Kersten had finished reading.

Kersten questioned Himmler the next time he saw him. Himmler answered with rudeness and violence, bursting out with obscenities against Venzel, which happened very rarely.

"He is one of the worst traitors, one of the Führer's worst enemies. He's a rat! He has no right to live," Himmler screamed.

Kersten calmed Himmler by reminding him that nothing was worse for his nervous system than his attacks of rage.

Then he said solemnly, "Reichsführer, I know my friend very well. He never said a word against you or Hitler. Everything that is held against him is the result of intrigue and slander."

"I am convinced of the contrary," Himmler answered. "My reports are from trustworthy and objective men."

The heated discussion continued throughout the treatment and afterwards. Himmler ended it by saying, "Anything we say can have no importance. Hitler himself personally ordered me to arrest Venzel. His aide-de-camp repeated it to me."

Kersten saw that he could not hope to free his friend, but at least he could try to save him from the worst.

"I understand you, Reichsführer. You cannot release Venzel. But you can spare his life. After the war there will be plenty of time to pardon him. You're still confident of victory, aren't you?"

"Good, then we're agreed." Himmler sighed wearily. He bent his head. "You really have the worst possible friends."

"How about you? Aren't you my friend, Reichsführer?" Kersten asked.

Himmler laughed. "Oh, well, you still have a few who are all right." He looked affectionately at the large man who gave him his health, and added, "I promise you that I will be generous in dealing with Venzel."

"Your hand and your word as a German leader to keep the promise," Kersten said solemnly.

"You have it," Himmler answered.

3

A week later, while Kersten slept in his compartment, Himmler's train lurched and got under way. It was taking the Reichsführer to his western headquarters in Berchtesgaden. Himmler lived there in a little chalet and it was there that Kersten finally got an answer.

"I consent to free the Danes and the Norwegians. We'll see about the Dutch."

Kersten thanked the Reichsführer effusively and added, "You can do one other thing which will make you glorious forever. Switzerland is ready to take twenty thousand Jews from the concentration camps. All it would take is your signature."

Himmler looked up toward the hill where Hitler was staying. It was almost a reflex.

"That's hard, very hard. Anything to do with the Jews is hard," he said in a low voice.

But Kersten insisted. He returned to the subject every day, tirelessly. Finally, Himmler half gave in.

"Let's wait until you come back from Sweden."

And so saying, he authorized the third trip to Stockholm without Kersten's even having to ask for permission.

"I plan to leave at the end of September," Kersten said.

It was the end of August. Himmler crossed Germany again to return to his eastern headquarters. Kersten stopped off at Hartzwalde, confident of the success of the great plan.

However, a new obstacle, the most dangerous of all, suddenly arose.

4

When he got back, Kersten told his wife that she and the three boys must get ready to leave Germany for good.

"You really have Himmler's permission for all of us?" Irmgard Kersten exclaimed.

"I'll have it," the doctor said. "He will let me do what I want, as long as I come back. That's all he asks."

Kersten and his wife then discussed what they would be able to take with them to Sweden, to set up house there. They also decided that Elizabeth Lube would be in charge of Hartzwalde.

Kersten took up his Hartzwalde life of long walks, large meals, deep sleep, and reveries. He had not felt so at peace for a long time, because he was now confident that he would be able to bring Gunther a favorable reply.

On his third day back he was about to go out for a drive, when he noticed that it was time for the news broadcast. As he listened, suddenly all his present and past projects seemed useless and absurd. Even before reading the news from the fronts, the announcer said that Finland had asked Russia for an armistice and had broken off diplomatic relations with Germany. It was the most important news of the day. Kersten's country was not only no longer allied with the Third Reich, it was on the other side.

The announcer continued: The Finnish ambassador, even though he was protected by diplomatic immunity, was under house arrest. This meant Kimivoki, Kersten's great friend.

Kersten looked out of the window and saw his horse in harness, waiting for him. He shrugged his shoulders. His drive, his trip to Sweden, none of it made sense any more. Nothing better could happen to Finland, but what will happen to me, to my family, to the plans I made with Gunther? he thought.

He went and sat at his desk, his head between his hands, and tried to think. He couldn't. One idea obsessed him: Kaltenbrunner would now have the last laugh.

Finally Kersten got up and telephoned Brandt. He was sure that the latter would immediately refer to Finland's about-face. But Himmler's private secretary talked to the doctor simply and affectionately as if nothing special had happened. Then he gave Kersten Himmler's regards and told him that Himmler was leaving on a trip in a few moments but that he requested that the doctor be at Hochwald on the eighth of September.

Kersten held the receiver, unable to decide whether to ask the crucial question. He was afraid of taking a false step and falling into a trap. Brandt understood what his silence meant.

"Did you listen to the radio?" he asked.

"Well, yes . . . yes, I did." Kersten hesitated.

"Good," Brandt said. "In Himmler's exact words, 'Don't worry.' He told me to tell you that."

Brandt hung up. The doctor looked at the receiver for a moment without moving. Himmler had wanted to reassure him; Himmler had said . . .

He went to sit in his armchair.

Yes, Himmler's cramps guaranteed his and his family's safety. But what was going to happen to the mission Gunther had entrusted to him?

5

On the eighth of September, 1944, Himmler's private train took Kersten to Hochwald. One of the Reichsführer's orderlies was waiting to drive Kersten to Himmler's barracks. The doctor was worried, for he knew how Himmler's moods changed with the state of his health. Since his last conversation with Brandt, Kersten had heard nothing about Himmler, and since then Finland had declared war on Germany.

He had the good luck to meet Brandt on his way to Himmler's barracks.

"You're here at last," Brandt said. "The boss is in bad shape."

"Thanks," Kersten said. "You couldn't have given me better news."

The doctor found Himmler lying on his uncomfortable wooden bed. The Reichsführer did not move when he saw Kersten. His body was tense and knotted up. He stared intently at the doctor, with his gloomy gray eyes. It made Kersten uneasy; he couldn't tell whether his look was full of hatred or pain.

Without a word of greeting, Himmler blew up. He poured a flood of abuse on Finland and its government.

"You Finns, what a dirty bunch of traitors you are! I'd like to know what the English and Russians paid those bastards, Mannerheim and

Rytti, to get them to sell out. I only regret one thing, that I didn't have them hung before all this." His voice was getting louder. "Yes, hung. And all the Finnish people liquidated. All, at once. That's all they deserve. Hitler said so to me tonight. Kill, kill!"

Kersten let Himmler rant and rave. He didn't answer. He knew that the angrier he got, the more his cramps tore him apart.

Suddenly, foaming at the mouth, his voice more hysterical than ever, he screamed, "You, what are you up to, sitting there like a log, deaf and dumb? Do something, for Christ's sake. I can't stand it. It's killing me!"

Kersten set to work to relieve his patient's torment. The magic, which had first helped Himmler during the last spring of peace in 1939, immediately spread throughout his body. The technique had its usual effect. Himmler felt his nerves relax, and he breathed more easily and after a while more freely. The pain gave way and finally receded. Again he knew the bliss of recovery. Tears of gratitude toward the man who had rescued him from his torture welled up in his eyes. Yet this man belonged to a nation of traitors. A pretty state of things! There was nothing in common between those dogs and the good Dr. Kersten who treated him with such success and devotion.

Himmler looked at Kersten's hands. Strong, soft, skillful, and capable of performing miracles, for five years they had rooted out his suffering. For five years the doctor had been his only friend, the only man in the world to whom he could speak freely and openly. What a doctor! What a person to confide in! Finland might prove herself a hundred times more base and treacherous, but Kersten would remain the healer, the friend, the Buddha. God help the man who dared harm a hair of his head!

Kersten sensed all of Himmler's devotion in the astonishing tenderness with which he asked the doctor, "Did you have a good trip, my dear Kersten? Is your family well?"

The doctor answered warily, "I had a very good trip, thank you. And when I left, my family was still free."

Himmler started up in his bed, as if he had been struck with a whip.

"Do you doubt my good will?" he asked. "I would rather die than hurt you or your family."

"I see that there are still people capable of gratitude," Kersten said gently.

Himmler dropped back on his pillow and said gaily, "Since the Finns have declared war on us, you are now allied with our enemies. Which means that legally you are on the same side as your dear Dutchmen. I am sure that pleases you."

Kersten laughed.

"You see, Reichsführer, one gets what one wants sooner than one would have thought possible. But also, from a strictly legal point of view, I no longer have the right to treat you."

Himmler shook his head and was silent for a moment. Then he said solemnly, "Politics have never come between us, and they never will, my dear Kersten. I care enough that even if every country were at war, and they were all slaughtering each other, we would still be friends. Do you agree to that?"

"Yes, I do," Kersten said.

"I am glad," Himmler answered. He closed his eyes as if more deeply to savor the moment of understanding.

Then Kersten continued, "Since things are like this between us, I am going to ask you a favor. There are two or three hundred Finns in Germany. They have families. They have worked honestly in this country and have never been involved in politics. Don't persecute them."

"I promise," Himmler said, without opening his eyes.

"What's going to happen to Hartzwalde's extraterritoriality?"

"It will continue, only it will be under an international title instead of a Finnish one." Suddenly he opened his eyes and added, "All this, on condition that you return from Sweden."

Kersten looked right at him and asked, "Do you doubt me?"

"No, not at all," Himmler mumbled.

When Kersten thought about their conversation later, he decided that Finland's about-face had, paradoxically, increased his power over the Reichsführer.

6

Kersten had only told Himmler half the truth about his family's going to Sweden. Not only was he going to take his wife and children to Sweden, but he was planning to leave them there. He could not do it and then inform Himmler of it afterwards. Not to tell him anything was too dangerous. The next day Himmler was as friendly as ever.

"It is very hard to raise children here these days. I'd like to leave my children—with their mother, of course—in Sweden, for a fairly long time."

Himmler did not react.

"They'll come back next summer," Kersten added.

Himmler looked at the doctor oddly. "I don't believe it," he said.

Did he mean to say that Kersten was lying? Or did he really sense, without wanting to admit it to anyone, that by the next summer his fate, and Germany's, would be decided, and the return of the family would have no importance? Paris had just been liberated, the Allied armies were advancing toward the Rhine, and an avalanche of countless Russians cascaded toward the eastern borders.

"I don't believe it," Himmler repeated.

Then he shrugged his narrow shoulders and to Kersten's great relief, said, "I don't care. I only need you."

"You can count on my return," Kersten said. "Besides, my old friend Elizabeth Lube is going to stay at Hartzwalde."

"That's what I figured," Himmler answered.

He felt surer now that he had a hostage.

7

But the Reichsführer was anxious about something else as well. He told Kersten about it the next time they were together.

"I am afraid of getting very sick while you are away," Himmler said. "That happened on your last trip; I thought I'd go crazy. I would have given anything to have been able to get in touch with you, if only to get your advice during my attack. I am sure even that would have helped."

"I think so too," Kersten said. "Nerves respond to mental influence."

Himmler thrashed weakly on his hard narrow bed. He groaned. "You see, just the fear of not being able to get in touch with you easily makes me anxious, and the anxiety starts the cramps. And you're right here! What will happen to me when you're in Sweden? Letters take days and days. And you can't explain symptoms by telegram."

Kersten suddenly thought of a way out which would be so perfect that he immediately felt it would be impossible to arrange.

"When I was last in Stockholm, I learned that Ribbentrop often calls the German Embassy there. Why don't you have Ribbentrop's office call me?" he said.

"Never, for nothing in the world," Himmler said. "I don't want that scum to know anything about my private life. I'd rather die of pain."

This obstacle only served to inflame Kersten's imagination. What he had thought of by chance a moment before now seemed absolutely necessary. He thought of all the quick decisions that would have to be made in Stockholm and of how they all finally depended upon Himmler. A direct line would be a great advantage.

"Is Ribbentrop's office the only way of telephoning?" the doctor asked.

"Yes," Himmler said. "It is impossible to telephone abroad in wartime. Hitler's headquarters and the Ministry of Foreign Affairs are the only ones who have the right to do it."

"Think about it, Reichsführer," Kersten pleaded. "Is it really impossible for me to call Hartzwalde from Stockholm, or to be called from Hartzwalde?"

"Absolutely impossible," Himmler said.

"Even if you are seriously ill?" Kersten asked. "A man in your position, a leader with all the power you have?"

The appeal to Himmler's conceit and fear finally began to get results.

"Give me some time to think it over," Himmler said abruptly.

The next day he greeted the doctor with a smile of triumph.

"Everything's arranged," he said.

He shook his head, full of self-congratulation and self-pity. "You see, dear Kersten, with all my responsibilities I care so little about my personal privileges that I don't know the extent of my powers. Yesterday Brandt learned that, as minister of the interior, I have the right to a private telephone line abroad. Since I've never needed it, I had not thought of it. It's number 145." The Reichsführer made a friendly gesture. "It's all yours." Himmler paused for a moment to let his words sink in. "When you telephone from Stockholm, either to Hartzwalde or to one of my headquarters—Berlin, Hochwald, Berchtesgaden, or anyplace else—first ask for number 145. When you have it, then give the specific number you want. You'll have any connection you want in less than half an hour. Brandt has informed the Gestapo and the telephone office that you have priority to call my headquarters or Hartzwalde from Stockholm."

For a moment the doctor couldn't answer; he was stunned to think how easy it had been to obtain such an amazing privilege. Suddenly he had become the only private person who could call Germany from abroad, and his conversations could not be overheard. It was even more fantastic than the use of Himmler's private postal number.

Kersten pulled himself together and leaned toward Himmler.

"It's wonderfully simple. I was sure that you must have had this among your powers," he said.

"Well, you knew more about it than I," Himmler said, laughing.

On the twenty-seventh of September, the day before Kersten was to leave for Stockholm, the Reichsführer declared, after a long and crucial discussion, "I agree with you. We must not let ourselves be too hard on the Germanic race; some must survive. The Danes and Norwegians in my camps will be spared. I know you are going to meet the Swedish leaders. When you return, I will do what they want."

"I want to ask you for one more thing," Kersten said. "It concerns my friend Karl Venzel. Do I still have your word, your word as a man and as a great German leader, that his life will be spared?"

"You have it," Himmler said.

His mind at rest, Kersten went to pack his bags.

8

Kersten's plane was so full of passengers that he had to leave alone. His wife, his three boys, and their nurse arrived twenty-four hours later. His happiest moment since the war began was meeting them at the Stockholm airport. From then on, no matter what happened to him or to Germany, his family was safe.

While his wife moved the few pieces of furniture which they had been able to ship from Germany into their small apartment, Kersten saw the minister of foreign affairs every day.

They went over everything. Germany's position became worse every day. As she became more desperate, the prisoners were treated more inhumanly. As the ground gave way beneath the masters, the lives of the slaves and living skeletons were worth less and less. They all had reason to fear the last convulsions of the dying animal. The time drew near.

In his race against death, Kersten was now sure of his alliances with Brandt, Berger, and Schellenberg. The enemies were still the same: Ribbentrop, and especially Kaltenbrunner. Kaltenbrunner had even tried to murder him in order to stop him, but his attempt had boomeranged, and Kersten's power over Himmler had increased. He had left Himmler well disposed toward the project. It seemed that Gunther's great plan had a strong chance of going through. The minister of foreign affairs was much more impatient than he had been when Kersten had been in Stockholm before. Public opinion in Sweden was bitterly opposed to the cruel treatment of the Danish and Norwegian prisoners; they would not stand for it much longer. They were, after all, of the same blood. Something had to be done, and quickly. Gunther asked Himmler to choose between two alternatives. The best would be to free all the Scandinavian prisoners. Sweden would be responsible for their transportation, and for feeding and housing them; it would be done under the supervision of the International Red Cross. The same would be done for all other prisoners Kersten could get released, especially the Dutch.

If he could not, or would not do that, then Gunther wanted Himmler to put all the Scandinavian prisoners in one camp which would be under the control of the Red Cross. This regrouping should be done as soon as possible. The Allied bombardments became more numerous and more devastating every day. They often hit the camps that were situated near the towns. Thousands of Danes and Norwegians were in danger of death.

Kersten telephoned all the details of his conferences with Gunther to Himmler. It was easy to get in touch with him. Kersten had told Gunther on his arrival of the privilege Himmler had granted him, and Gunther had immediately arranged for Kersten's calls to Germany to have top priority. The doctor had a telephone with two extensions put in his home. So that nothing would be lost of these historic conversations, even those with Elizabeth Lube, he always had an official listen in on them. Sometimes it was a Swedish official or a Finnish diplomat, but usually it was the Baron Van Nagel, the Stockholm representative of the Dutch government in exile in London.

These people were witnesses to an incredible paradox. They heard a man who was legally an enemy of Germany and whose country was at war with Germany exercise a privilege which was denied to commanders of armies and to all the ministers of the Third Reich except Ribbentrop. They heard this man talk daily to a man who was second master of Germany, and to the simple, courageous woman who managed his estate.

When Gunther had reviewed the objectives of the two plans, and Kersten had decided that he was ready to guarantee fulfillment of one or the other, the Swedish government convened and gave Gunther full power to go ahead.

The conference took place the third week in November.

As the ministers were leaving the conference, Gunther asked Kersten, "When do you leave?"

"I can take the plane immediately," the doctor said. "But I'd rather wait for Himmler to call for me so that my influence will be all the more powerful. Seeing how much time has already elapsed, I don't anticipate a long wait."

On the twenty-fifth of November the telephone rang in Kersten's

Stockholm apartment. It was from Himmler's headquarters. Himmler, in great pain, asked Kersten to return. Kersten told Gunther, and they met that day. The minister summed up Kersten's mission again: either to get the prisoners freed or to have them regrouped in a camp which would be safe from air raids. Then Gunther added another request. The Dutch government in London had begged Sweden to send foodstuffs to the parts of the Netherlands which the Allies had not yet been able to liberate. The inhabitants there, who made up literally half of the population, were dying of hunger. The Swedes had ships all loaded with foodstuffs and ready to leave, but the Germans would not allow them to unload their cargo. Gunther asked Kersten to get Himmler's permission to unload. Himmler was in charge of all the countries still occupied by Nazi troops.

The next day Kersten took the plane for Berlin, leaving his wife and children in Stockholm.

9

Kersten first went to Hartzwalde for a few hours. Besides Elizabeth Lube, he found Mrs. Imfeld waiting for him. This young woman had come previously, on the thirteenth of August, to speak about the possibility of sheltering twenty thousand Jewish concentration camp inmates in Switzerland.

"Himmler has done nothing. Instead, S.S. officers are swarming all over Switzerland, promising to free Jews for a price. It's five hundred francs per head for ordinary Jews, two thousand francs for the important ones. The Swiss authorities are highly indignant at this shameless trading in human flesh," she told Kersten.

The next day Kersten arrived once again, at Himmler's western headquarters in the Black Forest. The Reichsführer was depressed by his illness but very excited by the preparations for the offensive which Von Rundstedt was going to launch in the Ardennes. It was the end of 1944. This was to be the retreating Wehrmacht's last blow against the Allies.

Once Himmler was relieved by Kersten's treatment, he burst out in triumphant joy.

"All Hitler's calculations will be proven correct. He is still the greatest genius of all time. He knows to the day when we will be victorious. On the next twenty-sixth of January we will be on the shores of the Atlantic again. The American and British soldiers will have drunk their fill of sea water by that time. Then we will have enough divisions free with which to crush the Russians. We'll beat them to death. You'll see, wait till our secret weapons are brought into the fight," he shouted.

"In that case, it should be even easier for you to be generous. It's in triumph that you can really tell a magnanimous leader."

The doctor began to outline Gunther's plan once more. He had given details of it every day to Himmler over the phone, and Himmler had, in principle, accepted them, so Kersten expected him to agree very quickly. But Himmler resisted him. Kersten was first stunned, then anxious. The Reichsführer refused to do what had been agreed upon. He categorically refused all Swedish suggestions. He was drunk with elation. Von Rundstedt's future success lifted him out of the fear and despair in which he had been living. He was now convinced anew that the world was promised to the chosen race, the great German Führer.

He prostrated himself at the feet of his idol, with all the vehemence of one who has reacquired his lost faith. It was as if he had to atone for his wavering by being inhumanly cruel.

"This is not a time for weakness," was the way in which he answered all Kersten's reasoning and pleading.

Morning after morning Kersten struggled for the lives of the men suffering in the camps. He couldn't persuade Himmler; he couldn't even shake him.

In the meantime, the doctor received a crushing blow; from a reliable source he learned that Karl Venzel had been hung. Venzel, for whom Kersten had so often and so warmly pleaded; Venzel, his old and dear friend. Himmler had sworn, even on the day before he left for Stockholm, that his life would be spared. As soon as he heard about it, he ran to Himmler. He did not think; he did not even inform Brandt of his intentions.

Roughly, he swung open the Reichsführer's door and stood before him, his fists clenched and his face red with anger.

"So, you had Venzel hung. That's what your word means. That's your honor. And you dared give me your hand as a guarantee of your promise. So this is the honor of a great German leader!" he shouted.

Kersten stopped. Scorn, anger, and sorrow choked him. For once he had acted without calculation; he had given in to the blind force of his emotions. It was much more effective than any manipulation could have been.

There was no way out for Himmler. He was exposed as a liar and a man who did not keep his word, before the one man in the world whose love and admiration he wanted and thought he had. The Reichsführer, who dreamed of himself as a second Henry the Fowler, broke up in grief and shame. His shoulders sagged, his lips trembled, his nose shrank; he looked like a sneaky and ugly child who is faced with what he has done and fears that he will be whipped.

He whined, "Believe me. I couldn't do anything. Hitler wanted it at any price. He gave personal orders for Venzel's arrest and execution. What could I do? When he gives that kind of order I have to go to him myself and tell him it has been carried out. Believe me, if the thing had been humanly possible, I would have let Venzel live. But I swear, it was more than I could do."

Kersten harshly turned his back on Himmler. Himmler's moaning and whining angered him even more. He felt he might do something irreparable.

"No. No . . . don't go away," Himmler cried. "Listen to me."

Kersten slammed the door behind him.

As he was leaving the car that served as a living room, Kersten met Brandt. He told him how troubled and angry he was. Brandt, whom the doctor trusted completely, confirmed what Himmler had said. It had really been impossible for him to disobey his master.

"Don't forget," Brandt said, "that Venzel was in the conspiracy against Hitler's life, or at least Hitler was convinced he was. Hitler was taking personal vengeance. In that type of thing Himmler's will and power doesn't count for much."

Kersten didn't speak.

"Come on, Doctor," Brandt said, with a sad half smile, "you know enough about things in our little club to see how it was."

"Yes, I see," Kersten said slowly.

He wasn't angry any more; he was only terribly sad. But little by little, out of this very sadness there came a strange hope. Kersten remembered Himmler's shamed and tearful face. He had been ashamed of what he had done and conscious that he had compromised his honor as a German leader. It was clear to Kersten that he had to take immediate advantage of Himmler's feelings of inferiority. The death of one man could be used to save ten thousand other lives.

"Thanks," Kersten said to Brandt.

He went back to Himmler and said, very calmly, "You can prove to me that it was in spite of yourself that you broke your word. I will believe that Hitler's intervention made it impossible for you to keep your word, if you keep it in the domain where you are master."

"Anything you want. I swear it," Himmler exclaimed.

So it was that on the eighth of December, 1944, Kersten got the Reichsführer's formal consent to the following: the regrouping of all the Scandinavian prisoners in one camp, letting Swedish buses into Germany to transport them; freedom for three thousand women (Dutch, French, Belgian, and Polish) as soon as Sweden was ready to receive them; immediate freedom for fifty Norwegian students and fifty Danish policemen held in the camps.

Kersten did not stop at that. He continued to play upon Himmler's feelings of shame and guilt. It was a memorable day.

"Then there is the question of foodstuffs for the part of Holland which is occupied by your armies."

"I'd like to see all the Dutch who are still in our hands die," he grumbled. He met Kersten's eyes, and hastily added, "But since you are half Dutch, all right, I agree. All right."

The doctor wasn't even satisfied with that. He then went on to the Jewish question. He described the ugly racketeering that the S.S. officers were carrying on in Switzerland. This was the corps of elite men of which Himmler was so proud. Now Himmler had still another thing to be ashamed of.

"Give me the twenty thousand Jews that Switzerland wants to shelter."

"Don't even think of it. Hitler would have me hung on the spot." Himmler sounded terrified.

"Hitler won't know anything about it," Kersten said. "You're strong enough and you have enough power over your men so that he will never find out it was done. This time it's not Venzel," Kersten said, looking Himmler in the eye.

"All right." Himmler groaned. "All right. But all I can give you is two thousand, at most three thousand Jews. I beg you not to ask me for more."

He put his hands on his stomach and said pathetically, "I am in great pain."

Kersten treated him.

10

The doctor spent very little time in the Black Forest. After a few days he informed Himmler that he was planning to return to Sweden on the twenty-second of December. To excuse his departure, he explained that he had promised to pass the Christmas holiday with his family. Actually, he wanted to see Gunther and to work out measures to turn Himmler's promises into realities. Kersten knew that there would be long and touchy negotiations.

He foresaw the hidden hostility of the Gestapo and the slow workings of the bureaucracy. Every day counted. The Reichsführer might change his mind at any moment; they had to work fast.

Himmler showed no annoyance at Kersten's desire to leave him so soon; in fact, he was lavish with his affection and gratitude.

"The only thing I ask of you is that you call me as often as possible. You still have priority," he said.

The doctor went to Hartzwalde to pack his bags. There he received a letter which he had to read twice in order to believe his eyes. As proof of his most sincere friendship, the Reichsführer was granting

Kersten the freedom of the three Swedes who had been sentenced to death for espionage. Their original sentence after Kersten's intervention, had been commuted to life imprisonment.

"Dear Kersten, this will be my Christmas present to you. Take these men with you in your airplane," Himmler wrote.

On the twenty-second of December, 1944, Kersten took off for Stockholm with a gift the like of which few men have ever received.

11

As soon as he was off the plane Kersten went to Gunther and made his report, without even stopping at his Stockholm apartment.

"Himmler informs the Swedish government that it may get in touch with the Gestapo in order to regroup the Scandinavian prisoners into one camp. It will have complete freedom to arrange for the transportation of these prisoners. The Reichsführer has already ordered his men to co-operate fully with Swedish representatives."

Gunther was overwhelmed.

"You've done a tremendous job," he told Kersten. "I will speak of it at the next ministers' conference. You may be sure that they will answer your message favorably. The country will spare neither money nor effort to help the concentration camp inmates. I'll see you immediately after the New Year."

The winter holidays in the northern countries have a special, fairytale quality all their own. Kersten enjoyed them quietly with his family. He had the great pleasure of entertaining his old friend Kivimoki and his wife who, after some diplomatic maneuvers, had been allowed to leave Germany.

On the eve of January 1, 1945, amidst the laughter and the tinkling of glasses, while the logs crackled on the fire, Kersten had a moment of anxiety. Hitler's Germany was in its death agony. The Ardennes offensive had been a flash in the pan. The Allied armies had just started to build bridges across the Rhine. The Russian avalanche was tumbling from Poland into Rumania, Hungary, Austria, and East Prussia. What would happen to the millions of prisoners when Germany was in its last convulsions? What wouldn't the Nazis do in their last hours? And where would he be, what would happen to him?

When the holidays were over, Gunther told Kersten, "The Swedish government has decided to gather the buses needed to transport the prisoners, and send them to Germany."

Kersten telephoned the news to the Reichsführer and got his approval without difficulty. Himmler even told him that he had chosen the place for the regrouping; it was the camp of Neuergamme, near Hamburg.

However, it took another month of preparation and negotiation between Sweden and Germany before an official move was made. It was only on the fifth of February that Gunther told Kersten: "Count Bernadotte, vice president of the Red Cross, is responsible for the fleet of buses. Before he can do anything, Bernadotte must go to Berlin and arrange all the technical details. It's essential that he see the Reichsführer personally, and he must be treated in a friendly manner by the Gestapo. Will you introduce Bernadotte to Himmler?"

Kersten asked Baron Van Nagel to be a witness to his conversation, handed him one of his telephones, and called the Reichsführer at his headquarters. Himmler was not there. The doctor spoke to Brandt. He was happy to hear that the Swedish convoy was being brought together and that the plan which he had helped Kersten with for so long was finally going through. He promised to repeat Kersten's request to Himmler.

The same evening, Brandt called Kersten.

"Himmler is ready to see Bernadotte and asks you to assure him that he will stick to all his promises."

On the nineteenth of February, Bernadotte flew to Berlin. The Swedish ambassador to Germany introduced him to Kaltenbrunner, who in turn introduced him to Himmler; this was the protocol. The vice president of the Red Cross conferred with the Reichsführer for two hours. Schellenberg was present. At the end of the interview Himmler confirmed his promises to Kersten.

The Scandinavian prisoners were to be regrouped in one camp, the camp at Neuergamme. Sweden was ready to receive the prisoners who had been freed as a favor to Kersten.

12

After Venzel's execution, Himmler was true to his every word. He even kept one of his promises without being pressured to do so; Kersten was away and didn't even know about it.

During the month of February, when Kersten was in Stockholm, 2,700 Jews, who had been imprisoned in the sorting camp at Therezienstadt up to that time, had been assigned to the death camps with their gas chambers and cremation ovens. Two trains were loaded with these unfortunates and put on a side line, ready to travel. The head of the convoy called Himmler's headquarters and asked permission to start the trains. Brandt received the message and repeated it to the Reichsführer.

"Two thousand seven hundred, you say?" Himmler asked.

He wrinkled his brows; the number reminded him of something.

Suddenly he exclaimed: "Two thousand seven hundred—that's just right. I promised Kersten I would free two or three thousand Jews whom the Swiss are ready to take. Have these trains head to the Swiss frontier instead of to the east. Inform the Swiss authorities, the Gestapo, the railways, and our frontier guards." Himmler shook his head, and added delightedly, "Two thousand seven hundred. One would think it had been done on purpose. Not too many and not too few." His smile was ironic but affectionate. "Just enough to satisfy one of the good doctor's whims."

An hour later, the two trains got under way. Men, women, and children were crowded into them to the point of suffocation. The jolts of the trains threw them against each other like penned-up animals. Hungry and thirsty, lungs aching for air, freezing in their rags, nevertheless they prayed the trip would never end. They knew death awaited them at the hands of the S.S. So on they went, emaciated, dirty, frozen, sick, and terrified. When they had crossed all of Germany, the mothers had not even enough strength left to pity their own children.

Then the train slowed down and stopped. The cattle wagons were opened. There was a company of S.S. waiting.

But why were they saluting and presenting arms, instead of grabbing their victims as they stumbled out? Why weren't they driving them with the butts of their rifles toward the gas chambers? What did it all mean?

It was like a dream. The 2,700 Jews, men, women, and children, the 2,700 skeletons in rags, walked right by the S.S. standing at attention and crossed the frontier where, instead of executioners, they found Red Cross nurses who met them with smiles and tears of welcome.

13

Jewish circles in Stockholm knew nothing about this when it happened. Neither did Kersten, who only heard about it a month later, when Himmler wrote to him. Meanwhile, by a strange coincidence, the Jewish organizations were approaching Kersten for the first time. Their intermediary was a Mr. Von Knierin, a Balt from Russia, a banker by profession, and a friend of Kersten's. In February he came to Kersten and asked him to see Hillel Storch, who was the Stockholm representative of the World Jewish Congress. Kersten agreed to see the two men on the same evening.

"The situation of the Jews imprisoned in Germany is horrible and hopeless. All those who are still alive will be killed. We have tried everything, in vain. We know about your work and what you have accomplished. Help us."

"Give me a memorandum stating what the World Jewish Congress wants," said Kersten. "I'll do what I can as soon as I get back to Germany."

He did not yet know when he would return; it depended on Gunther. Gunther needed him because the details of the rescue of the Scandinavian prisoners were being worked out in Stockholm, and Kersten was the only man who could get in touch with Himmler directly to resolve any difficulties.

On the twenty-fifth of February, 1945, the ministers of foreign affairs received terrible news from the Americans. Hitler had formally ordered Himmler to dynamite the concentration camps, with all their prisoners, as soon as enemy troops were within eight kilometers of them.

"The Nazis still have eight hundred thousand prisoners," Gunther told Kersten, "and the Allies are not very far off."

With effort, he mastered his feelings and gave Kersten a picture of the situation. The Americans had asked the Swedes to do everything possible to prevent this final horror, but Gunther's government knew very well that there was no way of influencing Hitler's insane rage. The Swedish ministers were terrified at the thought of this seemingly inevitable massacre. Only Kersten had some chance of stopping it, through Himmler: one chance in a thousand, but it had to be tried. He must go to Germany at once.

Kersten agreed. Gunther then gave him a triple mission: he was to try to prevent the dynamiting of the camps; to reduce the difficulties which, in spite of Himmler, Kaltenbrunner was giving Bernadotte in his attempt to assemble and evacuate the Scandinavian prisoners; and to advise Himmler to have the German troops in Norway surrender, fully armed, because the Allies were pressuring Sweden to fight against that still powerful part of the German Army.

Kersten decided to leave on the third of March. The day before his departure Gunther gave him an official government document outlining his mission and appointing him to carry it out.

On the morning of the third of March, Kersten was making his last preparations for his leave taking, when Hillel Storch came running in, all out of breath. He was waving a telegram sent by the president of the World Jewish Congress in New York. It said that the Germans were getting ready to blow up the camps where the majority of Jews were being held.

"In the name of the Congress, I beg you to intervene," he said.

When Kersten flew away, his main baggage was a big brief case, completely stuffed with papers. He was in effect private ambassador of the Swedish government and of the World Jewish Congress.

14

In Germany the vise was tightening. Himmler's eastern headquarters were no longer in Zhitomir in the center of the Ukraine; they weren't even at Hochwald on the Prussian border. They were now at Hochen Luchen, in the province of Berlin, only twenty-five kilometers from Hartzwalde. The Reichsführer had taken over an S.S. convalescent hospital for his staff. His room was bare and depressing; its paint had yellowed; it was a room for sick soldiers.

Kersten found him suffering but still not willing to face defeat. He was sustained by his fanaticism. At least he put up a good front, and just doing that helped him to fool himself.

"Nothing is lost," he declared when he saw the doctor. "We still have our secret weapons. The world was astounded by the V-2 and it's only a toy compared to what's coming. You'll see—the last bombs of this war will be German."

Himmler had often threatened this way and upset Kersten. He knew that they were working on terrible weapons in the laboratories. But this time he was not afraid. It was too late.

Himmler's nervous excitement as he was hysterically invoking an impossible victory had redoubled his pains. He fell onto his metal bed. His face was hollow, his cheekbones protruded, and he was covered with sweat. Kersten started to treat him.

When he had relieved the sharpest pains, he asked: "Is it true that you have been ordered to blow up the concentration camps when the Allies approach?"

"It's true," Himmler said. "Who told you?"

"Some Swedes," Kersten said.

"They already know over there?" Himmler said. "It doesn't matter. We'll do it anyway. If we lose the war, our enemies must die with us."

"The great Germans of the past would not have acted like that," Kersten said. "And you are the greatest German leader today. You are more powerful than Hitler now. Your country is collapsing. Her armies are overrun everywhere. The generals can do nothing. You have the only force left, the S.S. police."

Himmler did not answer. He knew that what Kersten was saying was true. But since it was his habit to obey, the thought of having to take the complete responsibility of leadership made him unbearably anxious.

"Be generous, then," Kersten went on, with bitter violence.

"And who will thank me?" Himmler said. "No one."

"History," Kersten said. "You will have the glory of having saved eight hundred thousand men."

Without answering Himmler shrugged his shoulders. He had, at that moment, other, more important, things to do.

Kersten didn't insist. But in order not to remain stymied, he broached the one mission of the three which he was surest Himmler would support. This was to get Kaltenbrunner to stop underhandedly holding up Bernadotte's convoy.

When Himmler learned that his orders were being disobeyed, he was furious with the head of the Gestapo and gave him precise and threatening orders to keep his men and services entirely at the disposal of the Swedish government.

That was the easiest problem. The next day Kersten returned to the dynamiting of the concentration camps. Himmler refused again, and absolutely, to save the lives of eight hundred thousand prisoners.

Then the same old struggle began. It is pointless to describe it again, especially here when the drama of which it was the essential, daily instrument is about to draw to a close. However, it must be noted that the balance of power had been completely reversed since the time Kersten had started to treat Himmler.

Himmler now stood for a dying regime. The only power he had left was to drag innocent people down into Hitler's abyss. Kersten's only means of controlling this desire for vengeance was his healing art. He had at his disposal an influence of five years' standing, and a trust and friendship which Himmler had felt for no other human being. The entire weight of the civilized world, symbolized by the Swedish government, was behind Kersten. He also had three allies in Himmler's inner circle: Brandt, Himmler's private secretary; Berger, commander of the Waffen S.S.; and Schellenberg, who was in charge of the espionage networks. Schellenberg had just been promoted to the rank of general, on Kersten's insistence.

After a week's work, all this combined might succeeded in saving 800,000 people from certain death. This victory was embodied in one of the most extraordinary documents to come out of the war.

On the twelfth of March, 1945, in a depressing room in the convalescent hospital for S.S. soldiers, Himmler, in the presence of Brandt and Kersten, drafted with his own hand, on a crude wooden table, an agreement which he himself called "A Contract in the Name of Humanity." It provided that:

1. The concentration camps would not be dynamited.
2. The white flag would be raised over them when the Allies approached.
3. Not one more Jew would be executed, and the Jews would be treated like the other prisoners from then on.
4. Sweden could send packages to individual Jewish prisoners.

Himmler signed the document first, and then Kersten added his name.

15

Two days after the signing of the "Contract for Humanity," Kersten, who continued to treat Himmler in the convalescent hospital, succeeded in preventing another mass extermination.

It was in The Hague. The German troops still held the capital of Holland, and one of the most beautiful sections, Klingendal, had been turned into a veritable fortress. In the first week of March, a liaison officer between Hitler and Himmler named Fegelein, brought the Reichsführer the following orders from his master: In the event that it was impossible to defend the fortress of Klingendal, the garrison should be evacuated, and a bombardment of V-2 would be let loose which would destroy Klingendal and The Hague. Its 400,000 inhabitants would not be warned.

Hitler had been precise: "This city of Germanic traitors must die before us, and to the last man."

Himmler had given the instructions to Brandt, and Brandt had told Kersten. The doctor had repeatedly tried to stop Himmler from following the orders of a madman. He failed until the fourteenth of March, when he finally succeeded. Himmler's resistance had been broken two days before.

On the fourteenth of March Himmler told Kersten: "You are right about The Hague. It is, after all, a Germanic city. I'll spare it. The city will raise the white flag and will be surrendered to the Allies. I have the power necessary not to carry out the order." The technicians and the V-2 bases, from which the attack was to be launched, were part of the Waffen S.S. and were under Himmler's direct control.

From then on it was easy for Kersten to get whatever he wanted from Himmler. On the sixteenth of March with Brandt's expert help, Kersten drew up a long memorandum on the capitulation of the German Army in Norway.

All Kersten's missions had been carried out. But before his departure for Sweden, he wanted to get Himmler to concede still one more thing. For Kersten it was a personal obligation. He was being true to what he had promised himself that terrible, sleepless night, after he had learned that Hitler had decided to exterminate all the Jews. "I'll save as many as I can," he had sworn.

He got Himmler to include five thousand Jews from the concentration camps in the Swedish Red Cross convoy.

This victory was still not enough for the doctor. He wanted the Reichsführer's personal, spoken guarantee to a representative of the World Jewish Congress that those Jews would be included in the convoy.

Kersten was well aware that he had never attempted anything this difficult. It meant bringing a madman face to face with the object of his mania. It meant overcoming Himmler's pathological hatred of the Jews, his fear of Hitler, and his image of himself as the executioner of the race.

But in this incredible game which had begun five years before, the

Reichsführer, the chief of the S.S. and the Gestapo, the minister of the interior, the head of the concentration camps and of the V-2 was no longer master. The master was a civilian, a foreigner, a big, good-natured man named Felix Kersten.

On the seventeenth of March, during one of his last treatments, Kersten asked Himmler casually, "What would you do if a representative of the World Jewish Congress came to see you to arrange the liberation of the Jews which you promised me?"

Himmler started from where he was lying and shouted, "You're crazy, you ought to be put away! Hitler would have me shot on the spot. The Jews are our mortal enemies, and you want me, the second man in the Reich, to meet one of their representatives?"

Kersten shook his head.

"You don't have time to distinguish between friends and enemies," he said. "The only thing that counts now is the world's judgment. Just think what people would say if you received a representative of the Jews, after what you have done to them in Germany. They will say, 'There was only one German leader in the Third Reich who was really intelligent and courageous, and that was Heinrich Himmler.' "

The Reichsführer, already unsure of himself, hesitated and asked, "You really think so?"

"I am sure of it."

Already, Himmler took the doctor's conviction for his own. However, there still remained his fear of Hitler, the king of madmen.

"How can I do it so that Hitler won't know about it?"

The doctor tapped Himmler lightly on the stomach. "I am sure you will find a way," he said. "You have the power."

The day before Kersten was to leave, Himmler made up his mind. He told the doctor, "Tell the World Jewish Congress that I will see their representative. I'll arrange everything so that his visit will be absolutely secret. He will have a pass. I give my word of honor that he will not be harmed. I make only one condition: he must come with you."

They decided that the meeting would take place at Hartzwalde, and that there would be two witnesses, Brandt and Schellenberg. Kersten had won again.

One might ask why he wanted this concession, for the reason he gave Himmler does not really explain his determination to bring about an almost sacrilegious confrontation between the representative of a persecuted people and its great persecutor. Perhaps Kersten wanted to prove to himself the extent of his power. Perhaps he wanted to realize the myth of the executioner who pays honor to the spokesman of the condemned.

And Himmler—why did he agree to this utter contradiction of what he stood for? Why did he let himself be humiliated? Was it fear for his world reputation, for the image of himself that he would leave for the future? Did he imagine that one brief and secret meeting could exonerate him in the eyes of history? He had finally opened his eyes to the disaster that was about to engulf his falling idol. Isn't it more likely that his inborn, chronic need to obey had driven him to submit completely to another all-powerful master?

MAZUR, THE JEW

1

On the twenty-second of March, 1945, Kersten landed in Stockholm. He saw Gunther that evening and summarized what Himmler had promised. The German Army in Norway would surrender; the concentration camps would not be dynamited, and had been ordered to raise the white flag when the Allied forces approached.

The minister of foreign affairs had Kersten repeat the news before he let himself believe it.

"It's extraordinary," he murmured finally.

"That's not all," the doctor said. "I have permission to take a representative of the World Jewish Congress to Germany to meet Himmler."

Christian Gunther was a man of great self-control, but when he heard this he leaped from his chair.

"Am I hearing things? What? Himmler is going to see a Jew, a representative of a Jewish world organization? Come on, it's crazy and absurd. I know you are Dr. Miracle, but even for you this would be impossible."

"We'll see," Kersten said.

The next day he had a conference with Hillel Storch and told him that five thousand Jews would soon be freed, and that the camps where the others were being held would not be wiped out.

"I have a message for you. Himmler invites you for coffee."

Hillel Storch's face, which up to then had been full of gratitude, suddenly hardened.

"I would be grateful to you if you did not joke. It's out of place. What we are talking about is too serious and painful."

"I assure you I have never been more serious," Kersten said.

It took considerable time and effort for Kersten to convince Storch that he was telling the truth. Storch did not really believe it until he had listened in on several conversations between Kersten and Himmler. Only then did he decide to cable New York to ask the World Jewish Congress for authorization to see Himmler.

"If you think it necessary, do it," was the answer he received.

In the following days, Kersten worked a great deal, both with Gunther and Storch, in order to spell out the details which each one wanted to settle with Himmler.

The first week of April Gunther said to Kersten: "I must ask you to go to Germany once more. We are again having serious problems with Kaltenbrunner about the convoy. It would also be useful to have some precise information about the surrender of the German Army in Norway."

"All right," Kersten said, "I'll take advantage of this trip to bring Storch."

Gunther put up his hands to object, "That, no. I can't believe that. I simply cannot swallow it. If you do it, it will be so fantastic . . . I cannot even say just how fantastic."

On the twelfth of April Kersten heard from Hartzwalde that Himmler was expecting him to come with Storch in exactly a week, on the nineteenth of April. Hillel Storch agreed to go on that date. A few hours before they were scheduled to leave, Storch telephoned Kersten, and in a voice full of sorrow and regret said that he was forced to stay. People were afraid for his life in Germany; he had already lost seventeen members of his family in the concentration camps. But, he added, Norbert Mazur, a Swedish citizen and a practicing Jew, had offered to take his place.

Kersten telephoned Mazur to make sure he was willing to take the chance.

He answered, "Because it might help the Jewish people, I have to take the chance."

Kersten immediately telephoned Himmler to say that another Jewish representative was coming instead of Storch.

"It makes no difference," the Reichsführer answered.

"He has no visa for Germany," Kersten said.

"That doesn't matter. I'll alert my men. Whoever comes with you will have free entry. But above all, don't get in touch with our embassy, because they would immediately inform Ribbentrop."

The two men took off on the nineteenth of April, in one of the last planes to carry the swastika. They were the only passengers. As they approached Berlin, they began to hear the roar of Russian artillery. Underground, below the Chancellery of the Third Reich, a trapped and raging Hitler was sending out the frantic orders of desperation and madness.

Because of the roar of the motors and the vividness of their thoughts, the two passengers in the plane did not talk. Mazur watched the plain of northern Germany stretch out before his eyes. Kersten sat in his characteristic position: hands crossed on his stomach, and eyes half closed. But he still kept an eye on the companion whom he was taking on this strange and dangerous mission.

Mazur was a young man, tall, slender, and well dressed. He had a handsome, dark, thin face which showed strong intelligence, energetic determination, and complete self-control. He'll be needing every bit of it, thought Kersten.

2

At about six-thirty in the evening Mazur and Kersten landed at Tempelhof. It was dusk, and nobody was around except the policemen on duty. Kersten showed his passport, but Mazur kept his in his pocket. He was not asked for it; Himmler had kept his word.

But the car which was supposed to have been there had not yet arrived. Kersten and Mazur learned later that the message from Stockholm giving the exact time of their arrival had been delayed. But they did not have to worry long.

Suddenly, a loud-speaker crackled in the room. Then a voice burst out which the two men recognized immediately as that of Goebbels; Goebbels, the best and most enthusiastic orator of Nazism, Hitler's herald, who had celebrated all the important accomplishments of the Third Reich and the party.

Kersten and Mazur looked at each other. If Goebbels was speaking, it meant that there was important news.

"German people, rejoice. Tomorrow, the twentieth of April, is your beloved Führer's birthday!"

As the speech on this subject continued, Kersten and Mazur grew more and more astounded.

The glorious exhortations came from the bunker where Hitler was at bay, and it was addressed to a starving, bombed-out, and defeated people. Nothing could be more insane.

Finally Goebbels stopped just as a car arrived for Mazur and Kersten. It was marked with the S.S. insignia and came from Himmler's own garage. Near the car there was a uniformed secretary who gave Kersten two safe conduct passes with the Reichsführer's seal on them, signed by Brandt and Schellenberg. They stated specifically that the bearers did not need passports or visas.

To get to Hartzwalde, they had to go through Berlin. Night had fallen. Only the moon lit the ghostly, ruined city. The S.S. chauffeur was in a hurry to get out of Berlin before the nightly bombardment began. Squadron after squadron of Russian, American, and English bombers came every night. They bombed methodically, without mercy or respite.

No matter how well the driver knew Berlin, he still could not go fast. There was debris everywhere. He had to drive very carefully, down narrow pathways made by armored cars through the rubble and destroyed buildings. Finally they were out of the trap of the city. Ahead was the open road.

After half an hour a patrol stopped the car and told them to put out the headlights. The air-raid alarm had been given. The first group of bombers flew overhead. The driver listened a second to the sound of the motors. "Russians," he said.

Searchlights swung in the sky and caught several airplanes. Mazur waited for the anti-aircraft to open up. He was fascinated by everything, for he came from a country that had had no war. But no batteries fired.

"They have all been taken to the front," the driver said.

The horizon flamed up. Berlin and its suburbs were being bombed. They drove into a forest and stopped under the shelter of the trees.

Kersten and Mazur didn't reach Hartzwalde until midnight. The doctor gave Elizabeth Lube the tea, coffee, sugar, and cakes he had brought from Stockholm. He wanted to receive his guests in the best possible fashion.

Schellenberg arrived at two o'clock in the morning, dressed in civilian clothes. He was weary, depressed, and anxious. Himmler was under fierce pressure from Bormann, the highest authority of the Nazi party, to carry out the orders for complete massacre which Hitler. already sworn to suicide, was sending out from his underground lair. Bormann shared Hitler's frenzy. All the enemies of National Socialism, at least all those within destruction's reach, must perish with it.

"I am afraid that Himmler will end by giving in," said Schellenberg. "I am afraid that he will go back on his word. He fears Bormann and is jealous of his relationship with Hitler."

It all seemed unreal to Kersten. While everything was falling apart, and their moments were already numbered, the important dignitaries were continuing their intrigues, their petty jealousies and rivalries, as they had done when they were masters of Europe and threatening the world with slavery. All of them, Goering, Goebbels, Ribbentrop, Bormann, Himmler, continued their crazy dance around the king of madmen. But their intrigues could wipe out thousands. Schellenberg's job made it possible for him to follow the steps of each one of them in their dance of death. His worries had to be taken seriously. Kersten's work with Himmler was not yet finished: the convoy had not crossed the German border; the concentration camps could still be blown up.

The doctor and Schellenberg went over the situation point by point.

Finally Schellenberg said, "It's essential that you get Himmler to confirm the promises he made you in my presence. Then if he goes back on his word after you leave, Brandt and I can do what is necessary to prevent his orders from being sent out." The chief of counterespionage smiled sadly. "The present state of our communications will be a good enough excuse."

At nine in the morning, Kersten introduced Schellenberg to Norbert Mazur. The Jewish representative explained what he wanted to the S.S. general. Schellenberg promised to support him completely. Himmler was to come to Hartzwalde with Schellenberg that night; he could not get away any sooner.

"He is being held up by Hitler's birthday. He's got to be at a delightful little family party," Schellenberg said sarcastically.

He went back to Berlin, leaving Kersten and Mazur to imagine the celebration deep in the fateful bunker. This was the last insane rite, the last black mass.

3

Kersten was astounded by Mazur's calm, or at least the appearance of it which he gave. He studied his papers, took notes, went over details, prepared his arguments for the discussion. He did not act as if he were in a country where his religion was a crime, where all around him reigned hysteria, insanity, and the most savage instincts.

A Jew, a foreigner, smuggled into the country secretly, he was completely at the mercy of Himmler's slightest whim or change of heart. Yet he was calm, while the doctor, who was responsible for Mazur's life, had a great deal of trouble keeping a hold over himself. Kersten felt a deep need for sleep, for rest, but he could not stay in one place He talked to Mazur, he ate, he watched Elizabeth Lube getting things ready for their trip. They were to leave for Stockholm the next day, immediately after the meeting with Himmler. The doctor's old friend was working with the efficiency and pride that characterized her whole life.

She knew as well as Kersten that this was the last thing she would ever do at Hartzwalde. They would never see the beautiful estate again.

The Russian tide was about to flood forever the house, the meadows, the fields, and the woods. The doctor had resigned himself to it a long time ago.

He feared that a sudden, unexpected break-through of the Russian Army would catch him there and turn it into a trap. For he had been born in Estonia, now part of the Soviet Union, and he had carried arms against Russia in 1919 as a Finnish officer. Lastly, he had been Himmler's official doctor. True, he had been able to save many lives, but who, except a very few people, knew about that?

The doctor walked from room to room, lingering now in front of a beautiful piece of antique furniture, now before one of his old masters or a piece of velvet softened by centuries. All these riches were lost to him forever. He would never be able to replace them; he was getting on toward fifty: his time of great reaping had passed.

But Kersten did not suffer from this knowledge. He wanted only one thing: to escape from the insane asylum in which he had been living, virtually a prisoner, for the last five years. He wanted to forget S.S. uniforms, Gestapo agents, Himmler's cramps, Hitler's syphilis, the sounds of torture, punishment, deportation, and execution. Now that he had accomplished the incredible task which destiny had given him, he wanted a normal life—peaceful, ordered, and productive—the kind of life for which he was made. If only Himmler had already come and gone. After that . . . the little apartment in Stockholm, with Irmgard, the three boys, and Elizabeth Lube . . . it was paradise.

Night covered Hartzwalde, and little by little the estate became silent. The animals were asleep in the stable, the chickens and ducks in the courtyard. The Jehovah's Witnesses had retired to the outbuildings where they read the Bible and prayed and dreamed of golden thrones where the saints sit next to the Lord. Inside the house there were only Mazur, Kersten, and Elizabeth Lube. The hours dragged on interminably. The doctor kept looking at his watch.

Waiting, responsibility, and fatigue had worn his nerves raw. For a moment he let himself fear the worst: Himmler would not come; he had changed his mind. Or he had been wounded, or killed by one of the countless Allied airplanes which constantly strafed the roads and crossroads. Or Hitler had given him an unexpected and urgent mission. Or he had been arrested. Anything could happen now that everything was falling apart.

Kersten looked at Elizabeth Lube; he thought he caught anxiety in her face. The doctor went to poke the fire which crackled in the big fireplace. Then he forced himself to think of nothing. Hours passed.

Finally they heard the sound of a car stopping in front of the steps. Kersten ran outdoors.

Himmler got out of the car. He was dressed in his best uniform and covered with medals. He had come directly from the Führer's birthday dinner. Brandt and Schellenberg were with him. They had been delayed by troop movements and by the Allied airplanes strafing troops and convoys at treetop height. More than once, the Reichsführer and his passengers had had to dive into ditches.

Kersten asked Schellenberg and Brandt to go into the house, but he detained Himmler outdoors. He wanted to find out what mood he was in. Now that the meeting with Mazur was seconds away, the doctor was sharply anxious. How would a man who had spent his life despising the Jews, and who had used all his power to kill them, react when he was faced with a representative of that race?

"Reichsführer, in welcoming you to my house, I beg you to remember that Mazur is also my guest. But that is not the main reason that I ask you to be friendly toward him and generous toward his requests. The whole world has been shocked at the way the Third Reich has treated its prisoners. This is your last chance to show that it is not this way any more, and that Germany is capable of being humane."

In the soft darkness, in the heart of this beautiful estate, each inflection of Kersten's familiar voice comforted and reassured Himmler, who had been badly frightened by the trip.

"Don't worry," he said to the doctor. "I am here to bury the hatchet."

Kersten brought Himmler into the house and led him to the room where Mazur was waiting alone. The doctor introduced them: "Reichsführer Heinrich Himmler . . . Mr. Norbert Mazur, representative of the World Jewish Congress."

The two men bowed to each other very slightly.

"I am glad you have come," said Himmler in a friendly tone.

"Thank you," said Mazur in a noncommittal voice.

They were silent, but not long enough to make it tense and difficult. Schellenberg and Brandt came in, and Elizabeth Lube appeared with the tea, coffee, and cakes which Kersten had brought from Sweden. She put everything on the table, and the five men sat down.

The familiar motions, the tinkling of cups, the triviality of the remarks, all made the scene seem commonplace and almost friendly. Himmler and Mazur were sitting across from each other. Mazur drank tea, Himmler coffee. On the table between them there were dishes of butter, jam, honey, and plates with cakes and brown bread.

But in reality, there were six million shades, six million skeletons between the two men. Mazur did not forget this for an instant, for in his work he had followed every step of the unprecedented massacre of the Jews. In Paris, Brussels, The Hague, Oslo, Copenhagen, Vienna, Prague, Budapest, Sofia, in Belgrade and Warsaw, in Bucharest and Athens, in Vilno and Tallinn and Riga, in all these cities, and in all the villages and towns of the countries of which they were the capitals—in White Russia, in the Ukraine and the Crimea, from the Arctic Ocean to the Black Sea—everywhere it had been the same: the Yellow Star which deprived them of the law's protection and subjected them to night raids, endless convoys where the living and the dead traveled together, to camps, whipping, starvation, torture, to gas chambers, and finally, the crematory ovens.

That's what the man seated in front of Mazur meant to him, the man who sat across from him at the abundantly furnished table. This puny man with sad, gray eyes protected by glasses with steel frames, with Mongoloid cheekbones, in the dress uniform of an S.S. general, studded with medals each one of which was a reward for a crime.

And he, who had pitilessly forced men to wear the star, given the signal for the raids, paid the informers, stuffed the cursed trains, run the death camps, ordered all the tortures and executions, he was perfectly at ease. He seemed, even, to have a clear conscience.

Having drunk his coffee, eaten several cakes, and wiped his lips with a napkin, he proceeded without any embarrassment to the Jewish question. He even took pleasure in it. He was not sadistic. He had a chance now, which lately he had not often had, to satisfy his passion for lecturing and pronouncing, in short, to be pedantic. He was not violent or coarse, as Kersten had often known him to be. Himmler was well mannered at Kersten's table. But he did not leave out any of the strongest anti-Semitic ideas. His speech lasted a long time. Often, as Himmler talked and grew more and more pleased with himself, Kersten glanced anxiously at Mazur. But he could only admire Mazur's self-control as he listened with scornful patience.

Finally, Himmler had gotten onto the subject of the eastern Jews.

"These men helped the Resistance," he said. "They fired on our troops from their ghettos. And, moreover, they carry diseases such as typhus. It was to stop epidemics that we sent them to the ovens. And now they are threatening to hang us for this!"

Again Kersten looked anxiously at Mazur. The representative's features had tensed. Kersten wanted to intervene, but Himmler was carried away by his lesson and continued:

"The concentration camps! They should be called education camps. Thanks to them, Germany had her lowest crime rate in 1941. It's true that the prisoners have to work hard there. But all Germans work hard."

"Excuse me," Mazur said abruptly. His face and voice showed that he could not stand it any longer. "You cannot deny that crimes were committed against the prisoners in the concentration camps."

"Oh, I'll grant you that there were excesses every once in a while," Himmler said graciously, "but . . ."

Kersten did not let him continue. He saw from Mazur's expression that it was time to break up this useless debate, which was taking a dangerous turn.

"We are not here to discuss the past. Our real interest is to see what we can still save," he said.

"That's right," Mazur said to the doctor. Then he spoke to Himmler: "The least that can be done is to guarantee the lives of all the remaining Jews in Germany. It would be even better if they were all freed."

There was a long discussion. Schellenberg and Brandt participated in it, but from time to time they left the room, depending on the secrecy of the concessions. Once even Mazur had to leave; the Reichsführer wanted only Kersten and Brandt to be present. Even in this eleventh-hour meeting, Himmler was afraid that Hitler would find him out. For several days, urged by Schellenberg, he had been considering taking power in order to sign an armistice with the Allies. He could not make up his mind; he was still as terrified of Hitler now that he was betraying the latter in his death agony, as he had been when the Führer was all-powerful. He hung back, afraid to sign his name.

He would remove some names from the list of people to be freed, and tell Brandt and Schellenberg, "You will add these names yourselves."

He allowed one thousand Jewish prisoners to leave Ravensbruck, but he said, "Record them as Poles, not as Jews."

Finally, on Kersten's and Schellenberg's insistence, Himmler agreed to Mazur's requests in the name of the World Jewish Congress. Kersten was impatient finally to achieve all he had been working toward, and Schellenberg was in a hurry to leave with Himmler for the last desperate negotiations of the war. They were going to Hitler's bunker to see if they could put an end to his power.

4

It was close to six in the morning, the twenty-first of April. Dawn was breaking. Kersten accompanied Himmler to his car. A cold wet wind shook the branches of the trees. The two men did not speak. They knew they were seeing each other for the last time.

It was only when Himmler reached his car—the driver was already holding the door open—that he spoke to the doctor.

"I do not know how much longer I will live. Whatever happens, I beg you not to think badly of me. I have undoubtedly made great errors. But Hitler wanted me to be hard. Without discipline and obedience nothing is possible. With us, the best part of Germany will disappear."

Himmler got into his car and sat down. Then he took the doctor's hand, pressed it feverishly, and said in a choked voice, "Kersten, I thank you for everything. . . . Have pity on me . . . I am thinking of my poor family."

In the early morning light Kersten saw tears in the eyes of the man who had ordered more executions and massacres than any man in history, and yet knew so well how to pity himself.

The door shut, and the car disappeared into the gloom.

5

Kersten stood motionless for a few moments, thinking. Then he walked toward the house. But when he got to the door he turned around. He needed to release all the feelings which had been inside him the past night.

It was light now, and the dawn wind had died down. Slowly and heavily Kersten walked through his estate, saying good-by.

He looked at the century-old forests which grew for kilometers, at the fields, at the orchards his father had planted. He stroked the muzzle of a cow, the nose of a horse that had been Irmgard's pride. He listened to the noises of the chickens and ducks as they awoke.

Finally, he turned toward the house. There his sons had been born, and he had hoped that his sons' sons would be born there, too. The house, like the land and the trees, no longer belonged to him.

Inside, the living room was empty. Elizabeth Lube, Mazur, and Brandt had gone to bed. The fire was still going in the big fireplace. Kersten pulled his favorite armchair to the fire and sat down. There, in a half-sleep, he saw all the images of his life pass before his half-closed eyes.

He saw a young man in a Finnish soldier's uniform . . . a second lieutenant on crutches . . . a student of massage . . . Dr. Ko . . . Prince Hendrik of the Netherlands . . . Auguste Diehn . . . Auguste Rosterg . . . and finally, Himmler. Thoughts floated in his head as in a dream. In this house, without my wanting or anticipating it, a little chapter of history has been written. Whatever happens, I can only thank destiny for giving my hands the power to help so many people.

The doctor rose wearily. Now, at last, he could sleep.

He had his last meal at Hartzwalde with Elizabeth Lube, Mazur, and Brandt. Brandt assured Kersten that all Himmler's promises would be kept, and that, for the last time, he would add all the names he could to the list stamped with the Reichsführer's seal.

When breakfast was over, Brandt * gave Kersten three safe conduct passes. An S.S. car came for them and took them to Tempelhof, where they could hear the roar of the Russian artillery.

When the airplane had taken off and gained some altitude, Kersten fell back in his seat, closed his eyes, and thought for a moment of the future. His entire fortune consisted of 450 Swedish crowns. He had three children to bring up. He was not far from fifty. But he felt at peace with the world and himself. He still had the tools of his trade: his hands.

From now on, his work would not be involved with history or its atrocities. It would be patient, modest, good work, the kind he had always wanted and loved.

The empire of raging madmen which, little by little, he had been forced to fight, almost in spite of himself, miracle by miracle, belonged to the past.

* See Appendix, Note 9.

Kersten sighed with relief and settled into his seat. In a few moments he was fast asleep—just another fat man, with his hands crossed on his belly.

—Versailles, 1959

APPENDIX

1. At Rome, Kersten also had as a patient Count Ciano, who suffered from stomach pains. They became intimate friends. Ciano tried to persuade Kersten to practice in Italy, but Kersten loved Holland too much to consider leaving that country.

Although he never actually treated Mussolini, he met him several times. He met him through Ciano, and they got along very well together. Mussolini received him more than once at lunch, privately, sometimes in his palace at the Piazza Venezia, sometimes in a restaurant. They conversed in German, which Mussolini spoke with a very strong accent, but fluently.

He was very anti-German. Less so than Ciano, however, who was unreservedly so.

Mussolini found the Germans too serious, too unyielding, lacking in any sense of humor. They had remained barbarians.

As for Ciano, he affirmed that when he was with Germans, his blood grew colder every minute. Mussolini and Ciano were both, on the other hand, much taken with Finns.

And even at the time of the Russo-German alliance, of the Hitler-Stalin pact which roused Mussolini's indignation, the latter promised Kersten that he would intercede with the Russians on behalf of Finland. Kersten does not believe Mussolini kept his word, but thinks he was sincere at the time. Indeed, he made many promises, but forgot them very quickly.

2. Prince Hendrik of the Netherlands, who had regained his health as a result of Kersten's treatments, was one of the first guests. He hunted at Hartzwalde in 1931.

3. The title *Medizinalrat* is the highest that can be conferred on a Finnish doctor. It must be given by the president of the republic and ratified by the legislative assembly. It has only been granted four times in the history of Finland.

Kersten had been given the title *Medizinalrat* for his exceptional services to his country in 1939–1940, during the war with Russia.

4. Kersten had no further dealings with Heydrich. The head of the Gestapo was involved with preparations for the war with Russia. In September, 1941, he became Gauleiter of Bohemia, and he was killed in Prague on June 9, 1942, by Czech patriots. Kaltenbrunner replaced him as head of the Gestapo.

Heydrich's death was a great blow to Himmler. He even told Kersten, "Losing Heydrich is more disastrous than losing a battle," adding that Heydrich's exceptional qualities made it impossible to replace him.

There was something about Heydrich which was very important to Himmler, and which he told Kersten only after Heydrich's death. This man who had been physically the prototype of the Nordic, the pure Aryan, had actually had some Jewish blood. "I learned about it when he was still chief of police in Bavaria," Himmler told the doctor. "I told the Führer. He called Heydrich, talked to him at length, and was very favorably impressed with him. He decided that Heydrich's talents should be used to the fullest, especially since his non-Aryan origins guaranteed that he would be blindly devoted and zealous. He foresaw that he would be able to ask Heydrich to do things which no one else would do, even against the Jews, and that they would be carried out to the letter."

5. Himmler had made this trip in order to get the Finnish government to hand over all the Finnish Jewish population, which Hitler wanted to liquidate. With the help of the Finnish ministers, and thanks to Himmler's poor health, Kersten succeeded in gaining time. In the end, the monstrous demand was never met.

6. Kersten wanted no part of the honors which Himmler wanted to bestow on him. He used all his ingenuity to avoid them.

One day Himmler solemnly offered to make Kersten a general in the Waffen S.S. It would have facilitated his trips to the front, where he was the only man not in uniform. Kersten thanked him just as solemnly and said, "I think it's better that I keep on dressing the way I do. If the starving people saw an S.S. general as fat as I am, it would give the S.S. a bad name. Let's wait until the war is over."

Another time when Himmler was in Finland with Kersten, he wanted to give him a very high decoration: the Ritter Kreutz for service in the war. "Thank you very much," said Kersten, "but it's wartime, why waste time with medals? Besides, I am already Commander of the Finnish White Rose, and my compatriots might be offended if I accepted an inferior award. Let's wait awhile."

The third offer was the most difficult to refuse. Himmler wanted to give Kersten the title of Professor of Medicine in Germany. Hitler himself was to sign the document. Kersten got out of it by saying, "I would be proud and happy to have the title. But if we did this, it would offend Finland. Don't forget that there I am *Medizinalrat*. That's a higher title than Professor. To match it, you would have to give me the rank of Super-Professor." "But that title doesn't exist," said Himmler. "In that case, let's leave things as they are," said Kersten.

7. Berger was the most important man in the Waffen S.S. after Himmler. His license plate was number 2, while Kaltenbrunner's was only number 3. Kersten was pleased with Berger's loyalty, but it was only in 1944 when there was the question of reprisals against the

prisoners of war that the doctor conceived a real admiration for him. Strafing Allied airplanes were wreaking greater and greater havoc. At the end of 1944, Hitler ordered the execution of five thousand British and American officers who were prisoners of war, as a reprisal for the strafings. Himmler transmitted the order to Berger. On the seventh of December, 1944, the following scene took place at Himmler's headquarters in the Black Forest. Kersten was there.

"Take five thousand British and American officers from the prisoner-of-war camps," Himmler told the general, "bring them to Berlin, and have them executed." "Never," answered Berger without a moment's hesitation. "I am a soldier, not a murderer." "These are the Führer's orders," said Himmler. "Then carry them out yourself, I refuse. It's not a soldier's job." "But those are Hitler's orders. The Führer . . ." "Then let him carry them out," said Berger. "Do you realize that you are refusing to obey the Führer's orders?" Himmler shrieked hysterically. "I will have you hauled before a council of war!" "I don't care," said Berger. "You can have me shot, I will not be a murderer. As long as I am in charge of the camps not one of the prisoners will be killed." "Then you are deserting Hitler?" "No, I am saving his reputation," shouted Berger, and he left the room. Himmler told Kersten, his voice trembling with impotent rage, "I can do nothing against him now. I need him too badly. But after the war he won't escape court-martial." Later, Berger told Kersten, "If the worst comes to the worst, I have enough guns to resist Himmler. The whole Waffen S.S. is with me."

At the Nuremberg trials, Berger was sentenced to twenty-five years' imprisonment. His general attitude during the war and especially his refusal to murder five thousand Allied officers (Kersten testified warmly for him) stood him in good stead. He was released after five years. He is now in charge of a curtain-rod factory.

8. Among Himmler's characteristics was an almost neurotic shyness. At big receptions he always avoided crowds and went from group to group. When important generals came to report to him, he humiliated and demoralized them by making them wait three or four days before seeing them. When he finally received them, he spoke in rapid bursts, not letting them get a word in edgewise. Often they left without having been able to give the information for which they had been summoned.

After each of these interviews, Himmler would say to Kersten, "Thank God, I won't have to see him for another two months."

He was only at ease behind his desk; he fought a paper war. He was pedantically proud of writing correct and cultivated German. Here is a typical example: It was at the Hochwald headquarters in 1942. Brandt came into the office with a very important report from a Gestapo general who was equal in rank to Rauter. "I'm sorry to bother you, Reichsführer," said Brandt, "but a new report has just arrived which needs an immediate decision." Himmler apologized to Kersten for the interruption and took the report. He started to read. Kersten heard him mumble, growl, and then scream, "*Donnerwetter!* Unbelievable! Impossible! It's an outrage!" The sheets of the report trembled in his hands. Kersten expected to hear news of considerable importance. Suddenly Himmler brought his fist down on the table with a bang. "Would you believe it, Doctor? There are at least twenty spelling mistakes in this report!" Himmler took a blue pencil and crossed out the paper from one end to the other. Then he handed it back to Brandt. "Send this report back. I'll read it when it's correct." It meant at least a week's delay.

9. The fact that Himmler had given Brandt the authority to sign for him proved to be fatal for the secretary at his trial. Himmler himself escaped Allied justice by committing suicide, but Brandt was held responsible for all the monstrous orders which he had drafted, transmitted, and initialed under orders from the Reichsführer.

Kersten did everything in his power to defend Brandt. He testified before the committees of investigation to the constant and invaluable aid Brandt had given him in his campaign to save lives. He even wrote President Truman, but nothing availed. Rudolph Brandt was hanged.